# The Bog, the Bahamas, and Beyond
## *LESLIE HUNTER*

DENVER, COLORADO

The opinions expressed in this manuscript are solely the opinions of the author and do not represent the opinions or thoughts of the publisher. The author has represented and warranted full ownership and/or legal right to publish all the materials in this book.

The Bog, the Bahamas, and Beyond
All Rights Reserved.
Copyright © 2012 Leslie Hunter
v5.0

Cover Photo © 2012 JupiterImages Corporation. All rights reserved - used with permission.

This book may not be reproduced, transmitted, or stored in whole or in part by any means, including graphic, electronic, or mechanical without the express written consent of the publisher except in the case of brief quotations embodied in critical articles and reviews.

Outskirts Press, Inc.
http://www.outskirtspress.com

ISBN: 978-1-4327-9701-0

Library of Congress Control Number: 2012946870

Outskirts Press and the "OP" logo are trademarks belonging to Outskirts Press, Inc.

PRINTED IN THE UNITED STATES OF AMERICA

*To my wife Ann, and all who follow us*

*It is highly likely that the destiny of the family of Ann and Les Hunter will play out in America, as our children and grandchildren will probably live their lives in the country of their birth. The story that follows will hopefully give them a sense of self that comes from knowing where they come from, who they come from, and the historical threads of time and place that provided a backdrop for the lives of their family.*

# Contents

Chapter 1:    Scotland's Past................................................................1
Chapter 2:    The Watsons................................................................13
Chapter 3:    The Hunters................................................................23
Chapter 4:    Life in the Bog ............................................................30
Chapter 5:    The Young Banker ....................................................49
Chapter 6:    Ann Louden................................................................ 60
Chapter 7:    Siblings .........................................................................79
Chapter 8:    The Bahamas ..............................................................97
Chapter 9:    The Cayman Islands................................................ 113
Chapter 10:  Banking Shenanigans............................................135
Chapter 11:  Beyond .......................................................................150
Chapter 12:  The Spanish Connection ......................................170
Chapter 13:  Family Times ............................................................ 180
Chapter 14:  The Blue Nile ...........................................................209
Chapter 15:  Our World Changes ...............................................218
Chapter 16:  Real Estate and Stuff.............................................. 232
Chapter 17:  All's Well That Ends Well .....................................253

CHAPTER 1

# Scotland's Past

FRIDAY, SEPTEMBER 13, 1946 was a rainy day in Edinburgh, Scotland, and a lucky day for me. I was born without complications, into a complicated world.

Edinburgh was dealing with the effects of six years of war, and was still coming to terms with the new reality of a peacetime economy rising from the ashes of a war driven economy. All economic activity had been directed to the need for weapons and materiel demanded by the military. Now there was a return to the status quo ante - production of food, provision of housing, healthcare services for a peacetime population no longer traumatized by the war, and jobs for the returning service-men and women.

The first seven months of World War Two are known as "The Phony War" because the main actions of armies against armies on the continent had not yet begun, and there was not yet significant bombing of civilian targets in England and Wales. However, for central Scotland armed conflict from the air commenced on October 16$^{th}$ 1939, and although the primary targets were the British naval bases in the estuaries of the Forth and the Clyde rivers, both Edinburgh and Glasgow were periodic targets in the following months.

Bombing is designed to damage infrastructure and kill and/or terrorize the population, but that was just part of the effect on Scotland's capital. It was the loss of life from a generation of young men killed in action in other theaters of war that was perhaps the most profound and negative effect of the war on the city. My birth was recorded as a plus to the gene pool, but was a small statistical victory overwhelmed by the pages of death over the previous seven years.

Both the first civilian casualty and the youngest military casualty of World War Two were citizens of Edinburgh. The first to die was Joseph McLuskie, who was hit by machine gun fire from a German Heinkel Bomber while he was painting from a ladder in Abercorn Terrace, Portobello, on the first Luftwaffe raid. The youngest British serviceman to die was Reggie Earnshaw, who was 14 years and 152 days old when German planes attacked his ship, the SS Devon, off the east coast of England on July 6, 1941. He lied about his age to get into the Merchant Navy, and was serving as a cabin boy.

These two sons of Edinburgh had come and gone before I put in my appearance on the front line of humanity in September, 1946, and beyond these few words about their manner of dying, the unwritten story of their living is really what counts. I see this as a subtle reminder of my aspiration to tell a story, not just my story, but a story about me and the people around me.

To the children of Edinburgh, the challenge of learning how to spell the name of their home town is to remember the rhyme "**E**dwin **D**ied **I**n **N**ovember **B**uried **U**nder **R**obert **G**raham's **H**ouse." Edwin was King of the English province of Northumbria around 616 AD to 633 AD, and was just one of the many rulers from the south who would aspire to control this strategic location close to the narrow waist of Scotland. As for Robert Graham, he could hardly have provided a final resting place for King Edwin, as the name Graham is of Norman origin, and so must originate after the 1066 invasion. But Scotland's story begins thousands of years before then.

Neanderthal men and women (then the extant species of Homo Sapiens) walked north into the land we know as Britain - a place that was the north-western peninsula of the European landmass. The last Ice Age began around 24,000 BC and would eventually cover Scotland with ice that was in places more than one mile thick. The early population were driven south by the onset of unlivable weather conditions and the disappearance of the animals on which they depended for food. The ice finally established a line from the coast of South Wales diagonally across to the Humber estuary in north-east England, and the first settlers vanished from history.

Although the last Ice Age yielded its grasp on the islands around twelve thousand or so years ago, it is likely that the local climate remained in a condition of arctic severity for another few thousand years. The onset of warmer conditions would attract hunter gathers from the continental landmass, and these early pioneers of North Britain kept on coming. We can reasonably assume that the further back in time the more likely it is that they were nomadic hunters, comprised of small population groups, who would hunt and fish on the coastal plains of the north-east, the east coast, and across the central belt into the south of the land that we know today as Scotland. The land bridge that connected the British Isles to the continent now lies below the waters of the North Sea, but the settler traffic continued to bring new immigrants to these lands. Hunter Gatherers eventually realized the benefits of farming, which resulted in settlements of population groups, giving rise to villages and towns. The oldest stone house still standing was occupied from around 3,500 BC. If it is possible to accord them ethnicity and culture, then this must be ascribed to their ancestors from what today would be continental Europe. Even in the several thousand years from the retreat of the ice until the arrival of the Celtic people a few hundred years BC, groups of people would have been able to travel across bodies of water such as the (English) Channel. Their journeys westward eventually took them to the most north-westerly part of the continent, and they simply ran out of land, so they stayed.

The Celts originated somewhere in south/central Europe and their cultural pedigree has been established by two major archeological discoveries, the "Hallstatt" site in the Austrian Alps, and the "La Tene" site at Lake Neuchatel in present day Switzerland. The art work of designs and motifs that characterize the "Celtic" art form in the British Isles can be attributed to these earlier concentrations of Celtic culture in mainland Europe. The striking difference between the indigenous people (Picts) and the next wave of immigrants (Celts) is their choice of preferred location in the British Isles. Whereas the Picts tended to live on the southern side of a diagonal from north-east

### THE BOG, THE BAHAMAS, AND BEYOND

Scotland to south-west Scotland, the Celts kept moving west, and it is to Wales and to south-west England (Cornwall) that we find the concentrations of language and culture that derive from the waves of Celtic settlers. Further yet, across the Irish Sea, is another claimant to the Celtic blood-line, and it is easy to contemplate some ancient Celt gazing westward from the coast of County Kerry, the most westerly part of Ireland, and wondering what it would take to reach the land on the other side.

The next significant historical events were unquestionably the Roman invasions, which began in 55 BC under the command of the future Roman Emperor, Julius Caesar, and are more likely described as military expeditions. However, they set the stage for invasion proper, which happened in 43 BC, and which essentially created the imperial province of Britannia. The Romans ultimately established their northern border at a line roughly consistent with the modern day border between Scotland and England, and in 118 AD built a defensive structure, Hadrian's Wall, as a barrier to the barbarians in the north, whom the Romans called the Caledonni, and is the origin of the name "Caledonia" for pre-Roman northern Britain. Why this wall was built is explained in an inscription at its eastern end – "necessitas." Around 142-143 AD this defensive line was moved a further 100 miles or so north, across central Scotland, with the building of the Antonine Wall. This strategic defensive structure was the furthermost northern point of the Roman Empire, and perhaps as a tribute to the military guile and persistence of the enemy, the Antonine Wall and its connected forts and military camps were abandoned within a mere 5 years, with a retreat to Hadrian's Wall. Roman occupation continued in the southern parts of the Isles for a few hundred years, but by the year 500 AD the Romans had pulled their legions out for service in other parts of their declining Empire, and the vacuum was filled over time by a contentious bunch of Angles, Saxons, Jutes, and lesser tribal groups, all from continental Europe. History has identified them by the generic term "Anglo Saxons" and in the period we know as the Middle Ages, they eventually created a nation, England, that would one day color the atlas red, with two thirds of the world under the control of the United Kingdom. However, the early years, decades, and centuries of the English monarchy were spent in military adventures much closer to home, and the border with Scotland, as always, stood as a convenient outlet for their compulsion to expand and conquer.

While the Middle Ages saw the establishment of Scotland, England, Wales, and Ireland as constituent parts of a geography that would one day form a political unity, they were all fair play for the Vikings, who were frequent visitors to the Isles. When the Vikings turned their attentions to the western seas in the early 9$^{th}$ century AD, they quickly determined that control of the Shetland Isles and the Orkney Islands had great strategic advantage as safe havens, permitting more effective raiding ventures around the north of Scotland and down the Hebrides into the Irish Sea. The Viking Harold "Fair Hair" annexed both Orkney and Shetland in 875 AD and they remained under Norwegian rule until the thirteenth century, and Danish control thereafter. In 1469 Scotland's King James the Third married Princess Margaret of Denmark, and both groups of islands were pledged by her father as a dowry. In due course the failure of King Christian to make the dowry payments enabled King James to acquire the islands for the Kingdom of Scotland, and the geographic entity we know today as Scotland was now complete.

However, the fluidity of the border between Scotland and England was in earlier times the primary source of contention between the rulers of both countries. The victory by Scotland's King Malcolm the Second at Carham in 1018 did delineate a southern frontier of Scotland along the line of the River Tweed, but in due course the hegemonic claims by England were not so much about the border as about the right to control the monarchy, and hence the country.

During the first two hundred years or so of the second millennium AD, the monarchy of Scotland came to be united into a single line of succession, known as the House of Canmore, and the Scottish nobility was infused with the blood of many of the great Norman families who came with Edward the Conqueror in 1066. The frequent inter-marrying of royal families and nobles of England and Scotland during this time provided legitimacy to subsequent claims of the English monarchy to the crown of Scotland. When the last Canmore, Alexander

### THE BOG, THE BAHAMAS, AND BEYOND

the Third, died in 1286, his grand-daughter and direct heir, known to history as the Maid of Norway, was but three years old, and did not survive the voyage to Scotland. The subsequent impasse among the Scottish nobility on the right of succession gave King Edward the First (subsequently known to history as the Hammer of the Scots) the opening to act as referee in the deliberations of the nobles. Through less than subtle diplomacy, King Edward maneuvered his preferred choice, a malleable and pathetic figure, John Balliol, into the Scottish monarchy. His reign lasted almost four years. When King John finally quit in misery at his ignoble condition, having failed to command respect from the key constituents of nobility, clergy, or the people at large, the stage was set for King Edward to enforce his majesty upon the Scots. So began the Wars of Independence, and the call to greatness of a commoner, (Sir) William Wallace, and his successor, and Scotland's savior, Sir Robert the Bruce.

The Battle of Stirling Bridge in 1296 was a great victory for Wallace against the English, and the subject of a major film in modern times, Braveheart, which tells the story of the life and death of Scotland's patriot. So disgusted was King Edward by his commanders in the field at losing this battle that he took personal command of a mighty army, and traveled north to confront Wallace and his insubordinate Scots at the Battle of Falkirk, in 1298. Despite a gallant stand, that could have been an unlikely victory had the Scottish nobles not turned their horses away from the field, the Scots were decimated, and Wallace was on the run. It was not until 1305 that Wallace was betrayed near Glasgow, by the Scots knight Sir John de Menteith, and conveyed to London to stand trial before King Edward and his government at Westminster Hall. Readers who saw the movie will remember the manner of his death - hung drawn and quartered, with his body parts distributed along the road north to hang on the walls of the King's castles and garrisons. This was the punishment for treason, and the provider of entertainment for the people. Of such deaths are martyrs created, and Wallace, whose title in real life was the Guardian of Scotland, is in death the guardian of one of our sacred myths, the desire to be free, "for which no man gives up but with life itself." All the lakes in Scotland are known as "lochs" being the Scottish word for the

English word "lake". There is only one lake named as such in Scotland, the Lake of Menteith - a subtle and eternal reproach to the memory of the man who betrayed Scotland's patriot.

And so the baton was passed to the man who would lead the Scots to victory over the English at the Battle of Bannockburn in 1314, Sir Robert the Bruce. The Norman family of "de Brus" was part of the Norman diaspora that came with William the Conqueror and settled in bequeathed lands in northern England and southern Scotland. His father was one of the claimants to the throne when the Canmore line came to an end, and ultimately Bruce prevailed in the complicated process by which an eventual kingship was bestowed upon the young Sir Robert. He proved to be a man for the times, and has a place alongside Wallace in the story of Scotland's hard won independence from England. In time, his daughter Marjorie would marry Sir Walter the Steward, and their son, Robert, would be the first of the Stewart line of succession to the throne of Scotland.

In 1320, the 'three estates' of nobility, clergy, and the people, came together in the writing of a remarkable document, signed by eight Earls and thirty one Barons, that represented at the time the hopes and aspirations of the Scottish nation, in the form of a petition to the Pope to recognize the reality of a free Scotland - a nation not beholden in any way to the King of England, or to any nation who would seek to conquer and rule the people of Scotland, and the land of the Scots. Indeed, the Declaration of Arbroath, submitted to the Pope in Rome, was primarily a request for Papal recognition of the rights of the Scottish people to be free, not just from annexation by others, but also to be free of their own monarch, if the people so determined. The document, while praising the beneficence of King Robert the Bruce as leader of the Scottish people, also attested to the right of the people to remove a despotic monarch, should the actions of the monarch be contrary to the interests and well being of the people. This was leading edge stuff, and in more recent times the founding fathers of the United States would look to this document as a resource in the formation of their own Declaration of Independence.

With the accession of a Stewart to the throne of Scotland from the bloodline of Sir Robert the Bruce, the issue of claims to the throne

◂ THE BOG, THE BAHAMAS, AND BEYOND

from competing noble families soon disappeared, leaving the House of Stewart free to get on with the business of kingship. However, the proclivity of the monarchs to affairs of the heart, as well as affairs of State, ensured a steady supply of claimants to the throne during the next 100 years of the monarchy. After King Robert the Second died he was succeeded by the new King James the First, and so began a line of five successive Kings of Scotland, each a King James, ending with the death of King James the Fifth in 1542. The job of King proved not to be a sinecure, as evidenced by the outcome of each of their reigns. This first King James was murdered by plotting nobles. James the Second had an interest in the machinery of warfare, and died when the siege gun that he was operating exploded. James the Third was murdered after his son had taken over the monarchy. This new King, James the Fourth, was so troubled by his involvement in his father's death, that he wore a heavy penitential chain around his body all his life. He was killed at the battle of Flodden in 1513. The fifth King James somehow managed to live a full life, but was given a cruel farewell on his deathbed, when he was told that his latest wife, Mary of Guise, had delivered a daughter, thus ensuring that the Stewart line of accession would come to an end. His sole heir was the child who would become Mary, Queen of Scots, and she spent her young years in France, represented as Queen by various Regents from Scotland's noble houses. It was 1561 before she took the throne as such in the most trying of circumstances, a Catholic Queen in the midst of a country turning Protestant. These were the times of the Reformation, and she was forced to recognize the reformed religion in her public life, and to practice Catholicism as a private prerogative. She eventually was caught up in the armed conflict between those who would establish Protestantism and the defenders of Catholicism, and escaped imprisonment to take refuge in England, where her cousin, Queen Elizabeth the First reigned as the Virgin, and Protestant, Queen. Mary spent the last nineteen years of her life imprisoned in England as a guest of Queen Elizabeth, and was finally beheaded in 1587, after she was implicated in a plot to overthrow her cousin. These two powerful women, related by blood and by history, never met each other. Mary's death preceded by sixteen years the death of her cousin. In life there was never an opportunity for rapprochement between these two monarchs, or if there was, it was never taken. And yet, as a present day visitor to Westminster Abbey, one can look through the iron gates of a majestic crypt, and see, lying side by side, not fifteen feet apart, the sarcophagus of each of these Queens. Their bodies lie so close to each other in death, it is as if they were sisters.

Her protestant son, King James the Sixth of Scotland, became the first in line of succession to the throne of England, and was duly crowned at Westminster in 1603 after the death of Queen Elizabeth. After centuries of conflict over English claims to the throne of Scotland, how ironic that a King of Scotland took the throne of England, in essence without firing a shot. Crowned in London as King James the First of England, he quickly settled in to his new surroundings at the English Court, and it would be 14 years before he returned to visit his northern kingdom. His enduring legacy is derived from his authorization of the "King James Bible" that was printed in 1611. He is generally considered to be one of the most learned and intellectual monarchs of Scotland or England, but his private life was clouded in controversy over his sexuality. It did not take long for the couriers and courtesans of the Royal Court to pronounce upon the transition "Elizabeth was King, now James is Queen!" He did father several children by Anne of Denmark, but his close relationship with men over his lifetime would suggest that he was at the very least, bisexual. He died in 1625, and was succeeded by his son who became King Charles the First of England, Scotland, and Ireland. King Charles was never a popular monarch, and as head of the Church of England he was too close to Catholicism for a country that had turned its back on the old religion. The reign of King Charles would show that Catholicism in England was a difficult malady to cure, although the eventual execution of the king was deemed a necessary and salutary course of treatment, after he was tried and found guilty of High Treason. The country would briefly have a Lord Protector (Oliver Cromwell) as a civilian ruler before the Monarchy was restored with the accession of King Charles the Second in 1660. He died in 1685, having stayed sympathetic to the Catholic cause during his monarchy, but the stakes were again raised with the accession of his brother King James the

◄ THE BOG, THE BAHAMAS, AND BEYOND

Second, who made no bones about his Catholic beliefs. This was tolerated in England for three years until he was forced to flee the country with the advent of the claim of the Dutch Protestant William of Orange, which was recognized by his coronation in 1689. Thus was Catholicism purged from the throne of England.

The Jacobite rebellions of 1715 and 1745 sought to restore a Catholic Monarchy to Scotland, as a first step towards a similar goal in England. The first campaign in 1715 began with some of the clans rising in support of the "Pretender" to the throne, James the Third, but by the time he landed in the Highlands of Scotland, the war was effectively over, and he quickly left, never to return. For a short time his son, "Bonnie" Prince Charlie gained military ascendency in Scotland after making landfall in Arisaig in 1745, mainly due to the support of the Highland Clans, many of whom had remained Catholic. However his military adventures into England could not be sustained, and he reluctantly turned his army round at Derby, having got to within 130 miles of London. Even in retreat he was able to win a military victory at Falkirk, but his army was finally cornered on Culloden Moor near Inverness in 1746, and slaughtered. The Prince managed to escape his pursuers, at one point by dressing up as an old lady, and made his way to France, and eventually to Rome. He died an alcoholic, in ignominious circumstances, with syphilis a primary contributor. In death however he lies rather magnificently, in a vault inside the Vatican, Catholic to the end.

The city of Edinburgh is located comfortably south and east of the Antonine Wall, about one days march from the front line of the Roman defensive wall. Its location and topography would ensure that any invader who covets the land of the Scots would do well to secure the Heart of Midlothian, as Edinburgh came to be known. The Salisbury Crags, supporting the high point known as Arthur's Seat, provide clear lines of vision to the north, south, east, and west. The ascending line of today's High Street, from the bottom of the Crags to the castle ultimately built on the volcanic plug of rock, is a defensive jewel, so it is no surprise that history has much to say about the life and times of the people who gathered around this small piece of land that became the center of government, of commerce, of society, and for a period of fifty years or so in the late 18th century, the intellectual capital of the western world.

The Act of Union in 1707 joined the Scottish and English Parliaments into political union, and although controversial from a political perspective, the economic benefit of free trade within the burgeoning British Empire was a primary driver of the growth of Scotland's economy in the 18th century. As her capital city, Edinburgh was at the center of things, and her university a magnet that would attract young Scottish students who were already molded academically by a public education system that was national in scope and academic in substance. By 1750, Scots were among the most literate citizens of Europe, with an estimated literacy level of 75%. There are many reasons attributed to this intellectual flowering, but it maybe it was just that time, and that place, and somehow it all came together for Edinburgh, and for Scotland. Consider the fields of arts and sciences where Scottish intellectuals were at the forefront - architecture, archaeology, agriculture, chemistry, engineering, law, medicine, philosophy, and sociology. Let's not forget Adam Smith, whose treatise "An Inquiry into the Nature and Causes of the Wealth of Nations" is generally considered the first modern work of economics. In all of these fields of study and practice, the outstanding Scottish thinkers and scientists of the period were to be found here. Their output of intellectual and practical accomplishments in the arts and sciences contributed significantly to the subsequent development of the modern world.

With the coming of the 19th century, the stage was set for a revolution, albeit industrial, which transformed the United Kingdom through the growth of trade in goods and services that was the outcome of the industrialization of the British economy. The transition from agrarian to labor based industry began in the mid 1700's but became much more productive with the development of machine based manufacturing in the 1800's. Investment in roads, canals, railways, and shipping enabled trade to grow nationally as well as internationally. Steam power fuelled primarily by coal, and water power co-opted to drive textile machinery, allowed for significant increases in production capacity. The central belt of Scotland, anchored by Glasgow in the

◄ THE BOG, THE BAHAMAS, AND BEYOND

west and Edinburgh in the east, was the heart of industrial Scotland, by virtue of its accommodating landscape, coal resources, deep river penetration, and the fact that 80% of Scotland's population lived in this heartland. While all this was going on, Queen Victoria was settling into her 63 year reign as Queen of Great Britain and Ireland, when the phrase "the sun never sets on the British Empire" captured the popular imagination.

However, when Her Royal Highness died on January 22, 1901, the sun was rising in South Queensferry, an historic port town just a few miles to the north and west of Edinburgh. Because of the location of the town, on an east/west axis on the south bank of the River Forth, any dawn that brought rays of sunshine to the town would pass through the cantilevered spans of the Forth Bridge, a railway bridge that was an engineering wonder when it was built in 1890. The town had an important connection to the kings and queens of Scotland for a thousand years, as its location at a narrowing of the river made it a major ferry point for royal pilgrims and lesser mortals who would make the journey to and from Dunfermline Abbey, on the north side of the Forth, and Edinburgh, on the south side. Like so many children of Scotland, I would throw pennies out of the train window for good luck as it crossed the bridge, on our annual vacation to the Fife coast. This act of superstition did more than make a young child happy. Most of the coins did not make it over the edge, and provided much needed cigarette money to the many local men who were employed to paint and repair the bridge, including many of the Watson men with whom I share the links, if no longer the bonds, of family.

CHAPTER 2

# The Watsons

AT A TIME when most babies were born in the house rather than the hospital, I was delivered in the Western General Hospital, not far from my mother's family home in the West Pilton district of Edinburgh.

My grandfather, John Watson, was from a prominent family in South Queensferry. His father, my great grandfather John Watson, established a Slater and Plastering business in the Edinburgh area, and all six of the Watson boys eventually worked there. My great grandmother's name was Elizabeth Moore, and she was from Jedburgh in the Scottish border country, one of thirteen children. All we know of her is that she was a lookalike to Queen Victoria, and the only photo in the family records that I could find is evident testimony.

My grandfather, whom I knew as Grandpop, had a moustache, a center parting in his hair, and always wore a waistcoat with clothes that were invariably black, or dark. He died when I was about ten, so I have clear memories of him, and remember him as fairly gruff and serious, who liked a snack of cheddar cheese and HP sauce that he would have me taste along with him. By all accounts he was a stereotypical Scottish working class father, which means that he worked hard all his life, smoked (Woodbine cigarettes) like a chimney, drank in the pub at weekends, and did not make it easy for his seven children, the oldest of whom was my mother. He was born in 1895 during the latter years of Queen Victoria, but his formative years would have been during the reign of King Edward the Seventh, from 1901 to the start of the First World War in 1914, a period of time that is defined by the term "Edwardian".

## THE BOG, THE BAHAMAS, AND BEYOND

My grandfather would have been a product of his time and his generation, and it is no different for me or for you. We are not only given a finite time on earth to make of ourselves what we can, but we are also born into a particular time in history that has much to do with our destiny. For most of us, how we think and act is determined by our environment, and defined by the particular world in which we live. The Edwardian era bridged the old rules of the class system, which were remnants of the aristocratic model of civil life in the UK, that yielded to the democratization of wealth and power that began after World War One. The growth of mass media in particular, in the first part of the 20th Century, and the increasing power of labor as a harbinger of social change, both contributed to the demise of the old ways and the establishment of a new political, economic, and social paradigm.

One way that I can shape an understanding of my grandfather, is to understand what the Edwardian world was all about, and in particular, how it affected life for the vast majority of my fellow Scots who lived at that time. For Grandpop Watson the magnificent celebrations of the 60th anniversary of Queen Victoria's reign that were conducted throughout the nation would probably have made him feel proud of his country. As the Watson's had their own family business, all the sons learned the trades from an early age. The many years of construction of the Forth Railway Bridge was a catalyst for local industry in South Queensferry, and even though working on exposed roofs and cantilevered steel beams was hard and uncomfortable work, it meant that paid employment was pretty predictable. Even after the bridge was built, having employed over 4,600 workers, the effort to maintain it required an ongoing team of construction workers employed and on call. The towns of South Queensferry and North Queensferry are linked with the railway bridge no less than the land on either side. Somewhere on the bridge is the last rivet, made of gold, and driven home by the then Prince of Wales in 1890, and the only rivet not to rust.

By the time Grandpop had served his apprenticeship and became a journeyman Slater, he would have watched the evolving political events of the time and wondered if the prognostications of a war in

Europe would come to pass, and what it might mean for him and his brothers. For the man in the street, however, it must have been all but impossible to rationalize a conflict such as that which arose with the advent of the "Great War" in 1914. This was the series of events that followed from the political assassination of the Archduke Ferdinand in Sarajevo by the Serbian Nationalist group known as the "Black Hand":

- *The Austro-Hungarian Empire issues an ultimatum to Serbia to bring the assassins to justice, knowing that Serbia has strong ties to Russia*
- *Austro-Hungary asks Germany for support in the event of war with Russia*
- *Germany agrees, and Austro-Hungary declares war on Serbia*
- *Russia begins to mobilize its army, so Germany declares war on Russia, knowing that France is bound by Treaty to Russia*
- *Germany invades neutral Belgium, signaling its intent to take the direct route to Paris*
- *Britain, allied to France, declares war on Germany*
- *The Colonies unanimously volunteer support for the mother country, thereby committing Australia, New Zealand, Canada, India, and South Africa to the cause, and a host of smaller "island' colonies, primarily in the Caribbean.*
- *Japan, which had a treaty with Britain, declares war on Germany*
- *Italy, initially neutral, then sides with the Allies against her former allies Germany and Austro-Hungary*

Thus began in a few short weeks the first "world" war, which would soon exact a catastrophic toll of dead and wounded over the following four years. Military casualties of over 8 million deaths and over 21 million wounded are generally accepted to be credible numbers.

The narrow straits of the Dardanelles in Turkey were strategically important to the Allied Powers, as they could provide a supply route to the Russian ports in the Black Sea, through the Sea of Marmara. However, they were protected to the north by the Gallipoli Peninsula and to the south by the shores of Ottoman Asia. Turkish fortresses

### THE BOG, THE BAHAMAS, AND BEYOND

were well positioned in the high ground overlooking the shipping lanes. The Allied Powers mobilized to execute a strategy of capture and control of the Straits, and it became a series of disastrous campaigns, where the enemy had the high ground, a secure supply chain, and replacement troops when needed. Almost half a million British and Colonial troops were involved in and around the Dardanelles Straits in a hard fought and ultimately losing Allied cause, as indicated by the heavy casualty list of over 200,000 soldiers. This was no Normandy.

Like so many soldiers of that era and right up to the present, Grandpop hardly ever talked about the war. We know that he was conscripted to the Lothian Brigade of the Royal Scots Regiment, and saw active service in Gallipoli. He came back physically intact, although he was wounded, but not seriously, and by all accounts no different a man than before. It seems hard to imagine. In later years I would come across a folk song written by a fellow Scot, Eric Bogle, who lived in Australia, and was inspired to write the song because of the deep national sense of grief and angst that pervaded his adopted country even decades after the Gallipoli campaign. "The Band played Waltzing Matilda" is a heartfelt and sensitive parody of the original song, and Australia's unofficial national anthem.

Now and then Mum will come up with some obtuse fact or story about her background, and sound surprised when we don't seem to know it. It turns out that my Grandpop not only had several brothers but had three sisters, and two of them emigrated to America in the early nineteen hundreds. One of the sisters was pregnant and unmarried, and emigration was the preferred solution to an otherwise unacceptable event in the provincial town of South Queensferry. My great grandfather was affluent enough to travel to America to visit his daughters from time to time, and, in an unlikely twist of fate, he was killed in a traffic accident in Washington DC, about three miles away from Pentagon City, Virginia, which is where my two daughters live today.

Grandpop was demobilized after the war, and was able to return to civilian life in Edinburgh and his sweetheart, Catherine Morgan Bews, whom he married in 1919. My grandmother brings a smile to my face just by writing her name. She lived into her eighties, and spent

## THE WATSONS

most of her life in and around Edinburgh and South Queensferry. "Grandma" Watson was very much a focal point of her large and extended family, truly a benevolent matriarch. She had a medical condition known as Essential Tremor, which in later years caused her head to shake slightly, but for most of her adult life she had the other symptom of the condition, which causes the voice to tremble. It is hard to describe the sound, but it made her words come gently from her mouth, and complemented her personality.

Grandma Watson was born in 1888 in Edinburgh, although the Bews family name originates in the Orkney Islands. Her mother, Mary Judge, was from Edinburgh, of an allegedly Irish father, John Judge, who came to Scotland with his family sometime after 1835. His father was a crofter, so it is likely that the Potato Famine of 1845 was the cause of the family's emigration. The connection with the Orkney Islands has some interesting implications for the genetic contributions of the Bews family to the descendant families. A study of the genetic heritage of Orcadian (Orkney) men was conducted in 2000/2001 for the BBC program "Blood of the Vikings" which shows that around 60% of the male population had DNA of Norwegian origin. The conventional idea that the Vikings were raiders rather than settlers no longer holds. They came to stay, brought their women with them, and their bloodlines run throughout the northern and western British Isles.

Grandma was one of eleven children, and their names are locked in the memory of me and my siblings, as we used to listen to our Mum reel off the names of the Bews siblings in about four seconds:

Tottie, Mary, Mimie, Nellie, Katie, Aggie, Wullie, Bertie, Davy, Robert, Freddy.

This was the cast of the Bews family, and they occupied tenement flats in St. James Square in the center of Edinburgh. Katie became my Grandma Watson, but of her ten brothers and sisters, only three married. The others stayed together and died together in the tenements in St. James Square. The last to go was Uncle Freddie, and he was the only one who lived long enough for me to be able to attend his funeral. I have a collection of Watson and Bews family medals from the First World War and the Second World War that were passed down over the years, and unfortunately the medals are mostly generic, so

17

they do not always have a name on the back. It makes no difference to me. I have them all displayed in presentation cases, polish them on a regular basis, and they take me back to a time and a place that I sense vicariously through the recollections of my Mum, now Grandma Hunter to one generation, and "GG" to the next generation, including my own grandchildren, Graysen and Callum.

My Mum was born in 1920 in Edinburgh, the eldest of an eventual seven children. For the first two years or so she lived with her Mum and Dad and younger brother John at 24 Guthrie Street, just off the Cowgate in the heart of the old town. They lived in a peculiarly Scottish type of dwelling place known as a single end, essentially a room and kitchen with an outside toilet, in a tenement block of flats. These multi-family buildings were the main form of housing available to the broad mass of the (working class) population in Scotland from Victorian times, and were normally built in and around the center of towns. Sleeping was communal, and the tenement building, with its dark passageways, stairs, and corners, was as much a playground for children on a rainy day as it was a trysting place for young lovers on a rainy evening. It was during the early years of Mum's life that her father decided to try life in the United States, and went ahead of the family to Boston to seek work and a place to settle. Grandma was left with no reliable source of income, so she sold up their modest belongings and moved back in with the rest of the Bews family in adjoining flats at St. James Square, in the center of the "New Town" section of the capital.

Along the way my mother's given name of Mary was replaced by the name "Armis" as an acknowledgement to the Armistice that marked the end of World War One on November 11, 1918, as Mum was born two years later to the day. Her nickname paid tribute to this extraordinary event. She has been Armis ever since, and the only one I have ever known. For the first six months of her life she cried all the time, and then all of a sudden one day she woke up and smiled. Her mother was so surprised she took her to the hospital to see what was wrong with her!

Grandpop eventually returned home from America, after Grandma had a change of heart and decided not to go. When Mum was five the family moved to Pilrig, and then a few years later back to Guthrie Street, only this time to number 18. For the young Armis Watson, life in the inner city was simple and yet wonderful. A few hundred yards from her home was the Heart of Midlothian, a grouping of paving stones in the shape of a heart that marks the spot where the 15th century Tolbooth was located, which included a prison, and where public events were once held such as hangings and other forms of punishment for offences against the State, or more often, against the Church. It was the habit of Edinburgh's criminals to spit at the door of the Tolbooth as they passed by, a rather tame insult to authority. As she skipped past the Heart my Mum would spit on it, as Edinburgh's children have done for as long as anyone can remember. All the Hunter kids respected this tradition, as did my own two girls, and no doubt our grandchildren will once they are old enough to participate in this less endearing social habit.

A few more skips to the High Street and Mum had a playground that is today a tourist attraction for the thousands of visitors to Edinburgh, many of whom arrive from overseas in hopes of reconnecting with their Scottish roots. If she went uphill along the High Street she would reach the esplanade and battlements of Edinburgh Castle, the traditional military heart of the nation. If she turned downhill the road ends at the Palace of Holyrood, the official residence of the Kings and Queens of Scotland since the fourteenth century. In the grounds of the Palace lies the ruined Augustinian Abbey that was built in 1128 by King David the First. He was hunting on the Sabbath and narrowly escaped death from the antlers of a stag, according to legend. As penance to the church he built an Abbey on the spot, and named it Holyrood for his mother's Christian cross (rood) of ebony, ivory, and silver. Up and down the one mile length of the High Street, which connects the castle on the hill and the palace in the park, are the side streets, wynds, stairs and closes that give this old town center such presence. The tenements and flats of Guthrie Street today serve as dormitory apartments for students of the nearby University of Edinburgh, and were temporary places of respite for our daughter Cassie during her six months at the "Uni" in 2001 as part of her undergraduate studies. The Brewery at the end of the street is long gone, but the memories of the Coopers making barrels and the pungent smell of the beer still resonate with my Mum.

In time, Mum and her brother John would be joined by siblings Betty, Rita, Connie, Tommy, and Rae, and sometime after the war the family moved to their new council home at 23 Ferry Road Avenue in the West Pilton district of the city, where eventually I would live for a few months before we moved to Falkirk.

Mum can still remember with clarity going by bus on a school trip to a church on the outskirts of Edinburgh that had fabulous carvings and sculptures on the walls and roofs, and was located in the grounds of a ruined castle. This was the mystical Chapel of Rosslyn, which was to capture the popular imagination in the late nineteen nineties in the concluding scenes of "The Da Vinci Code" movie that was derived from the book of the same name by the American author, Dan Brown.

She had a couple of classmates who eventually managed to escape from the fairly austere background and circumstance of life that was inner city living in the nineteen twenties. Her friend Maidie Dickson was, even as a schoolgirl, an aspiring singer and dancer who later formed a comedy double act with a rising comedian, Chic Murray, and they became household names who were hugely popular in post World War Two Britain. Her neighbor in the tenement was a child of Italian immigrants whose original name of Eddie Paolozzi morphed into a more socially palatable Eduardo Luigi Paolozzi when he became an established Sculptor and Artist, and ultimately Sir Eduardo after his knighthood.

Within two weeks of turning nineteen years of age, Mum left school and got her first job in McKay's "sweetie" factory in nearby Fountainbridge, where she worked on the manufacturing line of the many kinds of chocolates and confectioneries that made the brand a household name. It was boring work, but the shop was full of like minded young ladies who got through their teenage years by learning to dance in order to attend the many dance halls that were the main places of entertainment for young men and women. They would also spend time in the numerous movie houses that showed the latest films from a place in far off America called Hollywood. With the outbreak of war in 1939 she left her job to enroll in a two month training

## THE WATSONS

course in munitions work at Ramsay Technical College, where she "graduated" at the end of the course as a "semi-skilled engineer". This qualified her for employment at the Scottish Motor Traction factory that manufactured parts for the Lancaster Bombers, and she worked a lathe to produce Breech Blocks for the aircraft. At some point she had a work related injury to the palm of her hand that kept her out of work for a while, and when she returned she was assigned to the filing room. That didn't last long, and she talked her way back on to the lathe in time to receive a commendation from a visiting Air Chief Marshall for her dedication to the war effort. In later years she would tell each of her children how she came to have a scarred hand, and the causes varied from being shot with an arrow by a Red Indian, to being shot by a German soldier, or some other impressive scenario that would capture the imagination of a Hunter child.

The early bombing raids against shipping targets in the River Forth as well as the Forth Bridge itself meant that the City of Edinburgh was in the direct line of fire, and the German Luftwaffe took the opportunity to bomb as well as strafe the city, although not in a sustained way. However, it was serious enough for Home Defence personnel to supervise street level civilian protection by establishing air raid shelters. In one of the early raids Mum was secured along with the rest of the street in an underground shelter, when she had a painful toothache and needed to retrieve the tincture medication that was back at the Guthrie Street flat. She talked her way out, ran home, picked up the medication, and hurried back to the shelter, all the while looking at an Edinburgh sky illuminated with flashes of color from bombing drops and the strafing of bullets across the city. Thankfully she made it back unharmed, and with one more story to tell her future children.

Although the strictures of living in a condition of war made social life somewhat hard to plan, difficult to commit to, and easy to make excuses for, the young Armis Watson was able to have some moments of laughter and fun around the time that she turned twenty one, and officially became an adult. The rest of her life would be determined by the first year or two of the nineteen forties, but she did not know that at the time. One of her pals at the factory announced that she was going to organize a "Mystery Tour" on an upcoming Sunday, to raise

## THE BOG, THE BAHAMAS, AND BEYOND

funds for the war effort. This involved hiring a bus and driver, filling the bus with factory girls, and heading out to a destination known only to the driver and the organizer. When she bought her ticket at work, one of the young men at the factory, who had a speech impediment sufficient to keep him from being drafted, announced to her works team that he would look after Armis on the trip, so in the interests of peace and harmony she humored her suitor by sitting next to him on the bus. When they finally arrived at their destination, the Inn at Currie, a small town in Midlothian, the troupe of mostly girls set up at the Inn for lunch and libation, followed by the selling of raffle tickets to raise funds for the military. There were two young Royal Air Force airmen in the pub that day, and she hit them up for a donation. When the party was organizing to leave, Armis stepped outside, to be met by Leading Aircraftman Peter Hunter, who saw an opportunity to ask for a date. This imposition was witnessed by her workplace suitor, who announced in a loud voice that the lady was spoken for, although the manner of proclamation left no doubt that there was probably room for negotiation with the subject. Sure enough, Armis was quick to point out that the other young man was not to be taken seriously, so arrangements were made for a subsequent evening together in Edinburgh. The first date took place on one of the nights when the Luftwaffe stayed home, and the rest is Hunter family history.

CHAPTER 3

# The Hunters

MY FATHER, PETER Shirra Hunter, was born in Falkirk in 1920 and lived with my Grandfather Hunter (Pop) and my Grandmother Hunter (Grannie) in Dalderse Avenue about a mile from the center of town. The rows of cottages, four to a block, were built in the nineteenth century and were fairly typical of working class housing stock of the times. Each cottage had one bedroom, a living room, a kitchen area, and access to an unheated outside toilet shared by their immediate neighbor in the block. There was also an alcove as part of the living room that had a double bed fitted in to it for Grannie and Pop, while my Dad and his step-brothers shared the bedroom. The only interior lighting was provided by a gas lamp in the living room, so reading in bed was not an option.

Pop Hunter was an iron-moulder to trade, just as his father James Hunter was. Pop was born in 1884 in the Falkirk area and like most of his contemporaries saw active military service in World War One. He was sent to the front line in France and Belgium, and although not wounded per se, he did suffer from Mustard gas exposure that left his lungs compromised for the rest of his life. He worked in one of the many Iron Foundries that were the core of the industrial base in central Scotland in general, and Falkirk in particular. I was travelling with my wife Ann in South Africa a few years ago, and we stopped to check out a small dry goods shop in the countryside a long way north of Durban. There we found a dusty black iron cooking pot, known as a Potjiepot in South Africa, stamped with the name "Falkirk Iron

◄ THE BOG, THE BAHAMAS, AND BEYOND

Foundry", where Pop Hunter used to work. Apparently these were produced in Falkirk going back to the mid 19th Century, especially for the South Africa trade, and the basic design goes back to the late Middle Ages.

Of the many foundries that established in the Falkirk area from the middle of the 18th century on, one was to become famous around the world because of its most important product, the Carronade. Carron Company was formed in 1759 by a group of Scottish and English businessmen, who saw an opportunity created by the ongoing war between Britain and France, which limited continental supplies of iron so critical to manufacture of iron products, particularly munitions. Various locations in England and Scotland had been considered by these friends and entrepreneurs, but the natural advantages of the location at Carron, by Falkirk, won the day. The area's easy access to raw materials and the neighboring rivers of Carron and Forth made it the preferred choice, and so began another significant chapter in the story of Falkirk. Within a year the foundry was producing guns and cannonballs for the Admiralty, and by 1773 the company was granted a Royal Charter. The government's faith in the company was rewarded by their most famous invention, a canon which they named the Carronade, in 1778. It had a large caliber relative to its overall size, and could be recharged and fired again much more quickly than contemporary weapons. By 1791 they were mounted on 429 British ships, and were being exported to Russia, Denmark and Spain. They were used by the Royal Navy in the Revolutionary War with the United States, and were still in use at the time of the American Civil War one hundred years or so later. Perhaps their finest hour was at the Battle of Trafalgar, where Nelson's ship the *HMS Victory* had been outfitted with two 68 pound Carronades in her forecastle. One single round shot with a keg of several hundred musket balls devastated the gun deck of the enemy ship *Bucentaure*.

The company manufactured iron and related products at the Carron Ironworks for over 200 years. In the end, the changing consumer preferences of post war Britain led to the inevitable decline of the company, as it did to all of the other foundries in the Falkirk area. However, during the life and times of Pop Hunter there was work to be done, and he was able to earn a living, although a hard one at that, in the foundries of his home town. It would have been dirty and unpleasant work, building moulds to shape the iron products, shoveling coal to feed the blast furnaces, handling the pans that poured the molten metal into the moulds, and stacking the finished product for delivery across the Empire. The coal dust and detritus from the materials used in the casting process would permeate the air inside the foundry buildings, and all in all it was a pretty unhealthy place to spend the majority of your working life. But for the sons of Falkirk, working in the foundry was where the young boys aspired to go after they left high school at fourteen or fifteen years of age. However, a life in the foundries was a reliable predictor of death. Three score years and ten was the biblical standard for a full life, and nineteen hundred years later in industrial Scotland it was still the standard. Pop died when he was seventy five, and the inevitable heart disease came with the job and the regular pay packet.

Pop's younger sister Mary, my great aunt but always known as just Auntie Mary, was never married, and as long as I knew her she lived near Victoria Park in a small tenement flat, and was considered the most genteel member of our family. She was someone that the family would visit from time to time, requiring us to observe a more disciplined protocol than normal. I was always trying to duck out of the occasional visits to her flat, as she would anoint my head with a smearing of butter or margarine to try and keep in place the reluctant locks of hair on my head. It made for some interesting walks home, as I had to outwit the neighborhood dogs, who were attracted by the smell. But for all that, she had dark brown eyes that twinkled, and would give us chocolate biscuits (cookies) with our cup of tea, so it was not all bad. In my late teenage years I went with her for a weekend at a seaside resort down the River Clyde, to Rothesay. We took a steamship from Glasgow to the Island of Bute, and stayed at a Boarding House. This was part of my rite of passage as a young man, learning how to be an adult, and although cups of tea, walks along the Promenade, and (yet another) game of putting made for a socially challenging weekend, I am happy that I was able to do something special for her. She died long after I had married and moved overseas, and her rather expensive and by now antique furniture has been spread around the family homes and ensures that her name is still part of the current vocabulary of the Hunter siblings.

Grannie Hunter was the grandparent that I spent the most time with, as she lived with Pop in a council flat close to my primary school (Victoria), and was a regular provider of lunch. I had a friend from school who lived a couple of doors along from Grannie, so I spent a fair amount of time there. Council houses were a distinct step up from tenement living, and most were built immediately after World War Two, becoming the government standard for social housing. In later years I found a copy of her marriage certificate and learned that she was born in the Camlachie area of Glasgow, as Elizabeth Keir Jack, in 1885. This is the same general area of Glasgow where Ann's mother and grandmother were born, and the surname 'Jack' is one of Ann's family names. We have speculated about a connection between our families, but more in jest than anything else. Jack is a fairly common last name in Scotland, although normally encountered as a first name. Grannie Hunter was a widow when she married Pop, as her first husband died sometime between 1910 and 1920, so it is easy to speculate that he was a casualty of World War One. She worked in a foundry in Falkirk, and this is where she met Pop. My father was born nine months to the day after her second wedding, and her surviving sons from that first marriage, Bobby, Jimmy, and Harry Malcolm were ready-made brothers to my Dad. Older brother Jimmy was killed on the island of Crete in the Mediterranean during the German invasion of that island in World War Two. By the time I knew my Grannie, she had lost a husband and a son, but not for many years would I realize that, or appreciate it. I will always remember her beautiful wrinkled face.

My Dad had three older step-brothers to mentor him as he grew up, and his progression through the Northern Primary School to Falkirk Technical (High) School would indicate that here was a young man who did his schoolwork, but did not excel. As a schoolboy of a working class family, his duty was to go to school then get a job at the earliest opportunity so that he could contribute to the household. He actually got his first job when he was about eight, at the Falkirk Greyhound Stadium, selling cigarettes from a tray to the local punters.

# THE HUNTERS

His abiding memories of his time as a schoolboy were his accomplishments as a footballer, and in particular playing in the Scottish Schools Cup Final at Hampden Park, Glasgow. This has been Scotland's national stadium since 1903, and is considered hallowed ground by Scots fans everywhere. To have played in a cup final there is quite an achievement, and only the score-line disappointed, as his team lost to the Glasgow opposition. The stadium in those days held about 150,000 fans but the wind and rain on the night of the game challenged the small crowd of family members and friends who braved the elements to see their favorites. I carried his runner up medal around for years as a young boy, but managed to lose it in London in the mid sixties, along with my own Scottish Cup medal that I won in 1958 playing for Stirlingshire, my home county.

Dad left school when he was fourteen years of age to become a Milk-boy, rising early in the morning to join up with the Milk-man, his horse and his cart, and deliver milk to the doorsteps of the Bairns (citizens) of Falkirk. His journey through High School had been interrupted for almost a year when he contracted Rheumatic Fever, a disease that is no longer prevalent in modern societies but was very much in evidence in early twentieth century Scotland. He was confined to bed for months in a room lit only by a candle, and it was a traumatic experience that he remembered all his days. He maintained that he contracted the disease by walking in the rain without proper shoes, and woe be-tide any of us during our own childhood if we came home with wet feet due to inadequate footwear. The disease would have a major impact on his health in later years, from a heart attack at age forty five until his death at age sixty one. It may be that this long time away from school made it impossible for him to catch up, and so as soon as he was of an age to leave school, he did so. When I was a child, I thought my Dad was really intelligent. He seemed to know so much about so much. As I got older, and developed a sense of my own knowledge base, it only confirmed that he really did have a breadth and depth of knowledge that on the surface was way beyond his social station. He was capable of much more, and in the way that history repeats itself, especially in families, I also think that I left a lot on the table when I left school earlier than my potential might suggest.

### THE BOG, THE BAHAMAS, AND BEYOND

I write this not from a perspective of hubris, but just from a lifetime of experience in business, where all my peers and challengers for success were way more educated than I was. Somehow, I made it through regardless and so did my Dad, in his way.

Although his job on the milk round was a steady pay packet and provided a modest contribution to the household, he kept looking for something better. He was finally able to join the local plastering firm of J.K. Miller, and began his five year apprenticeship on the way to becoming a "journeyman" plasterer. In the larger world, this was the time when America began to arise from the depths of the Great Depression, and the rising tide of world economic growth would certainly have reached into the construction industry in central Scotland, the guts of our country's economic base. However all that was put on hold, including his apprenticeship, with the outbreak of war in 1939 and his mobilization into the Royal Air Force.

He was enlisted in the RAF for the duration of the war, but spent most of it far from the military action, in Scotland, England, and Ireland. He was admitted with a health classification that precluded him from "active" duty, as a consequence of the Rheumatic Fever. This precursor of heart problems would become manifest later in his life, but for the period of the war it kept him away from danger, and he was assigned to work on maintenance and repairs to military aircraft. His enlistment shows him to be a Leading Aircraftman, but for all practical purposes he was a mechanic. He was also able to continue his passion for football, and represented his RAF squadrons as a tough tackling and creative midfielder. His photographs in the family album, or should I say the two or three cardboard boxes that held the photographic history of our family, show him to be fit and athletically built, with forearms that put my banker's arms to shame.

In 1942 he was transferred to Turnhouse Air Force Base on the outskirts of Edinburgh, and was able to bus it into town with his mates whenever they were eligible for some time off. He met my Mum on her mystery tour to Currie, and she tells me that they met for their first date at the landmark Duke of Wellington Statue outside Register House on Princes Street, a popular trysting place for young Edinburgh couples. They were married in 1943 and my older sister Katherine Watson Hunter (Rena) was born the following year.

For the rest of the war there were times when they could all be together and live close to where Dad was stationed, and other times when it was easier for Mum and Rena to stay with the rest of her family in Edinburgh. Of all six siblings, Rena has the closest ties to the Edinburgh side of the family, probably because she spent so much of her early years with the Watsons. Meanwhile, Mum had to come to terms with the likelihood that the town of Falkirk would play a large part in her life, since it was their plan to move to Falkirk once Dad was de-mobbed from the RAF unless the Edinburgh City Council allocated them a house, in which case they would stay in Edinburgh. That did not happen. For a city girl like Mum it was probably like moving to the country, and a far cry from the "Athens of the North" as Edinburgh is popularly known, at least by people who have never been there. In some respects this was pre-ordained by the election promise of the post-war Labour Government that required employers to make the same job available to military personnel as they had when the war began. For Dad, this meant a job back in Falkirk as a plasterer, and in due course he fulfilled his apprenticeship with the J.K. Miller firm, and was a skilled tradesman for the rest of his life.

The Hunter family, all three of them, moved into the row house at 39 Dalderse Avenue in Falkirk next door to Pop and Grannie Hunter. For Dad, it was a time of re-adjustment from six years of military service, and the renewal of friendships, as one by one his childhood pals returned to Falkirk. For Rena, it was a new life in a strange place, after the comfort and companionship of her many uncles and aunties back in Edinburgh. For Mum, it began rather inauspiciously when she sat down to have a cup of tea with her father-in-law, and he leaned over and asked "will ye tak' a wee tate?" He was asking if she would like a drop of milk in her tea, but not in any version of English that she understood. She got through the assault course that was her first few meals with the Hunters of Falkirk, and never looked back. Well, she may have looked back, but she never went back.

CHAPTER **4**

# Life in the Bog

MY EARLIEST RECOLLECTION is playing on a tricycle on the front pathway of our house at 9 Alexander Avenue, Falkirk. We moved into this newly built council house on my second birthday, in 1948, so it would have been some time not long after that. What is important for me about that memory is my then playmate, Ian Laurie, who had moved to number 13 Alexander Avenue about the same time. We were two doors apart, enrolled in the same nursery school, and subsequently tracked each other through primary school then on the high school. To this day we are as close as ever, the same two wee boys from Falkirk, as my Mum describes us. In 2010 we joined up in London, flew to Greece, and knocked on the door of our pal, Jim McLay, at his home in Kefalonia, on the eve of his 60th birthday. He had no idea we were coming, and answered the doorbell expecting a Greek friend from the village. In our boyhood days we would have rode our bikes to visit a pal, or walked. Today we fly a few thousand miles. Nothing else changes.

Our friendship has been a source of strength, inspiration, joy, and laughter for both of us these past 60 years or so, and the memories of the early years in Falkirk are never far from the discussion agenda when we meet up nowadays. We lived in a "housing scheme" at the edge of town, known colloquially as the "Bog Road" because of its location on an old marshy area of town. Post-war Britain saw a massive investment in the housing stock by local governments all over the country, which usually took the form of two story semi-detached houses, each with its own garden area, and with from two to five bedrooms. Each eligible household, meaning every family unit, was entered on a list at the town council offices, and in due course given a new house, with perpetual tenancy, subject to paying a weekly rent to the town council. Our street was at a far corner of the scheme, between farm fields and a railway line. A tunnel under the railroad track enabled the neighborhood kids access to a countryside of streams, woods, fields, and an old Army camp. For us it was Disneyland, a place to hang out with friends, spy on other kids, light fires, and be boys.

The neighborhood kids were all shapes and sizes, but the streets were our playground and created a sense of community that we took for granted, as we literally grew up with everyone around us. Nobody moved house. Nobody new moved in, after the last of the council houses in the Bog Road were completed in the early fifties. Once you got that council house there was no way it would be given up. Our group of regular chums included Claude "Cozzie" Frater, Jock Thompson, Gus Braidwood, Balfour Braidwood aka "Our Hector", Ian "Jinko" Jenkins, Alec Haldane, George "Custard" Cunningham, and Ian's next door neighbor, Tommy McAleese. Quite apart from that group, united in propinquity and loyalty, there were kids in every street, most of whom were from Protestant families and so attended our schools. Catholic schools in Scotland are still separate, even although they are part of the state school system, so we tended not to know the Catholic families as well, but there was no real animosity, just a lesser degree of familiarity. Odd characters come to mind, like Jim "Sneeger" McGregor, who was playing tag and made an escape up a stone railway bridge, only to fall off and break his arm. He stood up, shouted "ha ha, you never got me!" and promptly fainted. Guy Fawkes Night was always a major event in our lives, since we had in essence state sanctioned bonfires that were lit and burned for hours on November 5$^{th}$ each year. The "Guy" who is burned in effigy on top of the huge bonfire is in celebration of the Gunpowder Plot in 1605, when this Irish recalcitrant tried to blow up the Houses of Parliament in London. Every housing scheme or neighborhood had its own bonfire, and there were always enough public undeveloped patches of land around to accommodate the occasion. One year the zany flight

### THE BOG, THE BAHAMAS, AND BEYOND

path of a squib, which is a small controlled explosion, or firecracker, was lacking somewhat in control but not in explosive content, and it ended in an attack on my nose with the resulting scar a proud and lasting memory. Injuries in the line of fire, so to speak, were considered a badge of courage, and we treasured each one, especially if they required stitches.

My first such event was as a four or five year old, standing on the toilet bowl so that I could reach up to pull the plug, which hung down from the suspended water tank on the wall above the bowl. I slipped, and the inside of my thigh caught an exposed bolt and punctured my skin enough to visit the Infirmary for stitches. Next was a gash in my head when I fell backwards off a garden rope swing and struck the edge of the kerb. Six stitches for that one. Then I fell while running at speed down the hill at Thornbridge Gardens, and landed on my right knee on a road that had just been re-surfaced with gravel chips. Ouch! - more stitches. Ian and I were practicing our backward dives at the Municipal Swimming Pool, and again I struck my head on a ledge of solid stone. Off to the Infirmary for another repair job on the back of my head. The next one was a bit more creative. We had built a bogey out of old wheels and planks, and four of us were perched on the planks as we raced down the hill through the tunnel. My leg became stuck against the rotating wheel, and the side of the tire just bored a hole in my right leg, and there was nothing I could do as it was jammed there from the pressure of the other body parts all trying to preserve balance on the bogey. Several stitches for that. Stitches meant scars, and scars were badges of honor to be displayed from time to time whenever we were trying to impress a new visitor to our part of the universe.

Before our family began taking annual holidays at the seaside we always spent a couple of weeks each summer at Grandma Watson's house at 23 Ferry Road Avenue, Edinburgh. I remember meeting an American girl on holiday there, whose mother had married an American soldier and moved from Edinburgh to Memphis, Tennessee. Her name was Kay Dinkins, and to this awkward and shy young lad from Falkirk she was like something out of a movie. She was pretty, with long blonde hair, and a way of speaking that was radically different from the vernacular sing song of a Falkirk Bairn. Nothing ever came of it, not even a Valentine card. It would be thirty years or so later that I took my own pretty blonde daughters from Virginia to Scotland on holiday, and they probably had to run the gauntlet with the local boys somewhere along the line.

It may be that the speech impediment in the form of a lisp that I had for the first ten years of my life trumped my otherwise adequate appeal. Anytime I said a word with the letter "s" it came out sounding like the letters "th", and it was a pretty daunting disability for a would-be Lothario from the Bog Road. Fortunately, my school saw fit to organize one-on-one speech therapy for me every Thursday afternoon, and Mrs. Robertson was able to cure me by the time I got to High School.

Every housing scheme had its gang culture, and we were fortunate to live around the corner from one of the most notorious families in our town. The two youngest boys, Angus and Balfour, were close to us in age and for years we played together with our other contemporaries and managed to stay out of serious trouble. Crime for us meant stealing apples from gardens, turnips from the farmer, trespassing on farmland everywhere around, and playing cards for pennies, which was technically gambling. We were arrested only once, so I can't claim to have much of a criminal record. The older brothers, however, were well known to the local constabulary, and we younger lads sheltered behind their reputation, making sure that everyone knew that we were protected by the gang. Billy, the second eldest son, was often in serious trouble with the law. He was a "Teddy Boy" and dressed accordingly, with a long jacket, thick suede shoes, and Elvis style slicked back hair. Razor blades (the old fashioned kind) were the weapon of choice, and fights against other gangs were nasty affairs. However, even in this far corner of the Bog Road, a confrontation between the Soviet Union and Hungary would have repercussions, and at least temporarily upset the balance of power in the community.

The arrival of dozens of refugees in 1957 was a memorable event in the life of our town. What began as a student uprising in Hungary caused the pro-Soviet government to fail. For a few months in 1956 it looked as if Hungary would withdraw from the Warsaw Pact, and sever its political links to the Soviet regime. However, the Soviet President, Khrushchev, after initially sending accommodating signals to the Hungarians, ordered the tanks into Hungary on November 4, 1956. By January 1957 it was all over, and a new pro-Soviet government was in power. Thousands of Hungarians were displaced by the armed conflict, most of whom were young men. The British Government offered temporary asylum to the refugees, pending their absorption by other, mainly Commonwealth, countries, such as Canada and Australia. Suddenly the old Army Camp through the tunnel was temporary home to dozens of young Hungarian refugees, in their teens and early twenties, and each of them was provided with a brand new racing bike as a welcoming gift from the people of Falkirk. My sister Connie was the first of our household to register dissent and prejudice, as she would look up the street towards the tunnel for any sign of them entering the Bog Road, and when she saw them she would rush into the house, screaming "the Hungarians are coming" and head for her hidey hole in the cupboard under the stair.

Although there was lots of goodwill initially towards these young men, the language difficulties were hard to overcome, and communication was all but impossible. Natives of Falkirk have their own brand of the English language, so even for those Hungarians with a command of English, there was no way for them to connect our pronunciations and colloquialisms and make sense of it. The ways of romance, however, can find expression even when words fail, and the only population group in Falkirk that formed relationships with the Hungarians was the young women of the town. This was also a time when the country of Hungary had some of the best and most famous football players in the world, so the newcomers were able to outplay the locals in sport as well as love. This did not go down well, and there gradually built up a real animosity between the various Falkirk gangs and the Hungarians. Billy and his gang had a number of skirmishes with them, but eventually matters came to a head with a fight that saw Billy's gang and another local gang unite in opposition to the visitors. It was mayhem in a cow pasture, and Billy was badly beaten up after a number of his allies fled the field, thereby aligning himself by legend with the Scots Army of Sir William Wallace at the Battle of

Falkirk in 1298, who suffered a similar let down by his allies. Billy's short but infamous life was brought to a sad end when he died in a fire at the house when he was in his early twenties.

The illegal activities of our own group of kids were rather tame compared with those of the Teddy Boys around Falkirk. Corn fields are an amazing venue in which to play, given the scope for what seems harmless destruction of some long grass. About six of us were cornered by two policemen as we were running through a fully ripened field of corn, making tracks just for kicks, and putting a dent in the crop yield of the local farmer. We were all charged with the appropriate category of offence, and I learned later that the menu of choices for the Procurator Fiscal when contemplating the charge is long, impressive, and a bit scary. I had to go home and fess up, and I suspect I got a taste of physical medicine from Dad, which didn't happen often but when it did it made a mark. As trial day approached I succumbed to a strange illness, breaking out in all sorts of sores around my face and neck. A visit to the Doctor's office rendered a diagnosis of Impetigo, which has always seemed to me to have a name more threatening than the disease itself. The treatment was a liberal application of a purple medication that had the required effect on my face. It turned purple, and stayed that way for several days due to regular and comprehensive application. Anyway, I was quarantined for a week or so, which happened to be when I was due at Court with my fellow reprobates. My Mum was advised to deliver a Doctor's Certificate to the Magistrate so that I could be tried "in absentia". This is, I believe, the only thing that I have in common with the Great Train Robbers. Word came back that we were all "Admonished", which essentially meant that we were let off with a warning not to do it again. This was still the time when telephones only lived in telephone boxes, rarely in houses, so the word got to me by sign language when the lads came off the bus and ran by my window with their thumbs up in the direction of my purple face. My pals quickly converted their thumbs ups to pointing fingers, and had a group laugh at the invidious condition of their mate.

Ian and I decided to clean up our act, and joined the local Wolf Cub group, the 40th Stirlingshire. Weekly meetings were held in a church hall and we both enjoyed the regimentation, and the chance to wear a Cub cap, similar to a baseball cap, and a green kerchief round the neck. The whole point of the Wolf Cubs was to groom young lads for graduation into the ranks of the Boy Scouts within a couple of years. This was never part of our mission, and the lightly regulated Cubs were all Ian and I needed to acquire a sense of pride and accomplishment, and a chance once a week to bring some mirth and disorganization to the troop. We began by standing at attention for an inspection by the Troop Leader, a fellow Bog Road resident with the famous name of Jim Bowie, who had an impressive steel knife in his belt, as if to make folk wonder if he was the real thing. As we stood at attention I realized that I had a wad of chewing gum in my mouth, at maximum pliability. I quickly removed it and stuck it behind my ear, but not quickly enough to escape the attention of our distinguished commander. I had also managed to get the gum tangled in the short hair sticking out from my Cub cap, but this proved no obstacle, as he removed his knife and cut away the offending corsage. Apart from my infatuation with the teenage female Cub Leader (Akela) that is as much as I remember about the Cubs.

We had a death in the family that came out of the blue, when my not yet teenage cousin Bobby McGee died, in Edinburgh. He was the only son of my Mum's sister Rita and my Uncle Bobby, and a brother of Fiona and Connie. Such a bright young lad who was full of promise, yet for him the bell tolled, as it sometimes does, for no good reason.

On the other side of the bus station in the center of town was an old street that succumbed to a shopping development a long time ago, but in those days (the mid fifties), was the location of the Roxy, Falkirk's only live theatre. This was the scene of a continuing attempt on the world record for non-stop playing of a piano by a man from Bolton, Lancashire who went by the stage name of "Syncopating Sandy." At a time when television was still a rather rare commodity in the homes of the good people of Falkirk, here was a chance to see some real live entertainment. Ian and I made our way to the Roxy one afternoon, but lacking the sixpence to gain admission we had to be content with listening to the sound of Syncopating Sandy's piano from the loudspeakers positioned near the theater door. Naturally, we all wondered how he managed to keep playing and still attend to the call of Mother Nature, and allegedly he had a one armed assistant who, on hearing Sandy play "Lady of Spain" would draw the curtain with his one arm to shield Sandy from the audience, while he attended to his needs. Of course, he continued playing the piano while all this was going on, and eventually the one armed assistant would open the curtain again, and there was Sandy, syncopating away, and never a lost note. Rumor had it that the assistant actually had his second arm hidden in his loose clothing, and that he would take over playing for Sandy for the duration until Sandy made it back to the piano. This also held true for sleep breaks in the night. Anyway, it was fun to hang around the Roxy and listen to the patter of the local worthies against the background of a tinkling piano that just never stopped.

Something very rare happened to our small town in 1957. The local First Division football team, Falkirk FC, won the Scottish Cup, for only the second time in our history. It was in 1913 that we first won the trophy, which has a huge pedigree as a measure of achievement by the winner. It is the oldest national sports competition in the world, and is the same trophy that was awarded to the first winner in 1874. I listened to the last few minutes of the Cup Final with the bus driver and conductress who were on a ten minute break, wishing I was one of the 80,000 fans who attended the match at Hampden Park in Glasgow. Later that week the team bus went on parade in the streets of Falkirk, and when the bus stopped across from our house Dad lifted Connie up to kiss the Cup. Even today the memory of that occasion lives on through the playtime sessions that I have with my grandson Graysen, here in America. When I give him the cue, he follows me with the words as I say the names of all the eleven players who represented Falkirk that day, and then when I ask, "who was the twelfth man?" (i.e. substitute, on the bench) he yells out "McIntosh!" Of course he is correct, as it was Ian McIntosh who had the unenviable task of sitting on the bench while his team-mates had the day of their lives. Ian McIntosh died while I was writing this story, but Graysen and I will make sure his memory lives on.

In my final year of primary school I actually had an official girlfriend, a classmate Margaret Benwell. After several months of general acknowledgement of our unrequited love, we shared my first kiss

### THE BOG, THE BAHAMAS, AND BEYOND

(it may not have been hers) at the back of a tenement building near school. My pal Ian was, as always, right by my side, as he had been elevated to boyfriend status by another Margaret who lived in that same tenement. Margaret Benwell was a class act even then, and she went on to become the Dux Medal winner for academic achievement at our school. However, this meant that she was headed for Falkirk High School, whereas I was destined for the lesser academic campus of Graeme High. I entered Graeme High footloose and fancy free, along with a whole new community of female classmates from all around our town. The future suddenly seemed brighter.

By 1958 the Hunter family was almost fully assembled, although it would be another two years before the birth of Lorna, the sixth and final child. Rena and I had been joined by our sister Elizabeth (Betty) in 1947, and then Constance (Connie) in 1953. Dad was out at 7am for his work as a plasterer and would get back around 7pm. Most of the time he worked in a neighboring town, Stirling, and his working conditions left much to be desired. His bench was in a large unheated shed with open doors at either end to allow access to the lesser skilled workers who would mix the sand and concrete to produce cement, which Dad would form into sills and other construction parts for residential housing. He was rarely unemployed, and I can only remember one time, around Christmas, when he was out of work for a few weeks. He never drank during the week, and always drank at weekends, in common with most of the working class men in town. Friday and Saturday nights were reserved for the local pubs, where he would meet his pals, all childhood friends who would grow old together, and drink pints of beer, the occasional shot of whisky, and play dominoes. He would stop off at Tony's Fish and Chip shop on the way home and bring in fish suppers and chips to assuage somewhat for his usual inebriated condition. The drinking would cause arguments on a fairly regular basis, and we kids just learned to put up with it. I remember so many times lying in bed listening to the arguments from downstairs, with occasional threats on either side to leave, and yet we kids never talked about it among ourselves. It was something that we all dealt with on the inside.

Grannie and Pop Hunter lived close enough and spent time with us often enough that I must have loved them both with an emotion that I may not have realized at the time. We were not a family who expressed love for each other by saying so. It is such a long way from the way my own children were raised here in America, when the words "I love you" were, and are, part of our daily vocabulary. I don't think we were different from anyone one else at the time growing up in Scotland, and it may be there is something in our national temperament that made us that way. The most important three words in the world were rarely said, and confined to Valentine's day cards, thereby giving much more weight to the emotion of romantic love, rather than familial. I am still a bit bemused here in America when Valentine cards are sent to family members as well as friends, but I must say that there is nothing more profound than these three words from someone you love. Many years ago I began to say these words to my mum, and my siblings, and it has been a bit of an uphill battle getting the same response.

I know how much I must have loved Grannie and Pop Hunter because of the grief I felt when they died, during my second year at Graeme High School, in 1960. Pop died of heart failure and was buried on a Friday afternoon at Falkirk Cemetery, in the family burial plot. Two Fridays later Grannie Hunter was buried in the same plot, having collapsed and died in our house just a few days before. I can still hear my Dad's voice breaking as he held her after a fall down the stairs in our house, where she was staying. I was a designated Pall Bearer for her, as I was for Pop, but I was too overcome with emotion to go to the graveside. The family grief was shared with my cousins from the High Bog, which is where Uncle Harry and Auntie Isa lived, with our cousins Harry, Barbara, and Robert.

It seems to me that the emotional bonds of our family relationships are somehow segmented by time and circumstance, and I can easily put all of my thoughts and memories of my grandparents into a neat parcel that is filled with about fifteen years of my life. It is a simple story with few moving parts, and yet it provides such contentment in the odd moments that I enter that world. The two shillings and sixpence that Pop slipped into my hand every Saturday morning after a bike trip to see them was a gift of a scarce resource, when everything

◄ THE BOG, THE BAHAMAS, AND BEYOND

they owned was inside the walls of their council house, and in their pockets. The emotional value of those memories is for me, priceless.

It is impossible to contemplate my formative years of family relationships without reference to the physical context of our life in and around our home town. Falkirk people enjoy being from Falkirk. It may be that life has found them in some other part of the country, the continent, or the globe, but there is something about Falkirk that sticks. The people of Falkirk are known as "Bairns" which in the Scots vernacular means "children." The appellation stems from an event that allegedly took place in our "Burgh" in the late 17th century, with the construction of a well in the center of town to provide water "to the Wives and Bairns of Falkirk." The construction and gift of the well, supplying running water that was conveyed on a line of wooden water pipes joined by lead, is attributed to the Earl of Callender, James Livingstone, whose estates are to the south and east of the town. However, the well was opened in 1681, several years after the death of the good Earl, but it makes for a better story so the legend remains extant.

Falkirk is a pleasant enough town on the eye, but was not always so, particularly when the smokestacks and foundries sprang up to surround the town center during the Industrial Revolution of the 18th and 19th centuries. My childhood in the Bog Road coincided with the transformation of the town to more of a light industrial base, and the old factories were gradually converted to whatever topical use could be made of them, or demolished by Pete Buchanan's demolition company, whose motto was "here today, gone tomorrow." It was the development of government sponsored housing schemes after World War Two that defined the current topography of the town. While there are pockets of gentrification throughout, it is the large housing "schemes" that give Falkirk its character, and a reservoir of working class families from which the later generations of more upwardly mobile Falkirk "Bairns" emanate. As a young lad growing up in the fifties there was a pecking order of workmen that was observed in our neighborhood. The lowest of those was the Pig's Meat Collector, and it was his job to drive his truck around our scheme once a week to empty the bins that each household maintained as a repository of all residual food leavings and parts that survived the dinner table. We all observed this form of recycling, although we didn't recognize it as such at the time. The slops were trucked to the Piggery, which was about half a mile away on the other side of the railroad track. At a slightly higher level of community presence was the Dustman, known colloquially as a "Scaffy" – short for Scavenger – and an employee of the Town Council. The Scaffies would tour the Bog once a week to empty the rubbish bins, and were generally looked down upon by the very consumers that they served. Another notch up the social scale was the Milkman, who was about the streets in the early hours every morning, picking up empties and leaving a fresh and much needed contribution to the health and welfare of the citizens. The milk runs were finely tuned examples of a repetitive distribution system that exceeded the efficiency of German trains. You could set your clock to the time of morning that your particular house was served, but the early wake-up call from the clinking and clanking of the bottles elicited many a curse from a sleeping resident of the Bog, whose alcohol inspired repose was interrupted. The Window Cleaner was the other of the common service workers who were denoted as less worthy than the everyday residents, and he would show up once every two or three weeks and make his way along the streets and up and down his ladders. Although self employed, he got no shrift from the mostly stay at home women who were able to afford a few shillings a month for his labors. It may be that because he was always looking in other people's windows, there was a distinct community bias against him. The men didn't trust him, and he did "women's work," so this was not someone who merited a beer and a conversation in the local pub. Other than those four grades of trades, everyone else was pretty much on the same level, and were mostly Trade's Union Members, and voted for the Labour (Socialist) Party.

While school and football took up most of my time as a young lad, I was also able to participate in some of the other pastimes that were generally available as a curriculum option in the school of life that was the Bog Road in the late fifties. We all had some money around us most of the time, whether it was left over from pocket money or otherwise acquired from siblings or a visiting relative, it being the custom

## THE BOG, THE BAHAMAS, AND BEYOND

for adults to slip a sixpence or two to nieces and nephews at the end of a visit. This enabled most of the young lads of the Bog to participate from time to time in gambling sessions that were held in various sites in and around the edges of the housing scheme. Our home ground was by the side of a stream in a small access field through the tunnel, and distant pals from around the Bog Road would know to find us there on a regular basis, ready to deal them in. A formidable stake was around two shillings in value, and with the then currency denominated in pounds, shillings, and pence, and various subdivisions of actual coinage, the clinking and jangling from the pockets of our blue jeans spoke to the several means by which the money was acquired. Thus a stake of two shillings, which could be represented by a single coin, instead was likely composed of something along the lines of seven pennies, four halfpennies, three threepenny bits, and a silver sixpence. The card game of choice was either Three Card Brag, or Pontoon, which were simplified versions of Poker and Blackjack (Twenty One) respectively. A typical individual stake was a penny, and while fortunes were neither won nor lost, there was a lot of pride in being seen to be a decent card player. If playing Pontoon, a much desired hand of the first two cards dealt were those that added to eleven, thereby setting up the hand to be blessed by the subsequent draw of a ten, or any face card, which had a value of ten in this particular game. The odds of drawing a ten and so hitting twenty one were pretty good if you were lucky enough to be dealt eleven, and in the language of the streets the owner of two drawn cards adding to eleven were said to have been given "The Wire." One of the neighboring villages at the other end of town was Carronshore, and in the normal way of things we tended to look down on the local villagers, to whom we attributed a communal faculty of being not too clever. One way of portraying this obvious character flaw was to designate a total of twelve from the first two cards drawn as being the "Carronshore Wire," which was a rather subtle put down on the arithmetical capabilities of our fellow gamblers from the other side of town. I have since played Blackjack in Casinos from Nassau to Hong Kong, and have drawn more than my share of Carronshore Wires.

Dad was also a boxing fan, and I vividly recall as a nine year old getting up at around three in the morning so that I could listen on the radio to a world heavyweight boxing championship fight between Don Cockell of England and Rocky Marciano of the United States. Rocky won, as he always did, but we all believed it was because he used head-butts in the clinch. For all the times that Dad's drinking brought unhappiness and stress to the family, there were so many more times of happiness and pleasure from the life we led. In the days before TV was ubiquitous, the normal weekday evening was spent together around the fireplace, and our favorite game was "Questions" where we were challenged by Dad on general knowledge. He seemed to know so much, even though he had at best a modest education. We all did our homework in the living room, on the floor, whereas today's kids need lap tops and elbow room. There was always some money found by summertime to enable us to rent a caravan or a holiday chalet in one of the seaside resorts in the Kingdom of Fife, a rather salubrious name for a Scottish county that had farm fields, beaches, quaint little fishing villages, and the home of golf, St. Andrews. After throwing the ritual pennies out the train window on the way across the Forth Bridge, we would arrive at Kinghorn or St. Andrews and make our way to our chalet or caravan. The pleasure was in the simplicity. We would swim around the rocks and coves in the chilly waters of the North Sea by day, visit the amusement park at night, and meals were whenever and wherever. Mum would often send Betty and me out to a nearby field to harvest enough potatoes for the evening meal.

Many years later, while I was working in the bank in Richmond, Virginia, I was introduced to a Scottish visitor who had a connection with a local company. John Purvis and I struck up a friendship, and kept in touch for many years. My wife Ann and I plus our two young girls were visiting John and his wife Louise for afternoon tea while in Scotland on vacation, at their family estate at Gilmerton next to St. Andrews. After a while, John took me on a walking tour of his estate, and as he was pointing to the various fields and meadows, or "policies" as they are known in Scotland, I noticed that they backed up to the caravan site at Kinkell Braes, our childhood vacation spot. Sure enough, his potato fields were right where they used to be forty years before, in striking distance of the caravan site. I did not have

# THE BOG, THE BAHAMAS, AND BEYOND

the gumption to tell John of how well I actually knew his fields, but when I told my Mum later she had a good laugh. John entered politics and was a Conservative Member of the European Parliament for many years, but now is a gentleman farmer. I hope his potato yields have improved.

The closest pub to our home was the Mill Inn, and it would eventually become my Dad's local tavern of choice, being a mile or two closer to home than his former haunts in and around Dalderse Avenue. The Mill Inn on a Saturday night is not for the faint of heart. The patrons are all local to our part of town, and arrive with the same agenda, namely, to have a right good bellyful of beer and / or whisky, and to engage in conversation with their pals. The language is blue, it being a convention in Scottish pubs, at least in the Public Bar area for profanity to be quite acceptable in the normal course of conversation. The Mill Inn is a neighborhood ecosystem of language and rhetoric writ small. I have observed (and participated) in scenes like these in many Scottish pubs, but not with the abandon and commitment of a Mill Inn regular to the sacred art of conversation. Here lives the species of the specious argument.

I often stop in at the Mill Inn on my trips back to Falkirk, and the last time I went there took the biscuit. It was a quiet Thursday afternoon around 4pm so the bar was beginning to get busy, when a patron came through the door and stepped up to the bar next to where I was standing. When the bartender turned to him, he immediately began to imitate someone ringing a bell, then he put his hands in the prayer position and acted out a diving motion. The bartender poured him a Bell's Scotch whisky, and added water, which the customer accepted with a silent nod of approval. It suddenly became clear to me that the customer was dumb and could not speak, and had ordered his drink by miming. I can't wait for my next trip home, and my obligatory visit to the Mill Inn to see life in the Falkirk style.

In 1960, I bought a new bicycle, on a hire purchase arrangement, paid for weekly by my earnings as a newspaper delivery boy. The bike cost thirty six pounds. It so happened that my Dad was in the process of buying a second hand car, and so we all gathered around to inspect this 1939 Ford Anglia, for which he had paid twenty nine pounds. Our sister Lorna was born shortly thereafter, and the family was now complete at eight Hunters, so while the car was an immediate object of envy in the neighborhood, it didn't do much for the family unit. First off, Dad had a provisional licence so could not drive solo. Secondly, the car was literally idle. It would rev up wonderfully well in the idle position, but when the gear was engaged, the engine was somehow unhappy to be summoned, and responded by not responding. If it sounds as if the car had a personality of its own, then you are beginning to get the idea. When it was time for our annual jaunt to St. Andrews we piled into the car, with Mum in the front passenger seat pretending to be the licence holder, and my Dad in control of the wheel but not the back seat of the car, where six of us including the baby were trying to get comfortable for the two hour journey. In the midst of our two week stay the household ran out of money, so Mum and Dad left us to it and made a return trip to Falkirk to acquire sufficient funds for the balance of the holiday, probably thanks to a loan from Uncle Harry back in the Bog Road. Once again they ran the gauntlet of illegal driving, and though it would barely make misdemeanor in any respectable American county, in Scotland in those days it was a serious offence to drive without a license.

The caravan sites were full of all shapes and sizes of caravan accommodation, and there was always a sense of excitement as we meandered through our site, trying to locate our home for the next two weeks. It mattered not how cramped our allotted space was - we claimed it as our own and made the most of it. In subsequent years, I vacationed all over the world, on the best beaches, in exotic landscapes, in the lap of luxury, but it is hard to top the Kingdom of Fife in the first two weeks in August all those years ago. It was wonderful.

I never did avail myself of the opportunities to play golf as a child, as there was only ever one sport for me. That sport was football. The love of the national game is no different if you are an American kid playing baseball, a Canadian kid playing ice hockey, or a wee boy from Falkirk playing football. It is an obsession for most of the male members of society in the UK, and an increasing proportion of the female population. I dreamt about becoming a professional player, and playing for Scotland, as did all my pals. Organized football began at primary school, with the school team normally composed of eleven year old boys in the final year. Victoria School was my first real team, with an actual strip (uniform) and a coach. We won our league, got to play at a professional stadium in the Cup Final, and I won my first Cup Winners medal. I managed to get selected for the County squad, and our team won the Wilson Trophy, which was the Scottish Cup of Primary School football. However, I may have been good but I was not good enough. My close pals Ian Laurie, Charlie Smith, and Jim McLay were all signed by our local professional team, Falkirk FC. Charlie in particular had a few years as a playing professional in the Scottish Premier League, and finished his career in Australia. Ian played for a number of local professional teams, and eventually moved to South Africa, where he was a player and a coach. Jim had a few games as a professional, and then went on to work for a bank in London. Football was for them, as it was for me, a life-long love affair. With a house full of sisters I would never have a problem finding one of them willing to shine up my boots before my weekend games. My subsequent involvement with the beautiful game as an active player would last until age 60, when I played my last game at a five a side competition organized by my wife Ann and our daughter Shona. I even remember with clarity my first injury, which occurred in 1959 at an away game in a small village called Alva at the foot of the Ochil Hills. We played on the public park, and during the course of the game I had to run about thirty yards or so to retrieve the ball for a throw in. A local dog had taken up the chase after the ball, and promptly bit me in the leg for spoiling his recreation. I was quickly taken to Stirling Royal Infirmary for medication and stitches, while the rest of my team-mates got on with the game. I subsequently played competitive soccer for fifty years, and had no serious injuries, so it turned out to be a false omen.

Academically, I did well enough at school, always in the top classes but never among the top students. High School began at 6th grade, and I was entered by my parents in Graeme High School, where I again made the top classes during my four years there. In the Summer of 1962, three months shy of my sixteenth birthday, I stepped out into the world ready to get a job, and be somebody. Actually, that is probably overstated, as I did not have enough self confidence then to think about being somebody. The usual outcome of a boy with reasonable grades and a four year education was to become an apprentice to one of the trades to be found in the many local industries. I had already given up my paper round to become a butcher boy, which really involved cleaning the shop after it closed each day, and delivering fresh butcher meat to our customers first thing in the morning. I had a special bicycle which had a square frame built at the front of the bike that would hold a large basket filled with packages of meat for delivery. It was good pocket money, and I liked the work, but I left the shop the same week I left school, ready to find full time employment. My dad had already made inroads on my behalf with a local TV repair shop that would be taking on a couple of apprentices in the summer. However, my older sister Rena, on break from Edinburgh University had found a summer job with a local bank, and told Dad that she thought it would be a good job for me, with the prospect of lifetime employment.

I duly sent off written applications to the head offices of all five Scottish banks, for which my four "Ordinary" level certificates from Graeme High School were the minimum qualification needed. Four of the five banks responded in the negative, including Rena's bank, but for some reason the Royal Bank of Scotland invited me to sit an entrance exam, at the local branch. I duly showed up for the test, and was led to a seat in the kitchen area of the bank. The Accountant (usually the number two person in the branch) stopped by to prepare his soup for lunch. He looked over my shoulder and saw that I was having problems with business abbreviations - something not typically encountered by a young lad from the Bog Road. He identified C.A. as Chartered Accountant, and suggested another couple of corrections to my work. Somehow between us I did enough to pass, and when the letter came to our house there was happiness in the family. I was told to report to The Royal Bank of Scotland, 2 High Street, Falkirk, on July 16, 1962, and to wear suitable clothing. Dad was required to accompany me so that he could sign a fidelity bond in the event that I made off with the bank's money, as I was not yet of legal age.

This was the time in my life when my childhood ended, and I stepped into the adult world with an educational level that had

## THE BOG, THE BAHAMAS, AND BEYOND

somehow enabled me to get a foothold in a real job, notionally above my station in life. With an annual salary of two hundred and twenty pounds from which I could now contribute to the family household, I was just another wee boy from the Bog Road that had found a way up, if not yet out. The Russian word for God is "Bog" and when that obtuse fact came to my attention in my later life, I would draw the appropriate conclusion that life in the Bog was indeed Heaven.

CHAPTER 5

# The Young Banker

I REMEMBER THE seat on the bus as if it were yesterday. I also remember vividly taking home my own set of keys to the bank and proudly showing them to my siblings, as if it somehow put me closer to the money in the safe. These were the days when the bank manager was a pillar of the local community, and a leader among the business community in town. He approved all of the loans, and merely reported them to head office once a week. My manager, Mr. Swanson, was intimidating to customers and staff alike, but I always found him to be fair and reasonable. He signed his name with a flourish, and finished with two small dots. I was easily impressed. To this day, I have two small dots after my signature, and now my daughter Cassie does it. Banking for me was the best job that I could imagine. My first job was to sit inside an electronic ledger posting machine, and record all the credits and debits to the customer ledger. Then, in the late afternoon I would take all of the day's checks to Mr. Swanson, and he would look at every one, noting who they were payable to, and for how much. In the UK banking system checks can legally overdraw a bank account and create an automatic loan, so if the customer had an approved overdraft limit then there was no problem. In the absence of a limit, then the bank manager had to make a decision about whether or not to pay the check, or bounce it back through the system. Knowing to whom the money was being paid was a form of due diligence, so a check to a pharmacy had a better chance of payment than one to a bookmaker. Hence the daily review by the manager.

### THE BOG, THE BAHAMAS, AND BEYOND

In those days Scotland had five "Clearing" banks, all of which issued their own currency, so at all times there were five different banknotes in circulation, in various denominations, plus notes issued by the Bank of England. Twice a week representatives from the banks met in a secure room and swapped their respective bank notes with each other. The bundles had all to be checked by hand, and so there developed in Scotland a unique way of counting twenty bank notes at a time, by folding them over one hand and flicking them with the index finger of the other hand. I was made to practice this using cut up newspaper, and quickly became proficient, to where I could flick three fingers at a time and count twenty notes in about three seconds. My fellow apprentice Bill McKay joined two weeks after me, and so we were joint equal at the bottom of the food chain. Bill eventually became the head foreign exchange dealer for the Royal Bank, and now we occasionally meet in Naples, Florida, where he has a vacation home. But back then, the ring of the wall telephone in the ledger posting room was one of the first things I had to deal with. Never having had a phone at home, I was terrified to answer it, and would always try to find a reason for someone else to take the call.

Being moved around local branches was part of the apprenticeship program, so within a year I was transferred to the branch in Bo'ness, about five miles from the bus stop at the end of our road. This was a small four person office, and when I met with the manager, Mr. Philp, he explained that I was responsible for lighting the coal fire each morning, while he made the tea. That was the deal. I spent a happy twelve months to the day in Bo'ness, doing book-keeping, handling cash, acting as teller on occasion, and any other task that befitted the low man on the totem pole. Bo'ness was at the eastern end of the Antonine Wall, and so would have been an encampment of some significance during the Roman occupation almost two millennia ago. These must have been the glory days, as there was not much going on when I worked there. Life was simple. I used to take my lunchtime sandwich and flask of soup to a seat by the old harbor, which was no longer operational, and read my library books. I was at a stage in life when my sense of patriotism was emerging from some inner compulsion, which had only previously happened when Scotland was

# THE YOUNG BANKER

playing England at football. Robert Burns, Scotland's national poet, was required reading for anyone with Scottish blood in his veins, but not content with his poetry I had to know more about Robert Burns the man. There is a series of books (five in all) by James Barke on the life of Burns, and they are a must read for those interested in the life of "The Bard", as he is known in Scotland. I devoured them.

As a young man of seventeen years, I had the fairer sex firmly in my sights, and my girlfriend of the time, Monica Lehman, had been a feature of my life since high school. She lived in the nearby village of Maddiston, and I was a regular visitor to her home. It was through her father, Willy Lehman, that I developed a keen interest in politics, to the point of joining the library and reading all sorts of books and articles about political economy. This was co-incident with my part time studies for the Banking Institute exams, so to some extent was another expression of an awakening interest in my own intellectual development, such that I was a much better student after I left school than I was before. Willy was born in a part of Poland that was annexed by the USSR, and had escaped by train, eventually making his way to Scotland and a job in Kinneil Colliery in Bo'ness. He was a fascinating man, and whatever it was that inspired his belief in communism, it was manifest in his eyes, his voice, and his logic when he talked about it. I was at an impressionable age and absorbed all of it, although I was very much a closet communist, since I was the only one that knew it. I can't recall a single overt move on my part that would have registered my political persuasion with anyone else, but to me it was real, and my way of supporting the cause was through books and articles, nothing in the least extraneous. The eventual break up with Monica inevitably led to a lessening of my political convictions, and somewhere along the way my interest in the politics of social welfare was subsumed by the demands of my job, my pals, and the social backdrop of the sixties. It was a great time to be young, and it would have been around this time that I saw the monthly ads in the Banking Magazine with a call to young bankers to "Go East, young man", and wondered if this was a path open to me once I passed my exams. The East in question was mainly the Middle East and India, where the banking systems were dominated by British owned banks, a product

### THE BOG, THE BAHAMAS, AND BEYOND

of Britain's colonial heritage. I would eventually heed the call, but in the opposite direction, to the Western Hemisphere. For now, my dreams were no more than just that.

Exactly twelve months later I was transferred again, to a larger branch in the town of Bathgate, West Lothian. It was in Bathgate that I saw for the first time how adverse economic conditions can proscribe the progress of a community. It was amazing how a small town, only a few miles away from my own, could be so different. High unemployment, no jobs for the young, for-sale signs everywhere, and entire factories in shutters. The mid-sixties in Scotland were economically challenging. The traditional industries were coal-mining, ship-building, steel, and heavy and light manufacturing. Central economic policy was to maintain a strong currency, and the pound was pegged at a rate that was not reflective of economic reality. Wages were high relative to other countries. Prices were high so that exports were falling. Because the pound was unrealistically high, imports were relatively cheap, and we were having a party not knowing that we were about to run out of booze. Coal mines were closing across central Scotland. Shipyards were being de-commissioned, and the entire manufacturing sector was in a slump. The Bathgate truck and tractor manufacturing plant of British Leyland Motors had just been shut down, and the Bathgate area was a rust belt thirty years before the term was even recognized in America. The local branch was located in Hopetoun Street, and never a place so aptly named. I still go to the branch now and then, more for nostalgia than any financial need, given the ubiquity of cash machines. Our vacation home in retirement is an apartment in a medieval castle, about two miles outside Bathgate. I now take my daily jog along quiet country roads that were once served by Alexander's Buses, and carried a young lad to and from work in Bathgate, dreaming about the future, and not knowing that he was already there. How strange.

After a few months in Bathgate I had a call from Bill McKay, who told me that he had been transferred to the main office of the bank in London. He would henceforth be working in the International Trade Department, on the "Inward Bills" desk, which had to do with Bills of Exchange, and other esoteric trade instruments, that would soon be

# THE YOUNG BANKER

displaced by technology. However, from that point on, Bill McKay was known as "Inward" Bill, and a more outgoing inward you could never hope to meet. Bill is a livewire, and it wasn't but a few days later when I decided that I should put in for a transfer to London, and catch up with Bill in the journey of life. My Mum and Dad were, in retrospect, surprisingly supportive, so I told my manager in Bathgate that I would like a transfer, and within a few weeks I was heading for The Royal Bank of Scotland, 97 New Bond Street, in the heart of the West End of London. All of the members of the "Temperance Seven" were there to see me off at the train station, as by this time Ian and I had managed to accumulate five other best friends along the way. Our café of choice in town had been the headquarters of the Falkirk Temperance Society in Victorian times, dedicated to keeping working men of Falkirk apart from the demon alcohol. My pals, plus an assorted bevy of local girls that were part of our entourage, saw me off in good style. My then girl-friend, Nancy Laurie, was still at High School, so the move to London was pretty much a relationship breaker.

My year in London was simply terrific. I moved in with Bill to a flat in Streatham, and spent the first Friday evening at the corner pub, drinking Coke and listening to the sing-a-long in the crowded bar. Shortly thereafter I discovered beer, and found that the sing-a-long was even better. I quickly settled in to life in the "Big Smoke." Every morning I would get the commuter train to Victoria Station, walk past Buckingham Palace, cross Green Park, and walk on up to the office in New Bond Street. The Royal Bank had seven branches in London, and there were somewhere around thirty or so young Scots bankers like me, all away from home for the first time, and determined to get the best of the experience. We were all buddies after a while, and within a month I had signed up as a Territorial Army private in the "London Scottish," a famous regiment in British military history because of their heroics on the front line of the First World War, in France and Belgium. For some reason it had become the tradition for young Royal Bankers in London to enlist in the Regiment. Thereafter, the British Government knew me as "Hunter, Private, 24054808" and I became proficient at shooting blanks out of a World War One Self Loading Rifle. It turned out that a two week fire fighting course in Wiltshire

### THE BOG, THE BAHAMAS, AND BEYOND

was mandatory, interrupted by evening marches along the hills and dales of England's West Country, and as we were actually being paid to do this it was all too good to be true. Some of the guys lived in a flat above the New Bond Street office, and were on the way home one evening when two men came running up the street with policemen chasing them. With no other thought than "country first" the lads gave chase, and Lt. Eric Osman caught up with one of the runners and wrestled him to the ground as the police arrived. Unfortunately Eric had just tackled the plain clothes detective. There was no long term damage to his career, however, as Eric stayed in the Territorial Army all his working life, retired as Lt. Colonel of the Regiment, and every year he is invited to dinner at Balmoral Castle, the Queen's summer home in Scotland. Meanwhile at the office I was relishing my new work experiences and my new work-mates, most of whom happened to be cute young London girls, in an era of mini-skirts and not much else. My assigned desk was in the Securities department, and it was this area of specialization that would later enable me to get a work permit for a job in Nassau, Bahamas.

Within a few months I had reached an acceptable level of competence on the Securities desk, and I was able to step in and run it when the manager was out sick for a while. The bank provided help in the form of a trainee, who was being sent around various departments as a learning experience prior to being elected to the Board of Directors of the Royal Bank. This was someone in a different socio-economic league than the rest of us. He was the son of a Duke, and so his title was Viscount, and he would one day succeed his father in the Dukedom of the ancient family seat in Scotland. This would entitle him to a seat on the board of the bank. He was a pleasant fellow, a few years older than I, and he carried his public school heritage and aristocratic persona like a blinking light, letting folks ahead of him know that he was coming through, and not to be stalled in his journey through life. The awkwardness of how to address him was felt by all the staff, but for some reason I got away with calling him "Bush". It was a silly name of the times, although it has hung around me all my life, and even now, I still use it. It was a shared nickname, as use of it entitled the other person to respond to you as "Bush". He seemed to

## THE YOUNG BANKER

thrive on it, and would throw it right back at me by saying "Bush, old chap" prior to conversation.

I was able to link up with the rest of the Temperance Seven for two weeks in July at a vacation cabin in the seaside town of Clacton, on the Essex coast of England. These were the early days of Mods and Rockers - gangs of guys with short hair on Lambretta or Vespa motor scooters vying for attention with gangs of long haired motorcycle bikers. We belonged to neither camp, but we were enough in number to dull any motivation the Mods or Rockers might have to create trouble with us, and our Scots accent gave us a cultural mantle of protection. We managed to negotiate our way through days on the beach and nights on the town without upsetting either camp to the point of violence. Groups like the Beatles, the Rolling Stones, the Hollies, and the Searchers, filled the airwaves, particularly the pirate radio stations such as Radio London and Radio Caroline. There were enough top class groups playing the clubs to satisfy each week's contingent of exuberant teenagers from the sticks. The great British Seaside holiday, a cultural norm of the British working class for decades, was on its last legs. From now on it was the Costa Brava or the Italian Riviera that would invariably be the destination point for British travelers, and would lead to an unlikely merger of interests between Mods and Rockers, as they channeled their combined energies towards the young Germans and Scandinavians now seen as the common enemy. For the moment, for us, it was all about connecting with the local female "talent," and in this respect the holiday was a success for all of the Temperance Seven, with varying degrees of accomplishment.

In late summer I was able to spend a few hours with some of my Edinburgh relatives who were passing through London on their way to the port of Southampton, to board a ship to Melbourne, Australia. Once they got to Australia, they were welcomed as Landed Immigrants, having completed the formalities in the Edinburgh Consulate and paid the ritual ten pounds per adult (children no charge) for free passage to the land down under. As a Commonwealth country with a shortage of people and a surfeit of space, it was Australian Government policy to encourage immigration from the Motherland, and the only commitment of the immigrant was to stay for at least two years. New

### THE BOG, THE BAHAMAS, AND BEYOND

Zealand had a similar program, which cost twenty five pounds per applicant, and so the prevailing sentiment was that ordinary folk went to Australia and the better off emigrants went to New Zealand. Uncle Ronnie and Auntie Betty, with cousins Douglas, Tom, and wee Ronnie, closed out their life in the Edinburgh suburbs and headed for Melbourne, along with my Auntie Connie. Within a few months they were joined by Uncle John, Auntie Rose, and cousins Sandra, Kitty, and Gordon. So, one Sunday morning in late 1965 I made my way across Westminster Bridge to the south side of the Thames, and along the banks of the river to Waterloo station, for an hour or so of precious time with my relatives. Even now, I can feel the emotion when I think about that day. Perhaps it was because I was young, on my own, and saying goodbye to family members whom I might never see again.

Almost five decades later they are still there, apart from Auntie Rose and Uncle John, who have passed away. Two more generations of Watsons and Browns have added to the family, and like so many other British immigrants, the dream was fulfilled. This is a small story writ large in the emergence of Australia as an economic and cultural force in the modern world. The use of immigration as a national policy had its beginnings in post World War Two, when thousands of displaced persons were given the chance to re-settle there, under the auspices of a federal immigration program. By 1947 a post-war immigration boom was under way, and a million more migrants arrived in each of the subsequent four decades. Today, nearly one in four of Australia's population of over 21 million people was born "overseas." Most of my immediate family members have visited, and my sister Lorna and my brother Jack have both lived there for a year or two at times in their lives. I have not yet made the journey, but it is surely in my future.

However, back then in 1965 Australia was very much at the forefront of family matters. I received a letter from Dad to say that he had applied for our entire family to emigrate. I honestly cannot remember how I felt about that news, so my assumption is that I took it in stride, and began the process of looking for a job in Melbourne, our destination. After an interview with the Australia and New Zealand Bank in London, I was able to secure a position that would be ready for me when we finally landed as immigrants in Australia. Rena was still

## THE YOUNG BANKER

enrolled at Edinburgh University so she would be staying behind to complete her degree, while the rest of us would forge ahead to begin a new life. About the only pre-requisite for the Australia immigration program, apart from the nominal fee, is a satisfactory medical examination for the principal provider of the family. The medical report for Dad highlighted his rheumatic fever condition that kept him off school for months in his first year of high school, which had resulted in a weakness to his Aortic valve. He failed the medical and the move was off. There was no appeal possible, so the family unit went with the flow and got on with life. The idea had sprung so suddenly, and then been punctured almost as soon as it began, that it never seemed real.

On Boxing Day of 1965 I received a phone call from home that changed everything. Dad had suffered a heart attack and was in intensive care. The medical examiner had diagnosed a serious problem just a few weeks before it became manifest and, at forty five years of age Dad was now looking at heart valve replacement surgery in the early months of 1966. I can't remember whether I decided to transfer back to Scotland, or if Mum or Dad asked me to, but I do remember telling my boss in the New Bond Street office what had happened. The bank was very responsive, and arranged for me to move back to the Falkirk branch of The Royal Bank. Within a few weeks I bid my farewells to my pals in London, and headed home to Falkirk. I had spent exactly one year in London, arriving as a young lad, and in many respects leaving as a young man. I had arrived as a Bank Clerk, and left as a Banker. To be in London as a nineteen year old in the mid sixties was just the best experience in the world, and I will never forget it.

I moved back into the "wee room" at home in Falkirk, which I shared with my brother Jack, and settled in again to life in my home town. I had been transferred back to my first branch, at 2 High Street, Falkirk, and took up my duties as Number Two Teller in a very busy branch environment. My pals Ian, Charlie, and Jim had all been signed by our local football club, Falkirk FC, and were trying to make the break through to full professional status. As for me, I soon signed on with a Juvenile League team, Bothkennar Rovers, and was playing decent football, but far removed from the professional ranks. My childhood dream of playing as a professional was

◀ THE BOG, THE BAHAMAS, AND BEYOND

no more than that, but I suppose I contented myself with the knowledge that the banking business was capable of nice surprises from time to time in terms of work assignments and job locations. I continued to scour the Banker's Magazine ads, and wonder if that was the way to go, once I had passed my final exams. I had got through the three years of intermediate subjects, and was part way through the final three years, leading to my professional designation as an Associate of the Institute of Bankers in Scotland. This might be the ticket to a new world.

I still had one piece of unfinished business to attend to, which was to participate in the two week summer camp of the London Scottish Regiment. This particular year the camp was to be held in Scotland. I was still an enlisted Territorial Army soldier, and so had no choice but to show up at a military camp at Penicuik, outside Edinburgh, where at least I had the chance to meet up with my pals from London. We spent several days marching behind the pipe band into and out of several small towns in the Scottish border country, following the pipes and drums of the regiment. It was all good patriotic stuff, and it would culminate in my honorable discharge from the Regiment, on the final Saturday at twelve noon. After breakfast at the camp, and packing up our kit, we had to hang around until the three ton Bedford Army trucks arrived to take the Regiment back to London. In my case, it was a five mile or so journey into Edinburgh and then a connecting bus for the remaining twenty five miles to Falkirk. For whatever reason, I was desperate to get back home, and was not satisfied with a forced internment of three or four hours before I could legally depart from camp. With the help of my pal Bill McKay I hopped into the back of a truck that was leaving camp about nine o'clock, and when the truck reached a point fairly close to the city center, I hopped off at a traffic light, and made my way back to Falkirk on public transport. Technically I went AWOL, but I left the camp no worse for the experience, and feeling rather pleased with myself.

That summer I met a local girl, Patricia Cockburn, who lived about a mile away from the Bog Road in another housing scheme. Pat worked as a secretary in an office, and I had known her by sight for many years, as we went to the same school. Within a few months we were engaged, much to the surprise of both families, and if truth be told, to ourselves as well. I was all of twenty years of age, and Pat was nineteen. It was a nice idea at the time, but the reality of our very different personalities and aspirations, not to mention our lack of maturity, inevitably led to a break up. As is the tradition in such cases, her mother returned the engagement ring to my mother, and no more was said about it. However, I must be one of the few people to actually make a profit on an engagement ring. I received a full refund of the purchase price of seventy two pounds having only paid fifty four pounds after my Bankers Association discount. I have pondered the ethical issues of this transaction many times, and can only put it down to inexperience, and a shortage of money. In July of 1967 I was transferred to the Chief Office of the Royal Bank of Scotland in Glasgow, to work in the Securities Department, so now I had a morning commute by bus then train through to the wonderful City of Glasgow.

CHAPTER **6**

# Ann Louden

IT WOULD NOT take long for me to become a great fan of Glasgow and its people. The city has such a rich and vibrant history, which is often overlooked within the larger story of Scotland. As is the case with most large modern cities, its beginnings were fairly humble. Celtic Druids were the earliest settlers to leave evidence of their being, and it is likely that the streams and courses of the river (Clyde) provided fish to supplement their food supply. The origin of the name, from the Celtic form "Glas Chu" meaning "dear green place" would suggest the suitability of the area for planting and growing by the early inhabitants. The Romans had a trading post in Cathures, the earlier name for Glasgow, around 80 AD, so there must have been enough people to trade with. The nearby construction of the Antonine Wall by the Romans in 143 AD would not have had much of an impact, as it was abandoned within a few years of completion.

It was the arrival of a Christian missionary, St. Kentigern, in 543 AD that gives us the first authoritative information of "Glas Chu". This monk, who would become generally known as "St. Mungo" settled his church on the banks of the Molindar Burn (stream), and allegedly performed four miracles before his death in 603 AD. Nothing definitive seems to be known about Glasgow until the establishment of an Episcopal See in 1145, so that the preceding period of the Dark Ages truly did repress any light on Glasgow's history in the intervening centuries. We do know that the population had reached around 1,500 by the late 12th century. Work on Glasgow Cathedral began in 1238, symbolizing the city's growing role as a major ecclesiastical centre, and by 1451 the establishment of the University of Glasgow denoted the importance of the city in the academic world, rivaled only by St. Andrews.

The exile of the last Roman Catholic Archbishop (Beaton) in the late Sixteenth Century marked a significant move towards greater civic power and the emerging influence of the city's merchants and craftsmen. By 1649 Glasgow had become the fourth largest burgh in Scotland, and by 1670 the second only to Edinburgh. In 1674 a ship berthed at the docks with a cargo of a strange new commodity from the colonies in Virginia - tobacco, and so began a market relationship between the old world and the new that transformed the city. Once Glasgow had turned her face to the west there was no stopping her. The business community quickly seized the moment and became the primary European trading partner with the New World. The Treaty of Union in 1707 between Scotland and England just enhanced Glasgow's role as an entrepot center, and by 1730 the Tobacco Lords of Glasgow had become Scotland's first millionaires. By the time the Revolutionary Wars in 1776 were causing massive disruptions in trade between the former blood-nations, the shrewd merchants of Glasgow had already diversified into trade with the West Indies. By the end of the 18$^{th}$ century, Glasgow was Britain's largest importer of sugar.

As Great Britain industrialized at the start of the 19$^{th}$ century, Glasgow's traders became industrialists, and expanded their manufacturing operations in products such as soap, whisky, glass, sugar, and of course textiles. In time the cotton industry employed almost a third of Glasgow's workforce, but once again the savvy industrialists were ahead of the curve, by turning to industries that could exploit Scotland's abundance of coal. Factories were the Blacksmith's forge of the new economy. Soon the heavy industries such as shipbuilding, locomotive construction, and engineering of all types were dominating the landscape around the city. To feed the beast that was the industrial revolution required a cheap source of labor. Glasgow turned to the West again and brought in thousands fleeing the potato famine in Ireland, and to the North in welcoming Highlanders deposed by the Highland Clearances. Even Jewish, Italian, and East Europeans

### THE BOG, THE BAHAMAS, AND BEYOND

began to arrive in large numbers, all contributing to the culture of this, the largest of Scotland's cities. After the two Great Exhibitions of 1888 and 1901, both held in Kelvingrove Park, Glasgow was truly the "Second City of the Empire." It was around the turn of the century that a group of four students from the Glasgow School of Art began to collaborate on art and design, and their work product was strongly influenced by the Arts and Crafts Movement, Symbolism, Japanese art, and Art Nouveau from Europe. Led by Charles Rennie Mackintosh, they emerged as pioneers of the Art Nouveau movement in Scotland, and gained an international reputation for "The Glasgow Style" of architecture, interior design, and art.

Glasgow entered the 20$^{th}$ century as a leader in manufactures, with an established reputation as a cultural and artistic center. The large fortunes that were created in the 19$^{th}$ century among the leading families of the city inevitably filtered through the mainstream economy into Philanthropy and Arts. This was a Victorian city at the top of its game, and in those early years of the new century it was hard to imagine that things could ever be any different. Alas, the cold reality of World War One, and the aftermath that saw a decline in prosperity throughout industrial society, was but a sign of things to come. The awesome power of Glasgow's heavy industry would thrive again with the advent of World War Two, only to revert to a steady decline in the post-war fifties and sixties. This time it was foreign competition that met Glasgow head on - Polish shipbuilding, Japanese automobiles, South Korean Steel, and any other number of developing countries who had cheaper labor costs and a can do attitude to doing business that the traditional Scottish firm, neutralized by powerful Trades Unions, just could not match. It would take a re-invention of post industrial Glasgow, based on exploiting her tremendous cultural and artistic resources through Tourism along with a Services based economy, to restore the national and indeed international profile of this famous city.

From day one I was on cloud nine, with a job that I found quite challenging, and an office environment that was just terrific. There were about two hundred people in this office, as it functioned like a head office for the West of Scotland branch system of The Royal Bank

- lots of young male and female staff members, and a place to work that exemplified the personality of Glasgow, and the Glasgow people. Glasgow humor is at its core no different from many other brands of humor all over the world, but at the margins it has subtlety and nuance that says something about the personality of the "Glaswegian," as the citizens of the city are known. It is often told at the expense of the person telling the story, as Glaswegians are not afraid to laugh at themselves. It is often pawky, another one of these strange words you won't find in spellcheck, but is common enough in Scotland. I can't define Glasgow humor, but if you spend enough time in Glasgow you will soon figure it out. It is often but not always sexually explicit, but no more so than a comparable tale told in Mumbai or Shanghai, so that does not make it different. It is the sum total of the characters, the plot, the circumstances, and the motive, which often takes the form of an everyday event with a twist. Here is a good example.

In 1967 Glasgow Celtic Football Club reached the final of the European Cup and played against Inter Milan in the final. Celtic won their most famous victory, and the thousands of fans who had travelled to Lisbon, Portugal, for the final had the mother of all celebrations for a day or so after the match. Inevitably, we find a Celtic fan walking along the highway north of Lisbon with arm extended to hitch a ride, having spent all his money, including travel funds, in the pubs and back alleys of Lisbon. He faces a journey of well over a thousand miles to get back to Scotland. After a while on the road a car draws up, the window rolls down, and the driver of the car asks in a broad Scots accent if he can give the Celtic fan a lift. The fan asks the driver where he is heading, and the driver says he is going to Edinburgh. The Celtic fan then tells the driver "Ach, you're no good to me pal, I'm going to Glasgow" and keeps on walking. The hidden truth that gets a reaction from a Scottish audience is that Glasgow people and Edinburgh people do not (officially) like each other, and for this particular fan, principle trumps convenience. Glasgow people like that story, because it speaks to what makes them just a wee bit different from the rest of us.

The Glasgow office was full of characters, and a wonderful place to work. Graham Kenny was one of my chums and he worked in the Tax Department, which was an odd type of specialty for such a witty and interesting chap as Graham. One day I passed him on the wide stairs into the branch, around lunchtime. I asked where he was going, and he replied "I'm off to Sicily to find the truth." Naturally enough, he wasn't, being destined for the Gordon Arms pub around the corner, but I was amused by it, as it seemed entirely in keeping with the rather urbane and intellectual side of Graham that I knew was hidden behind his normal air of gravitas and modesty. The story might have ended right there in 1968, except that I always remembered his response, and used it myself on countless occasions over the years when I had the opportunity to respond to a like question. It was something I would say to friends in the hope of inspiring a laugh, or maybe a questioning look without the confidence to ask the question. In 2003 we had a family holiday in Sicily, visiting my sister Lorna and her family. Her husband Ron was a fireman in the US Navy, and was stationed at the air base near the eastern port town of Catania. On the last day we stopped for lunch together before heading to the airport, and over lunch I asked for a bottled water. I was duly served with a bottle of "Veritas" to accompany my sandwiches, and was looking at the label when I suddenly realized that "Veritas" was the Italian (Latin) word for "truth". I had found the truth in Sicily after 35 years! So Graham, if you are out there reading this book, know that I carried your words for a long time and can now report "mission accomplished".

My work in the Securities department on the main floor of the bank was much more interesting than my previous duties as Number Two Teller in Falkirk. I had to trade the stocks and bonds in the accounts of our clients, and while not responsible for the actual choice of the investments, I was still very much involved with our customers in the stock selection process. The head of the department, Alastair Breingan, was a great teacher, and I learned a lot from him and his assistant, Gordon Mitchell. The secretarial pool in the department included four attractive mini-skirted young ladies - Christine, Janette, Sheila, and Sheena. They provided the scenic background to our daily toils in the machinery of commerce, and were involved in all the socializing and drinks sessions that were often the culmination of our day's work together. Their friendship with a young typist, Ann Louden, in the Overseas Department, would lead to my romance with Ann that became a love story, and a life story.

## ANN LOUDEN

Our feelings for each other, that had their origins at a farewell drinks night for a retiring banker colleague, quickly developed into yet another office romance among the young people who worked in the Glasgow office. Ann was one of the most popular of the female staff. She worked as a secretary in the Overseas Department, which was the department with the most interesting and compelling group of young professionals. Although the manager was a fairly staid and reserved banker, his staff was very much the opposite, and it is a tribute to his management style that he was able to keep it all together. My trips to Scotland in later years invariably involve a pint or two with my pal Iain Kay, who back then was a big framed, overweight, girl-chaser, and who today still has the frame but no longer the girth. He never did marry so I suppose the chase is still on.

As I write this memoir I have the benefit of around forty plus years of harmony with the Glasgow side of our family, which began with my courtship of Ann, and as a consequence of our engagement and marriage, allowed me to come to know her direct and extended family almost as well as I know my own. There is no robust family knowledge base of the distant composition of Ann's family, as her parents and grandparents have been gone for many years. Thankfully, we now have the ability to tap into modern technology to tell us something about our antecedents, and we are fortunate that Scotland has such a comprehensive data base of official records available through the Internet with which to fill in many of the gaps in our family trees that would otherwise be lost for all time. However, the wealth of standardized data tends to create more questions than answers about those who have gone before us. When researching the Louden family I noticed that Ann's great grandmother on the Louden side was Agnes Elder, born in 1862, and when she married Peter Louden in 1882 she had to sign her marriage certificate with an "X" as a mark of her name, as she could not write. Her witness, and presumably her bridesmaid, Susan Cameron, likewise signed with her mark.

Ann's father Archie (Archibald) Louden was born in the Govan area of Glasgow, a tough working class district that sits alongside the River Clyde, and was dominated by the shipyards that brought jobs

◁ THE BOG, THE BAHAMAS, AND BEYOND

and relative affluence to the community. When Archie was born in 1915 the former independent town of Govan had recently been incorporated into the City of Glasgow, and contributed over three hundred thousand people into the larger metropolis. It had grown and prospered throughout the Victorian era, and would continue to be a busy center of shipbuilding and manufacturing in the years between the wars, but the post war years exacted a toll in lost jobs and declining industry that informs the contemporary reputation of Govan. Archie served his time as a Machinist and worked most of his adult life for the Scottish Co-operative Wholesale Society in their local factory, making new shoes rather than repairing the old. By the time we met in 1967 he had been made redundant by the "Co-op" and was able to find employment with the Babcock and Wilcox Engineering Company at their factory in nearby Renfrew, He worked in the packaging department, and he felt lucky to have steady and dependable employment that provided a reliable wage for the rest of his working life.

For all the lack of material wealth, I believe that Archie had a satisfying and productive life. If he were here today I am sure he would agree, although sometimes getting Archie to verbalize was a bit problematic. In the summer evenings he would walk down to the (Lawn) Bowling Club after his dinner, and play a few games with his pals. When he came back home for the evening he would take his usual seat in the living room, and if I happened to be there spending time with Ann he would smile back and forward as the conversation required, but never really join in. After his cup of tea while watching the BBC News on TV he would often take his glasses off, place them carefully in the case, then place the case on his forehead which he stretched back to form a level base. Then we would all watch as he slowly raised himself in the seat to a standing position, and then nod his head forward so that the case slipped off his brow into his awaiting hands. At this point the four spectators, Ann's Mum, Ann, her sister Agnes, and I would give a cheer and a round of applause while Archie exited the room to get ready for bed. That was it. When we did talk it was more often than not about football, which was the other sport that he loved. He was a committee member of a junior football team, Benburb FC and would much prefer to watch his beloved "Bens" play on a Saturday afternoon than the Glasgow Rangers at nearby Ibrox Stadium. It would be pejorative to describe Archie as a simple man, but perhaps fairer to describe him as a man of very simple pleasures. He never owned property, never drove a car, never wrote a check in his life, and had no knowledge of Stocks and Bonds. His mother, Gran Louden, lived in a rented house about half a mile away, and he visited her every Sunday afternoon for his entire adult life. Archie and his brothers Jackie and Willie were around and about each other to varying degrees for most of their lives, as were the various cousins. Archie's sister Jenny never married, so she lived with and took care of Gran Louden until her own untimely death from breast cancer in 1971. This was a hard thing to bear for "wee" Gran Louden, who was a caring and loving mother and grandmother, and she lived but a few more years until her own death in the late seventies.

Archie met and married Ann McCalman when they were both around thirty four years of age, and so having a family was an early priority. The future mother of my wife Ann and my sister-in-law Agnes was born in the Kinning Park area of Glasgow, just a few miles towards the city center from the district of Hillington, where she would spend her married life with Archie in a modest three bedroom upstairs apartment in a row of "Factor" homes. These were mass housing projects where the rents were affordable, and proliferated throughout the suburbs of Glasgow as an alternative to Council housing. Her mother, who as a Grandmother would be known as "Mama McCalman" had six children who survived childhood – Margaret, Helen (Nell), Ann, Daniel, Donald, and George. Margaret went to South Africa during World War Two, married a Rowan Stewart, had a son who they named Donald, and never returned. His Uncle Donald was the darling of the McCalman family, but died when he was just eighteen, and George was born with Down Syndrome, requiring care from his family from cradle to grave. Ann McCalman and her sister Nell were the two of the group who stayed close their entire lives, living just around the corner from each other in Hillington. Daniel and his wife Sheila lived at the other end of the city, in Bishopsbriggs, but were ever present at any special family event or occasion. Uncle Dan and Auntie Sheila were on holiday in the Mediterranean when he had a heart attack while bathing in the ocean, having only recently retired, and so Ann's Mum and Aunt Nell were the only two McCalman's to live their lives to maturity.

There is little in the way of family history that is known, other than a connection through the maternal side of the family to a man who was the head gardener at Pollock House, a substantial mansion house and estate in the Pollockshields area of Glasgow. Through research I was able to find out about the man in question, a Solomon Blair, who emigrated to Glasgow from County Tyrone in Ireland, now Northern Ireland, and who was my wife Ann's great-great grandfather. He was born in 1837 and would have experienced the Irish Potato Famine which began in 1845, so it is easy to speculate that he would find a way out through emigration, as did so many other Irish families.

These were the people who were the backdrop to the early years of life for my future wife Ann and her sister Agnes. What gave their life extra meaning and joy was the propinquity of their cousins "round the corner" at Auntie Nell and Uncle Adam's house. Agnes and Helen Smith were the older and protective cousins who nurtured and entertained their two younger cousins in a close community of family in Hillington. Cousin Adam was ages with Ann, and has always been a colorful contributor to the family story, from his early days as a musician in a rock band. He eventually went into engineering and spent a lifetime in the oil business working all over the world, until he settled down in Scotland's oil capital of Aberdeen many years ago, with his partner Alison (Ali). Adam is a storyteller par excellence. He is named after his father, who was a wonderful man, and was just one of the people who blessed the small circle of family that I became a part of when I met Ann Louden. Uncle Adam was raised in an orphanage, and was taken in by Mama McCalman to her already full home in Kinning Park when he was about sixteen. Adam would later marry into his adopted family, to Nell McCalman, and would provide a wonderful blend of character and caring as a father, grandfather, and uncle for the rest of his life. He was a painter and sign-writer, and in his spare time would create landscape paintings from postcard views that people would provide him of their favorite scenes and places. He was easy to talk to, a pleasure to listen to, and he was a master of understated conversation. One day when his son Adam was in his early twenties, and had still not quite decided in favor of education over recreation, he arrived home at Hillington to announce "Well, Mum and Dad, I am going to China!" Uncle Adam immediately replied "Well, cheerio then son", and went through to the kitchen to silence the whistling kettle that portended his afternoon cup of tea. This was vintage Uncle Adam.

Uncle Jackie and his wife Nessie had two children, Ian and Janice, and Uncle Willie and his wife Maisie had a daughter, Helen, to fill out the complement of cousins that would cluster around Gran Louden's home on a Sunday afternoon, and while there were never enough seats for everyone, there were chocolate biscuits and home-made cakes to spare. In the nature of things, the opportunities for Ann and I to have regular and sustained interaction with the Louden cousins have dwindled over the years, and so it is to a memory bank of reminiscences that Ann turns to today, when she has moments of introspection on her life growing up in the wonderful environment that made her the person she is.

Ann McCaffery McCalman, who became the first Mrs. Ann Louden when she married Archie, and in due course became my mother-in-law, was a dedicated and caring wife and mother, whose only purpose in life seemed to be the welfare and happiness of her family. She had no outside interests. She was not in any clubs, nor a regular attendant at St. Nicholas, the family church in Hillington. Her mission in life was to look out for the welfare of her husband Archie, and nurture her children, so she never ever spent money on herself, other than the necessities of life. In her later years of widow-hood she would make the long and tiring journey every winter to Richmond, Virginia, so that she could spend three months a year with her American grandchildren, Shona and Cassie. I remember in the distant past that she would sometimes speak about her time working during World War Two as a machinist on the factory floor in nearby Hillington Estate, assembling munitions and armaments for the war effort, just like my own mother. She must have been good at her job as she had a supervisory role on the factory floor, and had a complement of young female machinists that she looked after like a mother hen. By the time she

### THE BOG, THE BAHAMAS, AND BEYOND

married Archie she was almost 34 years old and ready for a family, as she gave birth to Ann at their then first home in Innerwick Drive in July 1948, some nine months and two weeks later, followed by Agnes in 1952.

This was the family that came to be such an important part of my life as my relationship with Ann progressed over the course of the three years that I worked in the Glasgow office. However, while it may have been love at first sight, we had to go through the usual twists and turns of a young couple trying to find each other and not lose themselves in the process. We both had our closest friends, Ann's in Glasgow and mine in Falkirk, whom we kept close even as the intensity of our feelings for each other made for some difficult choices. We would spend alternate weekends in Falkirk and Glasgow, and I was eventually able to find a reason to stay over at Ann's house at least one night of the work week. Ann's social life in Glasgow had much to do with her friend Morag McDonald, whom she met when they both entered Cardonald College after high school to take courses in Short-hand and Typing. This skill set was a viable resource for young ladies when job hunting in the Sixties, until the advent of desktop computers in the Nineties proved to be the death knell of Pitman's Shorthand, and the careers of those who could perform this strange talent. Morag (now Cowper) and Ann are as close today as ever, and if no longer fixated by the Glasgow club scene that they conquered in the Sixties, they at least are enthusiastic in their reminiscences of those early years of friendship and experiences. When Ann stayed over in Falkirk she would share a bed with my sister Connie, who was about fifteen or so, and who relished the opportunity to smoke in bed with Ann as they swapped stories.

I still managed to maintain my special relationships with my pals Ian, Charlie, and Jim, and in 1968 we joined together in a social initiative that was highly unconventional at the time, and brought us even wider recognition in the small town of Falkirk. We rented an apartment in a tenement building close to town, with the sole purpose of having it available as a social center, primarily at the weekends. We each continued to live at our respective homes, but availed ourselves of the privacy and functionality of an apartment that was cheap to rent, easy to furnish with second hand products, and which soon became party headquarters in the provincial town of Falkirk. It cost us six pounds a month between the four of us, which even with our modest financial resources was something we could manage without breaking the bank. This was our version of the "Swinging Sixties," and we had some great parties in the two years or so that we rented it.

Earlier in the year of 1968 I sat and passed the last of my exams at the Institute of Bankers in Scotland, and was now the proud possessor of the letters "AIB (Scot)" after my name. This had required a fair amount of day release classes, night school, and correspondence courses over the first six years of my professional life, and I was anxious to get my hands on my graduation certificate to bolster my chances of securing a job overseas. The yearning for travel and adventure had begun with my spell in London, and with that initiative nullified by my return home, I had refocused my efforts towards the eventual goal of taking a job overseas in one of the many current or former Commonwealth countries, where the banking organizations were either British owned or British run. The ads in the monthly publication of the Institute magazine added grist to the mill, and I was increasingly pre-occupied with, if not a sense of urgency, then certainly a feeling of intent to someday make the move overseas.

Before I even had a chance to develop any sort of logical game plan required of such an enterprise I stumbled on to an overseas job possibility, in Nassau, Bahamas, and interviewed with the President of a private bank engaged in offshore banking and located in the heart of this (to me) exotic tax haven in the British West Indies. The President, an ex-Royal Banker, was in Glasgow to recruit a manager for his Securities Department. He had left Glasgow many years before, but maintained a friendship with the Secretary to the Manager of our branch office, having previously worked together before he went overseas. Beatrice had mentioned to him that there was a young banker in the branch who had told her of his interest in working abroad, and she obviously was complimentary enough about my aptitude and abilities to stimulate his interest. The next day Beatrice told me about her meeting, and I was, naturally enough, quite responsive. When I met with him a couple of days later he certainly got my

### THE BOG, THE BAHAMAS, AND BEYOND

attention. Heretofore my desire for foreign service had always been directed east, rather than west. The prospect of a job in Nassau had immediate appeal, and I was quickly off to the Library to add to my pretty limited knowledge of the Bahamas, most of which was learned from watching a James Bond movie. In due course he called me to let me know that he had filled the position with a more experienced banker from London. He told me that while I had enough practical experience of the Securities Markets, I did not have the management experience that the job required. I had no option but to get on with life in Glasgow, which was easy to accept. I had a fulfilling job and a relationship with Ann that filled my heart with joy, so I put aside my immediate aspirations for a life abroad, in pursuit of additional business studies to help round out my CV. Not that I gave up on my social life – it would have been impossible in that office. The early months of our courtship were that curious mix of expression whereby when we were together we were glued to each other, held hands everywhere, and shared glances in company, yet were still independent enough to vacation separately, and not give up the company of our close friends. Ann went to Austria with the bank girls, and I did not have a formal holiday as such. I just hung around town with Ian, Charlie, and Jim, and for some reason saw them off at the airport to a holiday in Palma, Majorca, while I stayed home. There must have been a good reason for this odd behavior, but the years have washed it away, and I can only presume that I had it in mind to save my money for some other as yet undefined intention.

It was not just any weekend, it was the "September Weekend" in 1968, and the Ardrossan to Arran ferryboat had aborted the first attempt at docking alongside the pier at Brodick. Just like an aircraft that misses the runway, the ferryboat had to transcribe a rough circle in order to line up for the second attempt at safe harbor. I know exactly where I was at that particular time in 1968. I was ensconced in the toilet on the ferry, making the proverbial phone call in the big white telephone. While I was sick as a dog, my travelling partners were jostling for pole position at the ferry bar, ordering pints of heavy and packets of crisps, in lieu of dinner. My fellow travelers were workmates and friends of Ann's, and I wasn't just the Alpha Male of the group, I was the only male. Somehow I had persuaded Ann and the girls to let me come along on a camping trip to the island of Arran. We had the worst of the weather and the best of times. After setting up camp in the rain we were flooded out by early evening, and had to take refuge in the streets, where we stumbled upon a guest-house, and prevailed upon the landlady to give us sanctuary. We dried out in front of a small electric fire, stretched out as best we could, and had a passable night on the floor. In the morning we had our full Monty breakfast. I had never heard of the term until that trip, but the full Monty breakfast in the UK has its origins in the African Campaign in World War Two, when Field Marshall Montgomery, in command of the Allied Army, insisted on a full breakfast every morning, regardless of where they were in the desert, and under what circumstances. The British Army full breakfast of bacon, eggs, sausage, potato pancakes, tomatoes, onions, and toast, plus copious cups of tea, was forever after known in the UK as the Full Monty. In other words, going all the way, which explains the parody behind the movie of the same name. That trip to Arran became the first of many visits to this beautiful island, and was the venue of our honeymoon when we married a couple of years later.

Another job opportunity that came up got me briefly excited when I responded to an ad for a job in Hong Kong with the Hong Kong and Shanghai Banking Corporation. I had to interview in London, so I travelled the four hundred miles south to take my place with the other candidates. After my interview I was asked to take a medical exam later that day, so I felt pretty good about my chances. When I got back to Glasgow I told my pals in the bank, and they reckoned that I was a sure thing. My conversation with Ann was a bit more serious, as we had always talked about going abroad together, and here was an immediate opportunity that had come up in advance of our personal agenda. We met on a Sunday evening at the West Port Hotel Bar in Linlithgow, just a few miles from Falkirk. We were completely unprepared for the prospect of a job that might require me to be on the plane in a few weeks. We couldn't even bear to contemplate being parted at so much distance, and yet we were emotionally and financially unprepared for any other alternative. All we could do was push

### THE BOG, THE BAHAMAS, AND BEYOND

back deeper conversations and decisions until I at least had the official word that I had the job. The letter from London that arrived later that week took care of all that. I didn't get the job. There was nothing medically that was problematic, otherwise the bank would have let me know. They must have focused on choosing from among a few candidates, and once again I came up short. Ann and I emerged from this situation with a deeper sense of commitment to each other, and from then on my search for overseas employment carried with it the reality of the obligation that we had to each other, for a life together in the future. We began to save up for an engagement ring by dropping sixpences (old currency) into an empty bottle of Muscatel wine that we had brought back from our vacation in Spain that summer.

Our holiday together in the Costa Brava was in retrospect a rather brave enterprise, and it occurs to me now that the name of this region of Spain that we travelled to is quite an apt articulation. After all, this was 1969, and although the "Swinging Sixties" were the years when societal norms about male/female relationships entered a new and more permissive paradigm, it was still fairly unusual for a young single man to go on holiday with a young single woman. I am still amazed that we managed to pull it off. Now, I have to admit that we actually booked two separate single rooms, and so were able to take the high road with our respective parents on the structural aspects of the trip, but nevertheless we did make it to Spain as two singles, spent our time there as a couple, and returned as two singles. Everybody won, and Ann and I had a fabulous vacation together in the lovely old town of Tossa de Mar, about sixty miles north of Barcelona. We met two young married couples from the London area in one of the local bars, and spent a lot of time with them on the beach and in the pubs and clubs. All in all, it was a wonderful holiday, and little did we know that within the year we would be packing our jointly owned bags to begin a new life together in an equally temperate part of the world.

It was around this time that my Dad decided to form a partnership with two other plasterers and long time workmates, and form their own plastering business – Quality Precast Ltd. They rented a Quonset hut in an industrial estate in nearby Redding, and went about the business of making concrete window sills as a sub-contractor on housing estates, which were now popping up everywhere. The post-war explosion of municipal housing schemes had tapered off by the mid sixties, and private developers were now building homes to meet the demand of the rapidly expanding middle class. But for Dad and his partners it was still a hard day's work to produce enough units to feed the bank account, which happened to be the first bank account that my Dad ever had. My sister Betty, who by now was established as a secretary in the British Petroleum plant in Grangemouth, took care of all the administrative aspects of the business, and spent many an evening turning out quotes for jobs that sometimes hit the right number but often resulted in a lack of response from the General Contractor. The business managed to eke out an existence for the three partners for a few short years, but my Dad's health became an issue again, and he had to give up the strenuous work in his early fifties. His partners were able to go back to paid employment in the work force, but for my Dad it was the end of the line, and the start of a steady decline in his health that would eventually result in his premature death at the age of sixty one.

During the winter my mother must have sensed in me a resignation that perhaps an overseas move was not in my future, and that I might be inclined to accept the status quo. She had seen me come close to marriage to the wrong person, and now she perhaps saw me more reconciled to a future in Scotland, which maybe would not bring out the best in her son. Early in 1970 she had a chat with me in the kitchen, for once empty of siblings, and asked me about my plans for going overseas. In fact, it was not so much a chat as an inquisition about my future plans. She was the one who said, "why not try again with the bank in Nassau, you have two more years of experience now?" Well, I listened to Mum, and dutifully sent a letter to the President of the bank, in which I reminded him who I was, and why I now felt qualified and ready to make a move overseas. In the last couple of years I had almost completed my studies to become an Associate of the Chartered Institute of Secretaries, which was a highly regarded professional qualification, and this surely helped. Of all things, I received a letter from him offering me a job in Nassau, to be Manager of the Securities Department, at a salary of $11,000 a year, with the

## THE BOG, THE BAHAMAS, AND BEYOND

caution to begin the work permit application process immediately. To say I was shocked and stunned would be an understatement, but I quickly realized that the game was on, and I had finally, in the most unlikely circumstances, managed to find a way overseas. My thoughts quickly turned to Ann, and what would have to happen before the work permit was issued.

There was no doubt in my mind – engagement, marriage, and departure, so when I met with Ann to talk about a new future for us, together, I must have been pretty convincing. There was no formal "will you marry me" moment. I had been head over heels almost from our first alone time in the bank elevator, between the Foreign Exchange department where she worked, and the Securities department where I worked. This conversation was all about formalizing our engagement, planning a wedding, and getting organized to leave home. The estimated timeline for obtaining a work permit was about six months, so that became our frame of reference for all that happened next. The engagement ring, a Victorian Opal stone with ruby surrounds, was bought in an antique jewelry shop just off the Royal Mile in Edinburgh, just a quick five minute walk from St. Giles Cathedral, where we went in as two and came out as one. This was Easter Friday in 1970, and our life was about to change. The wedding day was set for August 21, and over the course of the next few months we had to organize our lives to marry, quit our jobs, say farewells to friends and family, then fly away. It all came together over the course of the summer, and apart from a few nervous weeks waiting for word of the Work Permit approval, it was all good.

We were married at the family church in Hillington, St. Nicholas, on a pleasant Saturday afternoon. Ian (my best man) and I travelled through to Glasgow together by train, and had a whisky in the Club car for old time's sake. Once we got to Hillington we hung out "round the corner" with Uncle Adam while the bride did what brides do, and then made our way to the church. Apart from Ann adding a couple of extra "du,du's" to the word "dutifully," it went well, and the reception for about seventy friends and family members at the Renfrew Airport Hotel was memorable. At some point Ian, Charlie, Jim, and I sang a Tamla Motown number on the small stage, and in many ways it was our swan song.

We did find the time and the money to have a honeymoon in the Isle of Arran, off the south west coast of Scotland. It also happened that the President of the bank in Nassau kept a holiday home there, and was on the island, so we made arrangements to meet. There was no business purpose per se, just the opportunity to spend a bit more time getting to know each other before we actually settled in Nassau. We met his wife and his Bahamian adopted child, and spent an hour or so together. There was something not quite right about our conversation, as he was the nervous one, not me, but he told us a few stories of Nassau, and gave us a nice book of maps of the West Indies. We took our leave, and I assumed that we would see each other in Nassau when I reported for work.

Our honeymoon lodgings on Arran were at a guest-house in Brodick, where we had a re-union with the landlady who had come to our rescue a couple of years before on our camping trip. Ann and I felt a connection of sorts to the kind lady in Arran who looked out for us on a bad night, so, given our need for a low budget honeymoon with a bit of nostalgia thrown in, a weekend at her guest-house seemed like a good idea. It was, and we had our Full Monty breakfast again the next day, with the morning sun streaming in over the Firth of Clyde, and showing the distant promise of the golf links of Turnberry, Royal Troon, and Prestwick, back on the mainland. All of them have hosted the British Open Golf Championship many times since its humble beginnings in 1860, when eight golfers competed for the first "Open" title. There's a lot to see on the Isle of Arran, but most of it is somewhere else.

We moved in with my older sister Rena and her husband Pete, who lived just a couple of streets away from my home in the Bog Road. I had already quit my job, and Ann had taken a Temp position so that we had some income on which to live in the meantime. I was at the front window one morning, having just dropped Ann at work, when I saw my Mum rushing towards the house waving an envelope which had been mailed from Nassau. Sure enough, it was official confirmation from a Mr. McDonald, General Manager of the bank in Nassau that the work permit had been issued, and flight arrangements made. We had six weeks to organize ourselves for the move to Nassau, and our new life together.

## THE BOG, THE BAHAMAS, AND BEYOND

As I look back on those times, I can see that the primary focus of my thoughts was on what waited for us at the other end. It was less about leaving the past, and more about the future. This was less true of Ann, as her family unit of four was about to be severely dismembered, whereas I had a bunch of siblings who would still fill our small but comfortable council house with cross currents of noise, activity, entertainment, and friends. One of the most emotional things a parent has to deal with is when their children leave the familiarity and safety of the family home, to begin their own journeys through life. In my later years I developed a bit of a guilt trip about the circumstances of leaving home and family for a new life, as for me it was never as much about leaving as it was about arriving. My focus and attention was on our destination together, and not about the empty space at the dinner table in the Bog Road. When it was my turn to be the parent, and deal with the departure of my children to college many miles away, I felt the pain.

By the time Ian and I teamed up as best buddies I was sandwiched between my two sisters. Katherine Watson Hunter (Rena) was older by three years, and Elizabeth Jack Hunter (Betty) younger by one year, so life within the confines of our new home in the Bog Road was fun, with sisters to play with and fight with as the moment dictated. My recollection is that we were generally compatible throughout our childhood, including the three siblings that came along later. I wish I could say that this has held true throughout the passage of time, but I suppose our family is no different than most. Strife among siblings has been around since Cain and Abel so it seems that we all face a bit of an uphill battle in maintaining love and order within the family, and over the course of our lives.

October 1970 was a watershed moment in our lives, marking a major fork in the road that led Ann and me to the Bahamas, and beyond. Today, with the benefit of hindsight, I can look back on the lives of all my siblings, and see how much they developed in their journeys through life. This may be a good time to tell their stories.

CHAPTER **7**

# Siblings

## Rena

RENA SPENT THE first three years of her life with the Watson side of the family while Dad was on active military service, and her emotional connection to the Watsons, and to Edinburgh, has lasted all her life. Her first school was the Bog Road Nursery, just a five minute walk from our house, and she blazed a trail for the rest of us in that small enclave in the midst of the Bog Road Housing Scheme. As soon as we each became two years old, we were off to the care and comfort of Mrs. Gardiner and her nurses. Rena was never short of conversation, even as a child, and it is no surprise that in later years she would graduate from University with a degree in English, and teach at schools for her entire career. While Ian Laurie and I were becoming inseparable pals, Rena's best pal in the neighborhood was Norma Laurie, Ian's older sister. Norma was older by a year, and that small difference in age around high school time would ultimately force a social separation, but would never quell the friendship and camaraderie that Rena and Norma had. Once Rena got to Victoria Primary School she quickly established her abilities as a student, and went on to finish second in the school in her final year, thus being designated as Proxime Acessit. The big deal in Primary School is to win the Dux Medal, and Rena was pipped at the post by Ewan Robertson, whose only reason for staying in my memory bank for fifty years or so is because he won, and she came second. At the time it was a big deal. If the mantle was passed to me to pull it off in my final year, it was not communicated to me, as I

### THE BOG, THE BAHAMAS, AND BEYOND

never really felt any parental pressure to excel in my years at Victoria Primary.

Rena's strong academics qualified her to attend Falkirk High School, rather than the less regarded Graeme High School. Graeme High was the new name for what was the Falkirk Technical School, the same school that my Dad had attended from the very first day of its opening in 1931. For Rena, the ramping up of studies in reading, writing, and arithmetic were grist to the mill. She loved Falkirk High from day one, and pretty soon she was immersed in Latin, the Social Sciences, and of course her favorite subject, English. All of a sudden there was a whole new social world to discover which went with the territory of high school. Her school got the cream of the academic crop in the Falkirk area, and her girl friends tended to come from a background that was a nudge or two higher on the socio economic register. The road to a university education in those days began with attendance at Falkirk High, and so Rena became the proverbial new generation upwardly mobile student, who was first in the family to attend University. In her last couple of years of high school I was by then attending Graeme High, and able to warrant at least an introduction to her attractive girl friends, even though I was younger and of no great import to them in the scheme of things. One of her schoolmates was Bobby McGregor, who went on to win a silver medal in Swimming at the Tokyo Olympics in 1964. He later visited our house on one of the few times that our parents were away, which created the chance for a party and subsequent bragging rights out of our association with our local hero.

Acceptance by the University of Edinburgh for a wee lassie from the Bog Road was a major accomplishment in itself, and for Rena was a chance to return to her roots in Grandma's house at 23 Ferry Road Avenue. She took the bus into town for classes at the University, which was close to our Mum's old stomping grounds in the High Street, and had always been a "city" university since its establishment in 1582. Back then, it was merely the fourth university in our country, but became the standard bearer for teaching and learning over the centuries, so that today it is ranked in the top twenty in the world of academic excellence.

After graduation, Rena returned to Falkirk to begin her career as a teacher, and went all the way through to retirement in our local school system. She met a young man from Southend in England, on a holiday trip in the mid sixties, and pretty soon Pete Winfield brought himself and his accent to the Falkirk area in pursuit of my sister. He caught up, they married, and lived in the Falkirk area until their daughter Jennifer was accepted at Dollar Academy, when they moved to the small town of Dollar. This quiet academic and retirement community is nestled at the foot of the Ochil Hills, and guarded by Castle Campbell, the former lowland stronghold of the Clan Campbell. It is a beautiful spot, and the scene of many a Hunter family picnic and hill-walking day in the country. Their son Nick became my "keepie uppie" partner whenever we could put a soccer ball together with a spare piece of grass. Nick was in college by the time the family moved to Dollar, and now lives in London, working in the "tech" world.

Rena and Pete have kept a holiday home in rural France for many years, close to the area where our sister Connie lives, and they now live their retirement in a foreign country, but thanks to the conventions of the European Union, with full health and other benefits. The main attraction for them at this stage in their lives is cultural, and they are just one of tens of thousands of British couples who make the move to France, Spain, or Greece for their retirement years. Rena always kept up with the Australian side of the family, and is a regular visitor to her aunties, uncles, and cousins "down under." As a teacher of High School English for so many years, she loves the traditional authors whose writings in the eighteenth and nineteenth centuries produced some of the great novels of literature. Robert Louis Stevenson has always been a particular favorite, and as a Scots "man of parts" who excelled as a novelist, poet, essayist, and travel writer, his writings resonated with Rena and gave her much enjoyment as a teacher as well as a reader. On one of her trips to Australia, Rena and Pete had a stop-over in the Pacific island of Samoa, and made the pilgrimage to his gravesite on the crest of Mount Vaea, far from his native land. I know this was a thrill for Rena, and something that she could never have imagined as a young student prepping for her next examination on famous Scottish writers, of whom RLS is by popular acclaim among the greatest.

◄ THE BOG, THE BAHAMAS, AND BEYOND

We don't see as much of Rena and Pete as we do the rest of our close family members, as they are permanently resident in France and our destination tends to be Falkirk, Glasgow, and points in between. When we do, it as if it was yesterday. Rena learnt to speak French at school, had many holidays and trips to France, and when the time was right she and Pete made the commitment to spend at least the next significant part of their lives there. So now when she sends me an email and mentions of a close friend in the village, it may well be an eighty year old retired shopkeeper from Nesmy who loves to tell jokes and reminisce about a life lived in the Vendee, his service in the War, and the comings and goings of the widow down the street. Vive la France!

## Betty

NO SOONER HAD I celebrated my first birthday than along came another sister, Elizabeth Jack Hunter, to disrupt my routine, and turn up the level of demands on our parents, especially Mum. We were still living in the cottage apartment at Dalderse Avenue, but just about to move to the Bog Road, and the magnificence of our brand new council house. Till then, we continued to use the outside toilet and take a bath in a bucket in the kitchen. Fortunately, there are no photographs.

I have no memories that I trust of tenement life, so in retrospect life for us kids really did not begin until we made the move to the Bog Road, and were cognizant of what was going on around us. Suddenly there was the nursery school just a few minutes away, which became the Prep School for all the Hunter kids. Two minutes at a fast run round the corner would bring us to the Swing Park, located in a triangle of ground bordered by the railway line, the Westfield Burn (stream), and the last row of council houses. In our early years Betty and I would be chaperoned at the park, but as soon as we had graduated from Nursery School we were old enough to roam the streets, hang out at the Swing Park, and generally disappear until the rumblings of our stomachs steered us back home for lunch, or dinner. Around this time the traditional pairing of Hunter and Laurie siblings would create another "best friend" relationship in the street, with Betty and Ian's younger sister Kathryn. So far the Hunters and the Laurie's were three for three in relationships.

◄ 82

## SIBLINGS

Betty followed right behind me from Nursery School to Victoria Primary and Graeme High. Her academic record was pretty much the same as mine - always in the top class, but never top of the class. In high school Betty was enrolled in a "commercial" syllabus, meaning the she was pre-ordained to become a secretary, or do some kind of office work. I can look back now over a sixty year perspective and easily see how Betty, like me, was educationally capable of much more, but was never really put to the academic challenge. Within the family unit, Betty and I were most often paired up for activities, because of our closeness in age, and I am so happy that having been separated for a couple of decades when Betty lived overseas like me, we are today very much back in touch with each other, and part of each other's lives.

She met and married a local boy with the rather unusual first name of "Bede." He was from a Catholic family, and was born in Jarrow in the North of England. Hence the acknowledgement to Saint Bede, the most famous son of the town. Bede Ward lived in the Windsor Road Housing Scheme, another government housing project on the western edge of Falkirk. He worked in the British Petroleum Refinery in Grangemouth, a port town adjacent to Falkirk on the River Forth, which was the major employer in the area. The refinery is a massive complex of pipes, machines, enormous cooling towers, and offices along a two mile stretch of road between Grangemouth and Bo'ness. Betty found work as a secretary in the BP, and met Bede somewhere along the way. They were married just a few months before Ann and me, and their three boys, Christopher, Vincent, and Ashley, are part of the network of cousins that keeps our extended family as an organism that continues to procreate, grow, and prosper.

Sometime in the late seventies Bede got the bug to go overseas. By the very nature of his skill sets working in an oil and gas refinery, he was successful in obtaining a job opportunity in Libya, North Africa, working for Esso Petroleum, later to become Exxon. Their destination, the Libyan town of Marsa Brega, lies on the edge of vast oil and gas reserves, and the petrochemical complex was its own little town, with delineated housing, school, sports club, beaches, and supermarket, neatly contained in the fold of a blanket of Islam which covers

### THE BOG, THE BAHAMAS, AND BEYOND

the coast of North Africa. Their stay in Libya was to last twenty five years, until their ultimate repatriation in the late nineties. Although it sounds a fairly extreme existence, there were many aspects to it that made the totality a wonderful experience, from expatriate friendships that have stayed strong, to the many places they visited while they lived in North Africa. Bede was able to earn good money, tax free, and with full educational expenses paid for the three boys to attend some of the best private schools in Scotland, and then University.

When they returned to Scotland they bought a beautiful old house in a village on the outskirts of Falkirk, and have been based there ever since. Ashbank Cottage on Main Street, Redding has been transformed into not just a family home but a four bedroom guesthouse, which Betty runs as efficiently as if it was the Dorchester. It tends to be the social headquarters for all the resident and returning Hunter family members, and the view over to the Ochil Hills and the mountains of the Trossachs country is magnificent. With one caveat - when you can see the hills, it is going to rain. If you can't see them, it is already raining.

Betty is my rock. She is an intuitively smart business woman, and she has developed these skills without the benefit of higher education and training. Having had my mid life career change from banking to real estate development and business consulting, I would have loved to have had Betty as a business partner along the way. In her developmental years she grew up in the shadows of an older, academically inclined sister, and an older brother who had the attention because of being the first son. Betty had to make her way in her own way, and it happened to be later in life that she had the opportunity to create a business out of nothing, after her three sons were educated, graduated, and employed. We thought her work was done. It was just starting.

Once again the family curse of wanderlust has worked its spell. Two of the three sons have settled overseas, far from home. Christopher and his wife Catriona, along with their children Connor, Rachel, and Jamie, now live in the South Island of New Zealand, after going through the immigration process a few years ago. They recently adopted a young local boy (Dougie) and are raising him as one of their own. Vincent and his wife Susan, along with their children Alex, Ben, and Freddie, live in Dubai, and will no doubt continue to move around the world's oil producing countries, due to the nature of his work in the Oil Services Sector. Ashley and his wife Claire recently moved with their young son Sebastian into Bede's old home in Windsor Avenue, and so far at least Ash has managed to contain the wanderlust genes that are scattered throughout his immediate and extended family. In all likelihood Betty and Bede will spend a fair amount of their retirement years on trips overseas, but for Bede this is like hopping on a bus. He still works in the oil business, and is sent on missions all over the world, six weeks at a time, to instruct on the health and safety of Gas Plant operations. Some of these assignments take place on offshore rigs, and it is a long six weeks when it is twelve hours on and twelve hours off, with not much to do and no place to go in between.

## Connie

CONSTANCE WATSON HUNTER was born on March 27$^{th}$, 1953, and immediately had to compete for attention with the upcoming Coronation of Queen Elizabeth the Second, who had succeeded to the Monarchy with the death of her father, King George the Sixth, in 1952. Queen Elizabeth was crowned at Westminster in June 1953, an event witnessed for the first time on television. The only neighbor in our street with a TV set was Mrs. McAleese at number 15, so everyone crowded in for the event, while baby Connie sucked her thumb in the corner.

It was eight years since the end of the war, but rationing was still in place throughout the United Kingdom, although the only citizens not subject to this restriction were those young enough to be fed at the breast of a mother. It would be another year before the last rationed banana in Great Britain was consumed, after fourteen years of government control over food supply. The true test of a baby boomer in the United Kingdom is whether or not you can remember rationing. This puts Rena, myself, and Betty at the leading edge, and Connie just a whisper away. That gap of a few years made a bit of a difference in our attitudes about this new wee baby who had showed up rather unexpectedly. She was more of a toy than a sibling, and she would grow into a really cute little girl, and a lovely young lady. She also inherited the smart genes, so that when she made it to the final year of primary school she brought the Dux Medal home to Alexander Avenue, and made us all proud.

Somewhere along the way she picked up a new best friend in the street, and of course it had to be another member of the Laurie family. This one was Billy Spicer, a younger cousin of Ian's, whose mum had died, so Mrs. Laurie took him in and raised him as one of her own. Connie followed Rena to Falkirk High School, where she did very well as a student, and was accepted to Aberdeen University. This famous old university was established by Papal Bull in 1495 at the request of Scotland's then monarch, King James the Fourth. For all its history and pedigree, Connie did not take to the university life. This was the early seventies, and there was a growing anti-establishment movement in the student body of university campuses throughout the western world. Along with dissention came a lack of respect for social order, and a step up in other forms of protest, such as drinking to excess, and drugs. Connie was still motivated by academics, and really did not like the vibe on campus. Much to the consternation of the family, she came home one weekend in early 1972 to tell them that she was dropping out of university, and planned to go to France, and find a job. A university degree that would allow her to teach was in her future, but not just yet.

Within a few weeks she moved to Lisieux, a town about a couple of hours north west of Paris, and took a job as a chambermaid in a local hotel. Her school French was enough to get her in the door, and in no time she had improved her language skills from sufficient to proficient. Connie moved to Paris in December that year, and before long she had a job with the Sofitel Hotel Group, although now in an administrative position. The first day on the job she met Jean Phillipe Saim, who had a money exchange business with several hotels in the area. Jean Phillipe would in due course become known as "Sam" in the Hunter family. They were married in Paris a few years later, and raised a family of three children in various apartments in and around the center of the city. Sam's father is French, and his mother is Tunisian, and Sam and his brothers and sisters were born in the capital city of Tunis. He was fluent in Arabic, and this was a big advantage in Paris in the mid seventies, which was becoming the second home of choice for many of the Arab investors who were riding the wave of higher oil prices to new-found wealth. Sam got his real estate licence, and was successful in building a profitable business because of his ability to speak and think in Arabic. You really need both in order to conduct negotiations with Arabs, and this was a real plus for Sam. Connie continued to work in the hotel business for several years, including a year in the South of France, in Aix-en-Provence, until she joined the American Hospital in Paris, where she spent ten years in a senior administrative role.

By the early eighties the real estate boom inspired by petrodollars was cooling off, and life in Paris was not quite as easy as it used to be, particularly for parents of children who attended the local schools. The immigrant community had grown considerably, straining the ability of the local government to handle housing, schooling, and social services. Over the years Connie and Sam had spent a few vacations in the Province of Vendee, an agricultural area an hour from the principal city of Nantes, and some three hundred miles south west of Paris. They packed up their belongings and made the move to the hamlet of Le Puy Gaudin, a few miles outside of the market and administrative town of La Roche Sur Yon in Vendee.

Connie went back to university to become a Primary School Teacher, and taught in local primary schools in and around La Roche Sur Yon, while Sam started his own real estate agency and property management business. I had got used to seeing Connie on my annual business trips to Paris on bank business, so while I was sorry to see them leave the city, it was clearly the right move for the security and education of the kids. In future years there would be many family get-togethers in France, so that the cousins of all my siblings came to know each other, and form bonds together.

In the Fall of 2009 Ann and I had a stopover in Paris on our way to Scotland, and met up with Connie for a few days, while she visited with her friend Chantalle. We walked everywhere, and saw a few of the apartments where Connie and Sam lived during her many years in the city. On the last day we were walking back from the Champs Elysees towards her old apartment on Rue Jean Nicot, on the other side of the Seine. As we walked, I began to tell Connie of a French banker I used to know with the mellifluous name of Jean de la Porte des Vaux, who was such an interesting and charming fellow, especially for a French banker. When I used to travel to Europe on business most of the French banks were government owned, but his bank was privately owned and seemed to have a much more progressive attitude towards doing business. It had been more than thirty years since we tried to do business together, but nothing worked out so we eventually lost touch. As Ann, Connie and I walked along the streets of the Left Bank we spotted a café with one empty table at the end of a row, and headed over to have lunch. I looked at the next table to see if I could get the spare chair, and there he was. Jean de la Porte des Vaux. I recognized him right away, and spoke his name to him, and he said "My goodness, how do you know me?" When I told him my name and bank connection he remembered everything, so we had a nice chat with him and his son, and marveled at the coincidence. As for remembering his name, it means "Jean from the gate of the cows" and since the Cowgate in Edinburgh is the main street at the junction of my Mum's childhood home in Guthrie Street, it had stuck with me for all those years.

Later, while we were reminiscing over never ending glasses of wine with Connie, we got on to the subject of food. It turns out that this is standard protocol for any decent French conversation, which has to at some point turn inevitably to the art and science of cuisine, a la Francais. For some reason we challenged Connie to reel off the food that she had eaten in France that she had never tasted before in Scotland. She listed Courgette, Aubergine, Chicory, Sweet potato, Chestnuts, Pasta, Pork Chops (no kidding!), Veal, Sirloin Steak, and several types of Fish with the head still on. And of course there was no chance of snails on the menu at 9 Alexander Avenue, never mind baby eels. Just meat and potatoes, just about every day.

Connie is in her late fifties now, and will soon retire from the Vendee School System. Her oldest daughter Axelle and her new husband Saif just returned from Tunisia, where she worked in Tunis for the Government as an Art Historian. Connie's daughter Virginia is at university near Swansea, Wales, with her little girl Effana. Her only son Remi is still in the Vendee, working on his rap songs and producing CD's in the hope of breaking through to the big time. For all that, Connie is still very much a Falkirk Bairn, and loves to come home and head for the Western Highlands and Islands with our brother Jack, who is something of an expert in camping and living off the land and sea. Ann and I are not really into roughing it, but we are still up for the odd night in a tent, as we did last year on the sands of Morar with Jack and Connie. Our campfire on the beach, while the sun set to the west over the Isle of Skye, was a memory that will linger, to be recalled on those times in mid winter when the North winds and rain attack in tandem. At times like these, the only place to be is in front of a coal fire, with a wee Scotch whisky to sip while the embers sparkle and shimmer.

Connie can also claim to be tri-lingual, as she learned how to communicate in sign language when she was a child. This was taught to her by our Mum, who had learnt it in the McKay Works so that she could speak with some of the employees who were deaf, and so were ineligible for military service. In later years she taught my Dad, who became really proficient over the course of many years of working with hearing impaired Laborers on the shop floor. Our sister Rena also became proficient in sign language, but for some reason the other four siblings, me included, never did absorb it. Connie also picked up a phrase that Mum used to say from time to time, which sounded like "San Ferry Ann". It was after many years of living in France and using the language that she suddenly realized that the phrase that Mum used was actually "ca ne fait arien" which is colloquially "OK by me." Quite how our Mum came to use this verbal riposte is easy to speculate – she had so many uncles who served in France during the First World War, it was probably brought back with them and made its way into the Watson family lexicon.

In a strange twist of fate, it is Connie of the Hunter siblings who inherited the medical condition of Essential Tremor, so that her voice is reminiscent of Grandma Watson, and to her brothers and sisters is evocative of the times we spent in the Edinburgh home of the

Watsons. She has lived in France for close to forty years, and has no apologies to any of us for her love of being and speaking and acting French. It suits her personality when she projects emotion with her dominant language, French, even though it is acquired, and when she lapses into her Falkirk accent on the times that we meet up on holiday back home, she sounds as if she has just left high school. It is a lovely combination.

## Jack

WE ALL REMEMBER the day and month, if not the year, when Jack (John Watson Hunter) was born. It happened on a November 30$^{th}$ in the late nineteen fifties. His birthday, however, is November 29$^{th}$ due to a mistake in the registration papers. He shares his real birthday with St. Andrew, the Patron Saint of Scotland, but that is a family secret that he can never prove.

There was too much of an age gap between Jack and me for us to develop as brothers-in-arms. As a child he was a wanderer, and if ever there was good cause to invent the Global Positioning System, it was Jack. He was not into sports like most of his peers in the Bog Road, so he developed an ability to enjoy his own company. He was not interested in academics, and would finally get a college degree in his late thirties, when he studied Art, which had been a lifelong interest. He did attend a junior college in Richmond, Virginia, when he lived with Ann and me for a while, but had to give that up when his student visa was not renewed. Jack looked like our Dad, but was a bit taller, at just over six feet. I always felt that if I had Jack's build I would have greatly improved my chances of making the grade as a professional footballer, but that's the way of things.

Although Jack finally settled in the Falkirk area as his permanent home, he has always travelled a lot. He spent eighteen months with us in Virginia, a year in Australia where he got to know his relatives, and about a year in London. In between times he would go back to Falkirk for a while, save his money, then head off to the resorts of Southern Europe. Jack was the only one among all of us who did have a genuine artistic ability, and it showed in his drawings, paintings, and metalwork sculpture. He can get music out of an old guitar, and plays the piano by ear and feel. In his early twenties, after his stays in America and Australia, he became a bartender in a Falkirk hotel, and was able to make enough to fund his occasional jaunts to the Mediterranean, and eventually to his favorite destination in the Canary Islands. This was the early days of low cost airlines, and Jack was able to stretch his money better than anyone we knew. Of course, it helps when you don't have to pay hotel bills, as he always camped somewhere close to an available beach. On one of his trips, he found a spot in a cave and settled in for the night. Unfortunately it was one of the equinox days, when the tides are at their highest. He awoke in the early morning to find the cave filling with sea water, and had to quickly evacuate, leaving behind all he had including money and passport. He made it out the entrance to the cave but was battered against the cliffs with the high seas. He was saved by a local couple who had ventured out in their boat for the early fish, and saw him in time to pull him aboard.

Over the years he developed a pretty unique system for room and board on his trips to the sunshine. He takes his camping gear with him, pots, pans and all, so that he is equipped for whatever beach area he chooses. After his several days of sun and sand he packs all his gear in a tarpaulin, digs a hole somewhere private and close to the beach, and buries his gear before he flies home. Then, when he returns for a subsequent vacation he digs up his gear and sets camp for the duration of his stay. At this time he has gear buried in the Canary Islands, Mallorca, and Sardinia. Needless to say he buys new camping gear in the winter when it goes on sale, so all in all he stretches his pound better than anyone I know.

For the last fifteen years or so he has added a new dimension to his sources of income, by modeling for local colleges in the Art Departments as a nude model. Apparently there is a consistent demand for models, but very few people around to do the work, so for Jack it is a fairly reliable job. He tells me that sometimes it is hard work, when he has to hold a particular pose for a long period of time, but other than that it is no big deal. He has also developed a skill in house painting and wall paper hanging, and there is no shortage of work in and around town.

It is still not too late for Jack to have a permanent relationship with a gay partner, and if he does I am sure that he too will be welcomed within our family. We have all got over the anguish we felt when he first "came out" and I think we in the family have handled it quite well, although only Jack can know that. He is big, and loud, and a natural comedian, and looks remarkably like our Dad.

## Lorna

A STRANGE THING happened on the day of Lorna's birth (Lorna Jack Hunter) in our home at number 9. I was asked by the midwife who delivered the new baby to light a fire in the back garden area, and to make sure there was plenty of wood to keep it going. Sometime after the new baby was delivered the midwife came downstairs and into the back garden, with the afterbirth, which she proceeded to put into the fire, and told me to keep adding wood so that it would all be burnt up. I don't really know what I thought at that point. I was still a relative novice as regards the human reproductive system, and probably knew all about the front end of the process, but was rather lacking as to the physical consequences of the end result. Anyway, I kept the fire going, and destroyed the evidence to the satisfaction of the midwife. By the next day there was no trace in our back garden of the detritus that was cremated just one day before. Only my pal Ian can attest to the strange happenings that day, and I suspect that the National Health Service has tightened up its protocols on home deliveries in the intervening fifty years.

Lorna was the last of the litter, and was therefore the youngest of six kids spread over a period of about eighteen years. Our Mum was forty one when she had Lorna, and at least had plenty of experience in motherhood to make up for the physical and mental effort of mothering in middle age. Lorna's school track followed the rest of us, with nursery school at the Bog Road, primary school at Victoria, and then on to Graeme High for four years of fundamental education. She took commercial courses which enabled her to enter the ranks of the workforce as a secretary, and then moved on to banking, at a branch in the neighboring village of Denny.

She was only nine years old when I went overseas, so I more or less left a child behind, and we would experience the growth of our sibling relationship in the years to come. By the time Lorna was of an age to leave high school, four of her five elder siblings had left Falkirk behind. Only Rena had returned to the Falkirk area, to teach in the local school system. I was in America, Betty was in Libya, Connie was in France, and Jack was with Ann and me in Virginia. It seemed only natural to Lorna that once she was of an age to handle herself, she would head out of Falkirk and look for a life elsewhere.

She chose a road well travelled, that of the main road from Scotland to London, and quickly found herself a job in the offices of the Home Secretary, one of the most senior Cabinet level appointments in the Government. At the time, the Home Secretary was William Whitelaw, and Lorna's boss was one of his principal assistants, or Under Secretaries, Lord Belstead, who would eventually become the Leader of the House of Lords in the Thatcher Government. Working in the top levels of government was pretty heady stuff for a young girl from Falkirk, and Lorna made the most of it. During her time at the Home Office she met and married a young Englishman, and next thing we knew Lorna and her husband Alan, also a civil servant, were posted to Yaounde, the capital of Cameroon in West Africa. Alan was in the UK Embassy there, and Lorna was with the U.S. Agency for International Development. Cameroon is reputed to be Africa in miniature, as it has most of the geological and cultural diversity that prevails throughout the continent. At various times it was a dependency if not outright colony of Portugal, Germany, France, and the United Kingdom. Eventually the French dominated north and the British dominated south felt the winds of change blowing over Africa and chose to form the United Republic of Cameroon in 1961. Cameroon has the African disease – a large population of poor subsistence farmers, a wealth of natural resources, and a small political elite that competes for power and influence among one another, with no significant improvement in the lot of the population at large.

The young couple returned to London after their one year stint in Cameroon but were unable to settle to life together in the United Kingdom, and were eventually divorced. She took a year out and went to Australia where, like Jack, she lived and worked in Sydney, but was able to spend time with the Australian side of the family in

### THE BOG, THE BAHAMAS, AND BEYOND

Melbourne. After a brief return stint of six months in London, Lorna set her sights on another overseas destination, and was successful in landing a job in Bermuda, working for an offshore captive insurance company. We were all happy for her, especially with such a beautiful and pleasant place to live, and were surprised and delighted a year or so later when she told the family of her engagement to Ron Hall, a Petty Officer in the United States Navy. Ron was a fireman located at the U.S Naval Base in Bermuda, and came to be a much loved member of the family. They were married in a quaint old church in Hamilton Parish, Bermuda, and Ann and I and our daughters Shona and Cassie travelled from Richmond for the wedding. I was able to wear the new kilt that I had bought on a previous trip home, and our two girls were so proud to be there for Auntie Lorna, and included in the wedding party.

When Ron's time was up in Bermuda he was due for a State-side posting, and they moved to the Fort Worth area of Texas, where he was assigned to the local Air Force Base Fire Department. They bought a lovely house in the small town of Azle. Their first child Shelby was born in Bermuda, and her baby sister Kayleigh was born in Texas. Once Ron had served the minimum time needed State-side, he applied for another overseas posting, and he was assigned to the U.S. Naval Base at Chania on the island of Crete, in the Mediterranean.

One of the benefits of being part of a family who have the travel bug is that there are lots of opportunities created for the rest of the family to enjoy inexpensive vacations, and experience other cultures. Once Lorna and Ron were settled in Crete, it was time for us to make reservations for a family visit. In this case, Ann and I were joined by my Mum, and Betty and Bede, for a couple of weeks of fun in the Greek island. Our girls were in college back in the States, so this was a first for us in travelling without them. It was super, with lovely weather and lots to see on the island. While we were there I took the opportunity to visit the British Military graveyard near the port. My Dad's stepbrother Bobby Malcolm was killed there in World War Two, when the German Forces attacked the island and were successful in defeating the Allied Forces. The cemetery is just outside the port of Souda Bay and is, like most of the British War Graves sites, such a beautiful and evocative place to spend time. Uncle Bobby was one of the 791 British soldiers who were killed in action on Crete, and all were laid to rest in this cemetery. We searched in vain for his gravestone, but could only determine that he must have been one of the many soldiers who were unrecognizable in death, thereby warranting a gravestone for an "unknown soldier". On another day I plan to visit the War Graves center in Athens, where all the names of the fallen soldiers are commemorated, and say a few words to an uncle I never knew except as a sepia photograph on the wall.

Ron's next posting was to the US Air Force base at Catania in north eastern Sicily, and it was not long before a goodly representation of the Hunter clan made its way there for a visit. The first thing that comes to mind when Sicily graces a conversation is the Mafia, and we were not disappointed. The Hall's were settled in a house a few miles from the military base, and it was large enough to contain the rest of us for our two week stay. Just beyond the grove of olive trees that represented their back garden was a large house under construction for a local businessman. We were awakened each morning to the noise of the roofers hammering away at the task of installing the familiar orange Mediterranean tiles on the roof. By the third day the job was done, and the house looked to all intents and purposes a finished product, at least externally. Two days went by, and we were awakened by the sounds of roofers working on that same roof, only this time they were taking out the tiles that had been laid just a couple of days before. It appears that the owner had failed to pay off the right people at Catania's City Hall for the privilege of installing a roof, so all of a sudden the paperwork proved to have a flaw, and in the interests of public safety the tiles had to come down. We did not see the Godfather, but he must have been around somewhere. I think it is fair to say that we all loved our stay in Sicily, except Jack, who came down with a stomach bug and spent the week on a camp bed in the hall, sipping juice, with a free pass to the hall bathroom.

Sicily is a really neat place to visit. It has three principal coastlines. One faces the Ionic Sea and Greece, one faces North Africa and the Muslim world, and one faces the Tyrrhenian Sea and the western coastline of present day Italy. This construct has much to do with the

## THE BOG, THE BAHAMAS, AND BEYOND

way that Sicily progressed through history, as a strategic location for whichever polity happened to be in the ascendance. As for Catania, its larger history has always been tied to the presence of Mount Etna, and the periodic eruptions of this live volcano. The city has been rebuilt seven times due to earthquakes and volcanic damage, but continues to thrive as a port city and a commercial center for the eastern part of the island. We all loved our time there, and left Lorna and her family rather reluctantly to return to the rain and wind of Scotland, and in our case an onward journey to the ninety degree temperature and humidity of Virginia.

We just assumed that when the Sicily posting was over for Ron they would go back to Texas, as they had retained ownership of their home in Azle and in all likelihood Ron would be able to get a civilian Fireman job once he was out of the military. Then Lorna told us that she and Kayleigh would be moving to Scotland, and Ron and Shelby would move back to Ohio. They had decided to separate, and agreed that the best of a tough situation was to split the kids, and try and settle independently in a way that would keep the emotional bonds of the family in some sort of structure. Ron was able to get a job as Assistant Fire Chief, and bought a house close to his family hometown of Elyria, Ohio.

The girls are older now, and used to living apart from each other, but are still close thanks to the faculty of Facebook. Shelby has had the benefit of being close to Ron's Mum and his siblings in Elyria, and Lorna has moved with her partner Joe to Gibraltar, with Kayleigh, where they are making a life for themselves in this quaint and peculiar British enclave in the south-western tip of the Iberian peninsula.

Lorna has proved to be the winner of the wanderlust sweepstakes in the Hunter family, and yet I have the feeling that there is more of the world that awaits her presence. For all the times we have seen each other since we left for Nassau, when my baby sister was but nine years old, it is the memory of her in a red trouser suit on the front step at 9 Alexander Avenue that day that always comes to mind. For Lorna, the fork in the road doesn't require pondering, you just take it.

CHAPTER 8

# The Bahamas

THE DEPARTURE FROM our homes was pretty emotional, but tempered by the excitement that we both felt at what might await us at the other end. As I look back today at that moment, for which I have total recall, I now see a young couple who were so green and immature, but held it all together with the certainty of our love. We had ninety pounds of borrowed money from my father-in-law Archie, and the promise of a work permit and job at the other end in what we assumed to be a tropical paradise. We were so lucky. It was.

The BOAC (now British Airways) plane from London had a brief layover in Miami, then took off again for the short flight of 180 miles to Nassau. We arrived in the early evening on a Friday, armed with the name of our contact from the bank, who we believed would be waiting for us at the airport with our work and residency permits. For reasons that today are lost in the mists of time, we got there ahead of our paperwork, and had a pretty difficult time of it with the Bahamian Immigration officials. They took us to a room, which had the obligatory dusty fan, buzzing insects, and oppressive heat, and wanted to know why we had landed in Nassau without the proper visas. We were told that we would have to go back on the next plane, and nothing we said seemed to make any difference. After perhaps the worst hour of our short lives so far, we finally got word that the visas had been delivered to Immigration, thanks to the arrival of my new boss Mac McDonald, and his wife Alvena. They drove us out of the airport and headed east for the six miles or so journey to the Anchorage Hotel,

## THE BOG, THE BAHAMAS, AND BEYOND

where we checked in for the night, and slept well. When we pulled back the curtain in the morning it revealed a lovely sunny day, with cruise ships heading into the harbor, and a pure white sandy beach that on closer inspection was man-made, but for us a short walk along that beach was the perfect start to our new life.

Later that morning the McDonald's picked us up and within an hour we were skimming the harbor waves in a speedboat for the short journey round the eastern end of Paradise Island, and our destination of Cabbage Beach. The island, which for centuries had been known as Hog Island was acquired by the American investor Huntingdon Hartford in 1959, who was one of the early developers to see the potential for tourism in the Bahamas. He was the founding member of Resorts International, which negotiated the gambling rights for what would become the Paradise Island Hotel and Casino. The change of name from Hog to Paradise must have been the first marketing initiative of the new company, although for some reason Huntington Beach never did catch on, so Cabbage Beach remains as such. It is a mile long crescent that ends at a coral outcrop by the golf course, and that day the sea was flat, the sun was radiant, and I managed to get up and onto the water on my first try of water skis. It was also our first exposure to American style fast food, as Mac had stopped off at Kentucky Fried Chicken and loaded up for our picnic. I look back and see a nice day on the beach with friends, something we have come to take for granted over the years. At the time, we could not believe how lucky we were.

The bank in Nassau was owned by Lady Sassoon, the widow of Sir Victor Sassoon. She was formerly his full time nurse, who took care of him in his later years when he was confined to a wheelchair. Somewhere along the way the relationship turned romantic, or perhaps practical, and they became a couple. The former Evelyn Barnes was a Texan, with an accent to match, and lived in a beautiful home on Cable Beach that Sir Victor had built, and named it "Eve's." Sir Victor, who died in 1961, had lived the fullness of his life as the inheritor of the Baronetcy and the wealth of this famous Jewish merchant and trading family. Originally Sephardic Jews from Baghdad who expanded into the Orient, his family built a fortune in Bombay and Shanghai through shipping, cotton, and opium, and later investments in hotels, office buildings, and banking. He built the beautiful art deco hotel, The Cathay, in Shanghai, where it is said that opium could be ordered on room service. Sir Victor moved the corpus of his business out of Shanghai after the war, in 1948, having lost much of his real estate when Mao Zedong and his communists took over the city. He was still a wealthy man, and settled for a while in Hong Kong, before moving to the Bahamas. His legacy in Hong Kong is the annual horse racing event in his name, The Sassoon Stakes, as he was a dedicated follower of the sport. In later years he would win the Epsom Derby in England, his favorite race, and is quoted as having once said "There is only one race greater than the Jews, and that is the Derby." Sir Victor was crippled from World War One and walked with the aid of two silver handled walking sticks until eventually he needed a wheelchair and a full time nurse, and found his future wife.

The bank in Nassau was established after his death as a family owned bank that initially held the financial interests of his estate. Eventually it operated as a stand-alone bank, and most of its clients were from England, whose desire to avoid high income taxes in the UK led them to deal with accommodating bankers in the Bahamas, of which there were many. The first thing I learned in my first day on the job was that my sponsor, the former President of the bank, was no longer working there. Whatever it was that happened was serious enough that Lady Sassoon had felt the need to require his removal from the Board of Directors, and his resignation as Chief Executive. This explained his reticence to talk much about the bank when we met up on our honeymoon in Arran. Because of bank secrecy laws in the Bahamas, there is no way to know what actually happened. From subsequent conversations with fellow employees, it allegedly had to do with front running the shares of an Australian Nickel mining company, Poseidon, which had a spectacular rise in price on the London Stock Exchange.

A basic understanding of the way in which the London Stock Exchange settles trades shows just how this was possible. Each trading period of two weeks has a settlement day, which occurs on the first Tuesday after the end of the previous two weeks. Every trade effected

### THE BOG, THE BAHAMAS, AND BEYOND

in that two week period has to settle on that following Tuesday, so that all purchases must be paid for and all sales proceeds must be remitted to the seller. So, let's say you buy 100 shares of a company on the first day of the account period, and by the last day of the account period it has gone up in price. The buyer of the 100 shares simply has to sell the 100 shares at the higher price, and the net profit will be paid on the following Tuesday. If the trades create a loss, then that is when the buyer has to put the money up for the loss on the trade. In the USA for example, all trades settle in three days, so if you buy shares you have to put up the money before you receive the funds from subsequently selling them. In the early seventies there was no email confirmation of trades. The stockbroker in London airmailed Contract Notes to the client, which in this case was a Bahamian bank. The President, who originated the orders to buy and sell, could keep the Contract Notes in his office for the given two week period of trades. If the price of the shares that he purchased had gone up, so that their sale in the same account period realized a profit, then he could allocate the trades to his own investment account, or to an account in another name that he controlled. If on the other hand the shares went down in price after the initial purchase, he could allocate the trades to the bank's investment account. I don't know if this actually happened, but that's the way I would do it if I wanted to game the system.

In a rising market, most of the trades will be profitable, or if not then the losses may not be too drastic. In such an event, the bank losses would not look too serious. However, with the roller coaster that was the share price of Poseidon, there were significant opportunities for big gains and big losses, and needless to say the bank took the majority of the losses. At the front end of the process, even bank employees were allegedly encouraged to buy the shares of Poseidon, and the bank made loans available to them for that purpose. Inevitably, when the fairy tale of Poseidon and its fabulous profits from its Nickel mines never materialized, from a high price of one hundred and five pounds the shares dropped until they were eventually worthless. By this time the bank had absorbed horrendous losses that were enough to threaten its very viability, and when it became apparent to Lady Sassoon that there was a serious problem, she had to get involved, and the outcome was the resignation of the President. This situation never became public knowledge, but the adverse financial impact on the Bank from the investment losses severely impaired its capital. The rest of the Bank's management team was a motley crew of mostly British expatriates, and they would one by one jump ship over the next two years.

However, when I reported for duty at 9am on Monday October 23, 1970, I had no idea that all this had happened. The bank was run by expatriate employees, mostly British, and without any current leadership, due to the vacuum created by the removal of the former President. Mac McDonald was the General Manager, but did not have executive authority, so his role was to try and keep the bank functioning on a daily basis while Lady Sassoon plotted her strategy for filling the vacancy in the office of the President. In the end she hired her brother, a mild mannered and soft spoken Texan, Ed Barnes, and he brought to the table not much of anything professionally, other than the confidence of his sister. Within a couple of months Mac left to rejoin the Royal Bank of Canada in Nassau, and two other expatriate officers returned to the UK. Mike Lammas was promoted to General Manager, and he was a pretty smart guy who did his best in dealing with a tough situation. It was Mike who had been hired back in 1968 in the job that I had first interviewed for in Glasgow. My office pal was George Ansell, a handsome and debonair Englishman who was raised in South America in a life of privilege and affluence. For all that, he and I became the best of friends. I moved into George's office to share the space with him, and there was a fire escape door that led out to a small balcony, and a collapsible metal staircase. Pretty soon George and I would take our cigar smoke breaks out on the fire escape, and he would regale me with tales about his life growing up in South America, and his early years in Nassau, when things were really happening.

At the same time I enjoyed getting to know the Bahamian employees of the bank, and I tried my best to fit in and contribute to the well being of the office. As a general rule the expatriate staff did not interact much with the local employees, and I found this rather strange, and on a personal basis not acceptable. Algie Darville was the senior banker in the group, and he ran the bank branch on the main floor of Sassoon House. His deputies were Leo Bethel and Donnie McKenzie, assisted by a number of very black and very cute Bahamian girls, and I was always welcomed on the floor when I would make the occasional visit. Leo was the poor guy who had borrowed money from the bank to invest in Poseidon shares, and was left with an overdraft of over one hundred thousand dollars that he was obliged to repay. Donnie was a white Bahamian, (known locally as a "Conchie Joe") from Marsh Harbour in Abaco, one of the many beautiful islands in the Bahamas. The other local character I befriended was the Janitor of the bank office building, Fred Gleeson, whose nickname was "King." He would always be around the building somewhere, and would kick into action after 5 o'clock, when the offices were vacant and ready to be cleaned. I remember meeting him one day and asked him how things were going. He replied "times are a changing boss, Hopalong Cassidy don't hop anymore, he takes a taxi!" I always thought that this was a pretty incisive commentary on life at that time, in such a simple and cogent expression. I have used it many times since.

Algie and his wife Ruth became good friends, and we learned a lot about the Bahamian way of life from them. Algie was from Cat Island, and when he quit the banking business a few years later he started up a petrol station, and he can be found there today, filling petrol tanks and in complete control of his business and his customers, almost all of whom are black Bahamians, and from "over the hill" in Nassau. This section of main thoroughfares and cross streets of housing and commerce is where the majority of the black Bahamians live on the Island of New Providence, of which Nassau is the main town. The predominant housing units are small wooden shacks, and invariably a large American automobile stands in the front yard, and doubles as a spare bedroom if required. Ann and I would often drive through there to shop in the City Markets supermarket, and soak up the atmosphere. We spent one hundred dollars to buy Ann a Singer sewing machine for Christmas at City Markets in 1970, and she still uses it today.

We had our first experience of a drive-in movie theater in Nassau, and it was a great night out. You take your own garden chairs, and set up outside your car next to a loudspeaker outlet. Add a few cold beers chilling in the ice chest, and the stage is set for a lovely evening, with only the movie to disappoint. Having said that, the mosquitoes were always a challenge in the tropics, but a liberal application of repellant normally did the trick. Our apartment was in a new block located in a residential subdivision on the eastern end of the island, but no more than a twenty minute drive to down-town. The other tenants were mostly young expatriates like ourselves, and we quickly made friends with Karl Zahner, a Swiss banker, and his girlfriend Ursula, who did not speak English. Within a few months she was quite proficient, thanks to Ann, which meant that she learned to speak English with Ann's Glasgow accent. Many of the schoolteachers in the Government school system were also from the UK, and we had a few in our block that made for an active social life. Our first Christmas was also the first away from home for many of us, so we made a day of it together, starting with a couple of hours on Montague beach in the morning and then a barbecue in the afternoon. On New Year's Eve, we all headed to Bay Street for the Junkanoo Parade, which is the big social event of the year for the people of Nassau. It is a street parade with thousands of participants, who belong to groups of from as little as twenty or so to as many as a hundred. Each troupe has a theme which determines its costumes, and the groups sing and dance their way along the parade route, all the while doing the meringue dance step, and shaking cow bells and various assorted drums. It is a profusion of sound and color, and if you ever saw the James Bond movie Doctor No, then you might recognize the scene. Its origins are believed to be African, and it is celebrated throughout the Bahamas. There is big prize money at stake so the troupes take it seriously. That first time at Junkanoo was pretty special, with the sultry tropical night an accommodating backdrop to the pulsating beat of the drums.

My two years of playing football in Nassau were probably the most fulfilling of my entire lifetime of playing the game. I made a connection to the Clan McAlpine team early in our time in Nassau, and played most of my soccer with them in the two years that we lived there. The club was sponsored by a British construction company (Sir Robert McAlpine & Sons) and the Player/Coach was a company employee, Dick Wilson, who was good enough at the game to have played professionally had he stayed in England.

The games were played every Sunday afternoon on a pitch that overlooked the entrance to Nassau Harbor, and the view was fabulous. As it was an amateur league, there was no admission fee, so for many people going to the Sunday game was part of their weekend socializing. The crowd was always vocal, as there were three main groups of spectators - the Expats (mainly Brits), the Bahamians, and the Haitians. It was the Haitians who generated the most noise, excitement, and occasional acrimony. They loved to bet with each other on the outcome of the games, so this created a fair amount of tension from time to time, and required the odd involvement by the Royal Bahamian Police Force. They identified players by characteristic rather than name, and our team was notable for a few designations that stuck. Our center half was a big burly former weightlifter, Frank Coleman, who became "Double Man" as he was the size of two Haitians. Our full back always had two soft drinks at half time to quench his thirst from all the running in the heat, so he became Dave "Two Soda" Jenners. Mine was "Bungy Trap" because of a particular move that I liked to make whenever I had the break of the ball to make it possible. If there was a high lob from a distance I would anticipate where the ball was going to bounce, and turn my body and squat so that I effectively trapped the ball between my butt ( i.e. "Bungy" ) and the ground. Then when I stood up, the ball was at my feet ready to go. This is something they had never seen before, and on the odd occasion when I pulled it off there was much laughter and shouting from the Haitians, and no doubt a few dollars passed hands as well.

The standard of play ranged from really good to really bad, depending on the team, but it was a highly competitive league, especially among the top clubs. Clan McAlpine also became our main source of friends, as the wives/girlfriends of the players all knew each other, and it was our primary social network when we lived there. We would occasionally plan for a holiday weekend trip to play off the island, and the ladies all came with us. At Easter in 1971 we went on tour to Bermuda, where we played the national team to a draw, then squeezed in a victory over the Bermuda Police Force. This was our first of several

## THE BAHAMAS

trips to Bermuda throughout our life so far. It is such a lovely spot, with lots of quaint areas of the island to visit, all wrapped in a veneer of British-ness. Once back in Nassau life continued as before, with lots going on socially as well as in the office. Then something pretty significant happened to our bank. We were taken over by a bank holding company based in Richmond, Virginia, USA.

The sale was precipitated by a liquidity crisis over a period of several months when the ability of the bank to stay open for business was questionable. The senior management group, of which I was not a part but would become one by default, continued to contract in numbers, as people jumped ship from what they perceived as a failing enterprise. Ernest Barnes was well intentioned but just did not have the banking experience and management skills to right the ship. Even two of the senior Bahamian managers left at short notice, including my good friend Algie Darville, so I soon found myself running the retail branch downstairs as well as my regular job of running the investment portfolio.

Each morning I would sit with Mike Lammas and review the bank's mail and in particular, any requests for repayment of deposits. The offshore accounts owned by mainly residents of the UK were gradually being closed, as the customer base came to realize that their primary contacts for business in the bank were no longer around. It is a pretty sobering experience to manage a run on the bank, because that is essentially the position we were in. The local Bahamian customers who kept current and savings accounts in local currency were pretty much oblivious to our situation, but our overseas clients were much more financially astute, and the daily review of the mail showed a relentless trend of deposit liquidation of the various foreign currency deposits that made up the bulk of our deposit liabilities. Normally, in the event of a lack of new deposit money flowing in, a bank would liquidate short term liquid assets to generate funds to cover the repayment of existing deposits. Our investment portfolio of such assets was running out of liquidity, as each month saw a net outflow of funds to clients who would no longer do business with us. At around the same time Mike Lammas and George Ansell quit, and within a few short months I was the only expatriate employee left other than Ernest

### THE BOG, THE BAHAMAS, AND BEYOND

Barnes. I went through a few weeks of this rather tenuous existence, trying to manage the cash position as best as I could to keep the bank stable and operating while Lady Sassoon sought a buyer for the business. Then one day Mr. Barnes told me that there was an American bank interested in acquiring us. A few days later the Bank of Virginia, a multi-bank holding company based in Richmond, Virginia, sent a team of folks down from head office to undertake the "due diligence" examination of the books prior to finalizing an offer to Lady Sassoon. While this was going on, my work permit renewal application had made its way through the government channels, and was extended for another year, but with the proviso that it would not be renewed again. This was quite a shock, and we soon found out that the Government was pursuing a new and much tougher policy on foreign workers, which was part of the political process to gain independence from the UK and become an independent nation.

Even in the time that we had lived in Nassau we saw a change in the political and social landscape that did not auger well for the future of the offshore banking business. There was a new governing political party known as the PLP that represented the mainstream black Bahamians, who comprised about 80% of the population. Their leader was a charismatic former lawyer, Lynden Pindling, who had galvanized the black majority in seeking self determination for their country and political control by the majority black population. Having won the 1967 election and kicking out the former white controlled United Bahamian Party, he was now focused on independence for the Bahamas, and more opportunities for Bahamians in the better paid managerial and professional ranks within locally operated business. When we first lived there we would spend social time in and around the Casino on Paradise Island, as I played soccer for a few months for the Casino team. All the Croupiers and Floor Managers were Italian, and dressed in evening suit and bow tie every night on the job. Today the Croupiers are local, and the dress code is island casual, which means pretty much anything goes.

As our life in Nassau evolved, we came to know and understand the Bahamas and the Bahamian people, and realized that we were among the last group of expatriate Brits to enjoy the "offshore" life in this beautiful tropical paradise. The social structure that we found was but a remnant of the glory days of decades ago, when foreign investors brought capital and development ambitions to the islands, where they were welcomed by the white Bahamian establishment who ran the country. They came to be known as the Bay Street Boys, and it was their legacy that Lynden Pindling sought to overcome with his new brand of populist and democratic politics. The motto of the Bahamas during the years of the Bay Street Boys was "Expulsis Piratus, Restitutio Comercio" which referred to the conversion of the islands from a nation of pirates to a nation of commerce and trade. The local joke among the expats during the Pindling move towards independence was that the new motto of the country would be "Expulsis Comercio, Restitutio Piratus." This was humor much appreciated in the English style pubs frequented by the diminishing expatriate population, but not to be put about within Bahamian circles, lest there be recriminations. Our final work permit notification was but a small routine event in the administration of government, but the message was loud and clear that no longer would a privileged class of white professionals be permitted to usurp the rights and ambitions of Bahamians by what today we would recognize as a glass ceiling on promotions. Frankly, I had no problems with the motivation of the politicians to chart a new course for the country, and will always be proud of our association with the Bahamas. For Ann and me, it was something that we did not dwell on, as we were young enough to adjust our life to just about any circumstance, and that very condition of an end date to our life in Nassau would soon be pre-empted by another job, from our new employer, in another island paradise, the Cayman Islands. But for the moment, it was all about keeping the bank open long enough for a deal to be made with the Bank of Virginia, and finally the sale was announced in late summer of 1971, to be signed on November 30.

The first thing that happened was the arrival of an interim General Manager from Richmond, Al Davis, who arrived with his wife Fran and quickly assumed control of the day to day running of the bank. Al was at the tail end of his career, and had been head of the Internal Audit Division of the parent company. He came to Nassau sporting a crew cut of gray hair, which had been that way since his time in the

◄ THE BOG, THE BAHAMAS, AND BEYOND

Marine Corp. He was such a refreshing change, and I thrived on the new circumstances in the office. Bank of Virginia had bought 75% of the Nassau bank, and 100% of the Cayman bank. The inclusion of the shell Cayman bank in the deal would prove to be a fortuitous circumstance for Ann and me as the acquisition process developed over the next few months. There was much to be done to get the bank on a sure footing again, by quickly restructuring its balance sheet and business plans to reflect the strategic goals of our new owner. First of all, the local banking operations were dissolved, and all depositors were repaid and directed to other local banks. All of the British clients were advised of the change, and requested to close out their business, moving deposits and loans wherever possible to other offshore banks. We managed some two hundred or so offshore companies for those clients, and they all had to be transferred to other Trust Companies on the island. We also had a constant stream of bankers from Richmond who were sent down to review the loan portfolio and determine how best to exit the local lending that had been part of the business mandate of the bank in Nassau. I got to know some of them quite well, which made our eventual move to Richmond that much easier.

In addition to Al Davis, there was now a new President of the Bank, Tom Marshall, who was a former Citibank executive from New York. He had been hired to jump start the international banking business for the Bank of Virginia, so he came to Nassau ostensibly to chart a new course for the bank in executing a strategy to grow an international loan portfolio that would add revenues and profits to the parent company. Fortunately for me, Al was still effectively running the bank, along with myself and a hard core of about fifteen local staff who had stayed on board through all of the tribulations of managing a bank in its death spiral, only to be saved from failure by the new owners. Over the next few months I reveled in the new environment at the office, as I had a growing respect and admiration for Al Davis, and was gradually building up my contacts with the rest of the bank from the many visitors from head office who would find one reason or another to visit the new subsidiary in the Bahamas. It was in February or March of 1972 that Tom Marshall told me of the bank's decision to open a physical presence in Grand Cayman, and activate the banking licence of Cayman Banking Corporation as Bank of Virginia (Grand Cayman) Ltd. Although possessing a Class "A" Licence in Cayman allowing us to operate as a commercial bank on the island and do local business, the plan was to keep the office small, stay away from over-the-counter banking, and concentrate on commercial business locally, and international lending into Latin America. He asked me if I would I like to move to Cayman as the Resident Manager, and set up the new bank in George Town, capital of the Cayman Islands, on the island of Grand Cayman. This was wonderful news for us, as it solved the issue of the disappearing work permit, and provided for ongoing employment with an organization that I felt positive about. Since I would require secretarial help, the bank were quite open to having Ann appointed as my secretary, and so the offer to move from one tax haven to another, albeit to one that was quite a bit smaller than Nassau, was something that made a lot of sense, given the finality of our residence in the Bahamas.

At roughly the midpoint of what would be a two year stay in Nassau, we were comfortably ensconced in a place that we really liked, and part of a social group of young people just like us who were out in the world for the first time, and relishing the weather, the amenities, and the karma of life on New Providence Island. Our closest pals were John and Ruth Williams, from Chester in England, and Malcolm and Annie Davis, from the London area. John and I played for Clan McAlpine together, and Malcolm was the friend with the speedboat, so every Saturday morning we would head for Rose Island, which was just to the east of Paradise Island, and spend the day on the beach. Sometimes we just drove out West Bay Street to Caves beach, so that the three guys could don the snorkel and flippers and head out to the reef searching for Conch Shells, while the girls worked on their suntans. The larger soccer club crowd was mostly made up of couples of different nationalities, and were just the best of friends we could hope for to share our early life together as a couple. Our leader was Dick Wilson, captain of the soccer club and father of two young children with his wife Jill. We spent lots of time together, and Dick and I became lifelong friends. We also had a social relationship with a bunch of young British soldiers and sailors who were based in Nassau, and

### THE BOG, THE BAHAMAS, AND BEYOND

who played for the team. Seaman Jimmy Brown, our goalkeeper, managed to break his nose in the cup final, but played on until it went to penalties, then saved the last penalty to give us victory over Paradise Island, our nemesis.

The first few months of 1972 were quite hectic, with visits to Cayman to prepare for the move, and also to Richmond to begin to acquire a sense of the parent company, and also meet my colleagues in the new and growing International Division of the bank. This was exciting for both of us, now that Ann would be back in the work force, and contributing to the efficacy of the new bank, as well as a financial contribution from her salary as my Administrative Secretary.

For the Easter break in 1972 we went on a tour of Mexico, representing the Bahamas, and played three games against pretty decent opposition. The Mexican Olympic team beat us 6 – 1 although the high point for us was in the first minute, when we took the kick off, passed the ball four or five times, and scored without a Mexican player touching the ball. Eventually the altitude had an effect, so we at least had an excuse. We played and narrowly lost to a Mexican Division Two team in Morelia, and then had a memorable trip across the mountains to a town called Orizaba for our final game. The bus trip took several hours, and when we finally got there the Mayor of the town, Senor Guttierez, was waiting for us with a bus, so we reluctantly got out of our coach and into his for a journey up a mountain to a silver mine. When we got there he showed us a railway track into the mine that came from a village at the bottom of the mountain. It was a cable operated train, and would pull the miners up to the mine in the morning. During the day, if there were reasons for any of the miners to go back to the village, they would use their own form of transport, which was demonstrated by one of the miners. He put a metal clip over the rail, then a piece of leather on top of the clip, and sat astride it with a stick in each hand and his legs extended so that his feet were crossed and rested on the track. Then he pushed off the steep slope which gave him momentum, and his sticks gave him balance as if they were ski poles. He shot off down the steep track into the distance. When he finally got to the bottom, he stood up and waived, and all we could see was his colored bandana. Then we were back in the bus, and

# THE BAHAMAS

off to the main hotel in Orizaba, for a night's sleep before the game next afternoon.

It was a town straight out of an old black and white western movie, except the streets were narrower, and the population that strolled them for entertainment and social intercourse were pretty much representative of the Mexican diaspora. Many carried the features of the indigenous Indian population, some were much more Spanish in looks and style, and the majority were proto-typical Mexicans with men in big hats, ladies in shawls, and smiles that lit up the world. There was a background of Latin music from somewhere that inculcated the mind, and created an atmosphere that we all felt, and which provided a sultry background to our convivial congregation at the hotel bar. I still have a beer glass from that night, which deserves a more salutary description, given its contours and etchings. I did not steal it, although I probably would have if required, but a little negotiation with the waitress and it was all mine. In those days in rural Mexico money in the hand was a Yankee dollar bill, as the song goes. Anyway, that was the best of the night, as the hotel room accommodation was just awful. Ann was awake all night, worrying about tarantulas and related bugs, and I was less worried, but no better rested.

As for the game, I can't remember if we won, lost, or drew, but I do remember running to receive a long pass and glancing over my shoulder to get in the right position to control the ball. At that point the ground rose in the form of a mound, as the field doubled as a baseball stadium, and as I was looking the other way I stumbled at full tilt and went arse over elbow. The ball went sailing over my falling body and the two thousand or so people in the stadium were unified in their laughter and scorn. Not my finest moment on a soccer (or baseball) field. It was a long journey back to Nassau from Orizaba, and I had to deal with the revenge of Montezuma on the return journey, due to some errant culinary decisions while in Mexico. Actually, we later figured out that not drinking the water is no protection if you continue to drink Margueritas on the rocks. The rocks are dangerous, so be warned.

The earthquake struck in the early hours of the morning on August 28th, 1973 and the epicenter was Orizaba. Our friend Mayor Guttierez had his fifteen minutes of fame when he became the face

### THE BOG, THE BAHAMAS, AND BEYOND

of the ravaged city, and reported to the world media on the damage, destruction, and loss of life caused by this 6.7 Richter scale event. As the home of the tallest mountain in Mexico in the form of the Pico de Orizaba volcano, at over 18,000 feet, the occasional rumblings and gurgitations of the town's ensign were part of the constancy of life in this part of the country. On this occasion, the volcano signaled its discontent with its guardian, and those chapels and churches that escaped damage overflowed with the good people of the town, trying once again to make sense of this latest human tragedy.

When we returned from the Easter break, we were now firmly on the home stretch towards our relocation to the Cayman Islands. The transformation of the bank in Nassau from a full service local financial services organization to an offshore bank of convenience for a U.S. domiciled bank holding company was well under way, and one by one the personnel left to take up other employment on the island. We had lots of farewells to get through, and also the red tape of obtaining a work permit in Cayman, but the situation there was quite different from Nassau, and everything went according to plan. We decided to take our vacation for a full month in Scotland, for a wonderful reunion with family and friends. There was a host of them all waiting for us to exit through Customs in Glasgow, and we were pretty much overcome by emotion after our two year absence. Leaving again for the tropics at the end of our trip was a bit less traumatic than the first time, since we knew where we were going, and what we were going to.

CHAPTER 9

# The Cayman Islands

IN 1503 LEONARDO da Vinci painted the Mona Lisa, and King Henry Vii of England began building his chapel at Westminster Abbey. While this was going on, Christopher Columbus was sailing from Porto Bello (Panama) towards the island of Hispaniola (the present day Haiti and the Dominican Republic) on the fourth of his voyages of discovery in the New World. On May 10th he sighted Cayman Brac and Little Cayman, which he named the Tortugas, as the sea around the islands was replete with tortoises (turtles). Over the years of discovery and exploration of the Caribbean the name 'Tortugas' would be coopted by other seamen for another group of islands, and the presence of marine crocodiles on Little Cayman is the likely source of attribution for the name 'Cayman', which in due course came to be associated with all three islands in the group.

George Town, Grand Cayman was the rather run down capital of the Cayman Islands until the concerns about the viability of the Bahamas as a tax haven began to raise the profile of this small and politically stable British Crown Colony. Beginning in 1971 there was a deluge of licence applications from banks all over the world, looking to set up shop in Cayman as an alternative to Nassau. The down-town area of George Town was literally a building site, as all the major offshore players were in process of establishing their Cayman operations to cater to the growing needs of offshore banking clients. In our case, we had other reasons for opening the Cayman office, which had to do with the terms of the acquisition of the Nassau bank from the previous owner, Lady Sassoon. She maintained a minority interest in the Nassau bank, so it made more sense to channel our offshore business through Cayman, where we had a 100% ownership position, rather than share our profits in Nassau. Ann and I had already visited the island a couple of times so that we could lease office space, choose office furniture and equipment, and also negotiate the purchase of a condominium for the bank, as our local residence. These were exciting times, and although we had been really happy in Nassau we had no choice but to move because of the work permit situation. Anyway, for us it was an address change for another part of paradise, as we quickly settled in to life in the Cayman Islands, and welcomed several of our friends from Nassau, who were also transferred to Cayman. Joe Heavener came to Bank of America from Barclays in Nassau, and Ian Kilpatrick came to set up an office for Panatrust, a subsidiary of the Banque Nationale de Paris. My business mandate for the bank was to use our Class "A" licence to serve corporate clients on the island and also Canadian investors who dealt with a separate Canadian subsidiary of our bank, and were interested in offshore accounts. In addition, any international loans that were originated by our head office in Richmond would be allocated as assets of the Cayman bank, in order to build up profits offshore. Retail banking on the island was provided by the large American, Canadian, and European banks, all of whom set up impressive headquarter offices in George Town. We settled for a 500 square foot office in the West Wind building, on the shorefront, and our office had a beautiful view of the Caribbean Sea, and the general harbor area. Our neighbors in the building included Lloyds Bank Trust Company, and the Assistant Manager was my friend from the bank in Nassau, George Ansell, who had moved with his wife Janet and their two boys.

We arranged for the purchase of a two bedroom apartment in Harbour Heights, a condominium development about four miles along Seven Mile Beach. We chose an upstairs unit, number 25, which we had furnished from top to bottom on a trip to Miami a few weeks before we arrived. Our balcony overlooked the beautiful white sand beach, and a swimming pool and clubhouse. Many of the units had been bought by visitors as vacation homes, mostly Americans and

Canadians. Over time we would come to know just about everyone, and there was no shortage of social intercourse. We bought a huge American car, a Plymouth Fury, so that we had good air conditioning, and enjoyed the fifteen minute commute along the beach road each weekday to the office, and also at lunchtime when we would often come back to the apartment for lunch.

The total population of Grand Cayman in 1972 was about thirteen thousand, on an island that was about twenty miles long and seven miles wide at the western end, where we lived. The eastern end of the island was sparsely populated, although Bodden Town, roughly half way along the southern coast had a few hundred proud residents. Today there are about forty seven thousand residents of Grand Cayman, such has been the growth of this now famous resort and tax haven. The interior of the island is not particularly attractive, with the high point about sixty feet above sea level, at a place designated as "The Mountain." The beaches were historic nesting grounds for sea turtles, which attracted ships in search of fresh meat for their crews. The first recorded landfall was by Sir Francis Drake in 1586. The first recorded permanent inhabitant was Isaac Bodden, born on Grand Cayman around 1700 and a grandson of the original settler named Bodden, who was likely one of Cromwell's soldiers at the taking of Jamaica in 1655. The majority of Caymanians today are of African and British descent, with considerable inter-racial mixing. We found the Caymanians to be delightful people, and when we lived there in the early seventies there was no serious crime, and no evident discrimination. The Caymanians are a Crown Colony of the United Kingdom, and the Governor is appointed by the Queen. The Governor is titular head of the local Government, but in practice the Cayman Legislature is made up of elected Caymanians who sit in the House of Assembly, and control governance of the Colony.

The center of expatriate social life on the island was the Lobster Pot Pub, which was on the rocky shorefront on the outskirts of town towards Seven Mile Beach. In due course the Cayman Rugby Club was started, and team members were obliged to travel to Jamaica or the USA in order to play against a team other than themselves. They would ultimately build a clubhouse and social club at their grounds, and nowadays enjoy

### THE BOG, THE BAHAMAS, AND BEYOND

competition with teams from all over the globe, who are eager to make the trip to the island. Within a few days of arriving I answered a knock on the door and found a future friend and teammate, Bill Bissell, who had got word that there was a Scottish guy from Nassau just arrived who could play football. Bill was an architect, from Newcastle, and his wife Edna worked as a nurse for the local doctor. I was soon playing for the Eagles, and within a few weeks had persuaded Henry Propper, the Managing Director of the McAlpine Construction Company to sponsor our team, now known as Clan McAlpine, as it was in Nassau. Henry and his wife Nadia lived in our block at Harbour Heights, and although not much of a soccer fan, he was aware of my connection to the Nassau affiliate, and was happy to support our new team. We quickly became the team to beat on the island, and although it was not quite as exciting as playing at Fort Charlotte in Nassau, we had some really great competition from other Expat teams, and also local clubs that had a lock on the Jamaican players who lived in Cayman. The early seventies was a difficult time in Jamaica, with high unemployment, and the country had taken a sharp turn to the left in politics, leading to concerns about the Prime Minister's cosy relationship with Fidel Castro and Cuba. The relatively few Jamaicans who were able to get work permits for Cayman were glad to be out of their crime ridden island, and contributed to the diversity of the growing population on Grand Cayman.

There was no television, as this was before the advent of TV satellites. There was no radio broadcast locally, although a good short wave set would get you the BBC World Service for serious news content. A regular transistor set would provide access to the Miami radio stations, ensuring a steady supply of pop music and car dealership advertising. There was no fresh butcher meat and produce. Everything came from Miami, on the daily plane service, and certain items were only shipped once a week, and others less frequently. The shoppers, mostly the women of the household, soon got used to not having choices, and it was amusing to reflect sometimes on the fact that pretty much everyone across the island would be having the same meal for dinner. There was a weekly newspaper, The Caymanian, and a next day supply of a few British and American dailies.

The Cayman mosquito is a pretty mean specimen, and hence the existence of a Government run Mosquito Control Unit, with scientists from the UK and America plotting on a daily basis how to deal with the dreaded bug. Their specially equipped plane would fly around the island dispersing the repellant, and there was a fleet of vehicles that travelled the roads and byways across the inhabited sections of the island blasting out the gray smoke that contained the latest chemical recipe. I remember one evening Ann and I had gone down to West Bay for a pizza in a local restaurant, and the Mosquito Man happened to drive right by the window, causing clouds of gray smoke to fill the restaurant for a few minutes. There was no need to get uptight. That was just part and parcel of life on the island. Naturally, much of the social and sporting activities took place on and around the water. There was an active yacht club based at the Galleon Beach Hotel, which was a ten minute walk along the beach and a great spot to hang out on Sundays for the weekly barbecue. While we were there a new Holiday Inn opened, and the rather upscale lounge was soon home to Cayman's only resident calypso singer, The Barefoot Man, who to this day entertains the tourists with his songs and stories of life in Cayman. He is actually George Novak, who was born in Germany, married a Bahamian girl, and somehow pitched up in Cayman around 1970 and never left.

I had my first experience parasailing one weekend when a few guys showed up at the beach with parachute equipment rigged for use as a parasail. We gathered round to see what all the fuss was about, and I ended up volunteering to try it out. One end of the rope was affixed to a speedboat, and the other end was connected to a few belts and braces that were fitted around me, with a rope length of about two hundred feet. All the helpers held on to the ends of the parachute to keep it in the open position, while the speedboat took off parallel to the shore, gradually increasing speed. As the slack was taken up I began to run along the beach with the crew right behind me keeping the parachute open. As this happened, the parachute gradually filled with air and at a certain point there was a semblance of lift off, when I was lifted up and across the water, gradually increasing height as the boat opened up the throttle. I soon found myself way up in the air, with a view of the entire island, and lots of colored shapes on the beach, no doubt with thumbs in the up position as I headed along the shoreline towards George Town. Unfortunately, there was a storm brewing from that direction. The headwinds were all of a sudden in competition with the velocity of the parachute, and it soon became clear that the speedboat was slowing to a crawl as my parasail was acting like a brake. Then, as I looked down at the boat in the distance, I saw one of the guys hacking away at the rope in order to release it from the boat, which was taking in water. Suddenly I was jerked upwards, then the parasail began to increase in altitude with its new found freedom, no longer connected to the mother craft. I began to be concerned, as the winds were pulling me out to sea, but there was nothing I could do other than literally hang in there pending further developments. I may have given a fleeting thought to the fact that there was not much except open sea between me and the Yucatan Peninsula, or maybe I just dreamt it later. Anyway, the parasail began to gradually descend, and I noticed that the speedboat had turned in my direction and was heading out to sea with me trying to estimate where I would hit the water. My main concern was to get in the correct position so that as soon as I hit the water I would be able to release the straps and not be caught up in the harness. However, as soon as I hit the water my arms became caught up in the ropes, and I ended up on my back being towed behind the parasail, which was now skimming across the waves, propelled by the continuing strong winds. Someone in the boat had the idea to race past the parasail and then cut into its path so that it took the air out of the chute, and sure enough at that point the ropes got slack, and I eventually drifted to a halt. I clambered on board about half a mile or so out from the beach, and soon landed on terra firma with cheers and handshakes from a relieved group of spectators.

On one of our first trips home to Scotland after our move to Cayman, I was contacted by a local lawyer, Steuart Howie, who had read an article about me in the Falkirk Herald newspaper about our move from Nassau to Cayman. Steuart lived in the nearby village of Laurieston, but we went to different schools so never knew each other. He told me that he had been hired by a Cayman law firm, and he and his wife Diane were about to move to Cayman. When they did arrive a few months later we were able to welcome them to the island and introduce them around. We became great friends, and whereas our path eventually took us to the USA, they returned to Scotland a long time ago, where Steuart practiced law until his recent retirement.

I would drive out to the airport on a regular basis to pick up arriving Canadian clients, bring them to the office where we would get their accounts set up, and invariably entertain them to drinks and dinner in the evening. In some cases the deposit accounts they opened were funded by cash, usually U.S. dollar currency, and this was perfectly legitimate stuff as far as the Cayman authorities were concerned. As part of our application to the US Federal Reserve Bank for permission to engage in offshore activities, we specifically undertook not to open accounts for US citizens, but there was no such restriction against doing business with Canadians. I think the most we ever took in was around $100,000 of currency, but some of my colleagues who represented the other large international banks often took in cash in quantities much greater. I have seen a suitcase opened on the baggage line in the airport by the Caymanian Customs Officer with nothing but bundles of large denomination dollar bills, in aggregate surely more than a million dollars. Having perused the contents to make sure there were no consumer goods being smuggled in, the Customs officer closed it up again and marked the suitcase as checked with a chalk mark on the side. These were the good old days when pretty much anything was acceptable in a tax haven jurisdiction, but there is a concerted effort nowadays by the various bank regulators to clamp down on currency transactions, whether it be for tax evasion or for laundering drug money.

I also had to figure out what kind of banking business made sense for our Cayman bank. We obviously did not want to do local currency branch banking, as there were no company aspirations to build and operate a branch bank such as we might have back in Virginia. This led us to focus on commercial lending, where we could make a smaller number of loans but in larger amounts, and after taking stock of the local market I recommended to my boss Don Just in Richmond that we focus on lending to companies or organizations that were important to the growth of the local economy. Having sold the plan to

◄ THE BOG, THE BAHAMAS, AND BEYOND

Head Office, I then had to get out and market our bank locally, and see what business I could drum up. The largest private employer on the island was Mariculture, a company that farmed Green Sea Turtles at a location by the sea just outside the settlement of West Bay. The farm was run by an enterprising engineer but the financial aspects of the operation were handled by Keith Norman, who was one of the founding shareholders of Mariculture. Keith had an apartment at Harbour Heights, although at that time he was more of an acquaintance than a friend. He introduced me to his fellow board members, and we developed a plan to lend several hundred thousand dollars to the company, to help expand the plant and also provide marketing money. I also developed a lending relationship with an American businessman who had started Cayman Water Company, with a franchise from Government to build an infrastructure to enable fresh water to be delivered to houses and businesses, from a Desalination Plant. We funded loans to help him acquire state of the art desalination equipment from Israel, where there was pioneering technology in the business. Another client was a Florida Dredging operator whose company had important dredging contracts on the island, and needed working capital to support their business plan.

My largest local relationship was with a French Canadian banker, Jean Doucet, who had opened up a local bank in 1969 in the two car garage attached to his house opposite Seven Mile Beach, on West Bay Road. By the time we arrived in 1972 he was running a banking conglomerate with offices in London, New York, Hong Kong, Mexico City and Monaco. He was a long time client of our bank through our finance company in New York, who had made him a loan to start his bank in Cayman. Now that Bank of Virginia had a physical presence on the island, we were able to take over the lending relationship, and my job was to find ways to grow our business with this fascinating albeit controversial banker. Consistent with our overall strategy of lending to ventures that were important to the island, we developed a funding vehicle for his rapidly growing mortgage business through Cayman Mortgage Corporation, which concentrated on mortgage loans to Caymanians. This was a critical need not served by the large banks. We also provided commercial mortgage financing for his banking offices, as the original house and two car garage had been converted and extended in all directions as he grew his business and personnel. The complex was now known as Interbank House, and the Interbank Group was his umbrella corporation for his various enterprises. The other business of his that we financed was shipping, which was a key issue for an out of the way island such as Grand Cayman undergoing a huge increase in economic growth. He had purchased two ships, the Dominion Pine and the Night Train, which were already in service in the coastal trades around the Gulf of Mexico. I was able to structure ship's mortgage loans to help fund the shipping operations. Jean Doucet was no ordinary banker. Although he had his formal training as an officer of the Provincial Bank of Canada, he was really an entrepreneur in disguise. He was considered *persona non grata* by the establishment bankers on the island, but I got to know him quite well and always enjoyed our business and occasional social interactions. I also turned down a lot more loans than we made, as he was always coming up with ideas that were just not viable and justifiable loan proposals for our limited and focused appetite.

For our quarterly trip off the island at Easter 1973, Ann and I decided to fly to New York, which would be our first visit to the city. We stayed at the St. Regis Hotel near Central Park, and had a lovely weekend of sightseeing in the Big Apple, as it was called in the mid seventies. The popular song of the moment was "Killing me softly" by Roberta Flack, and when we went for a walk in Central Park on Sunday, we came upon a crowd of people listening to a young black singer/guitarist. He had just sung his version of that song, and the crowd were cheering and clapping and asking him to sing it again. We were lucky enough to hear it the second time around and it was a fabulous rendition of a great song that we experienced quite by accident. The memory lingers.

In the summer we had a visit from some of my family from Scotland. We flew over to Jamaica and welcomed my Mum, Rena and Pete. My Dad's health was in a gradual decline, and he was not well enough to make the trip. They stayed with us for a couple of weeks, and had a great time. We planned a day out on a boat over one weekend and hired the Ebanks Brothers from West Bay, who had a

### THE BOG, THE BAHAMAS, AND BEYOND

catamaran that was actually a houseboat, so it had a nice roomy interior and lots of space on top for lounging or fishing. The trip took us out into the North Sound, which is a large horseshoe shaped bay about five miles or so wide, and from the boat we snorkeled and explored the tropical reefs. The three Ebanks brothers went into the sea at their favorite spots to emerge in a few minutes with lobster and fish that they had speared. We then landed on the Beach at Rum Point, where we were served up cooked fish and lobster, on crackers, with a home-made spicy sauce. Throw in a few Heineken's, or "Greenies" as they are known in the islands, and it made for a lovely day out. The Ebanks brothers were rather special. There was Frankie, Jackie, and Crosby Ebanks, and their actual names were Frank Sinatra Ebanks, Jackie Gleason Ebanks, and Bing Crosby Ebanks. Apparently it was not uncommon for islanders to name their children after famous people, whom they only knew from newspapers and long distance radio. The Ebanks brothers were the top dogs in the weekend boat charter business, and we spent a lot of time with them in the three years that we lived on the island.

After our family left I had to make a quick business trip to the Bahamas to sign a contract on behalf of the bank in connection with the financing of a resort development in Andros Island, the largest of the "out" islands in the Commonwealth of the Bahamas. This was a deal that had been cooked up in Richmond by the President of the Bank of Virginia. I had met him a few times on my occasional trips to Richmond, and would later spend a fair bit of time with him as the deal progressed. He was a smooth and sophisticated guy in his late thirties, and obviously on a fast track within the bank. He was the executive who had pushed the bank's expansion into international banking, which would ultimately lead to his downfall, but in these early days he was seen as the man with the golden touch within the company. As the inspiration behind the Nassau acquisition, he had to make sure that the investment would pay off, but it soon became apparent that a large real estate development loan on the books at the time of acquisition was in deep trouble, and represented a potential loss of around two million dollars. He was approached by three Florida real estate developers who had a plan for the acquisition of the project, and its subsequent development into a large resort community on the north-east coast of Andros. The bank committed to lend the new group almost three and a half million dollars, to improve the infrastructure of the resort and finance the sales of the residential building lots through a real estate brokerage distribution system in the USA and Canada. The pitch to potential buyers was that for around one hundred dollars down payment and one hundred dollars a month for about five years, a buyer would own a quarter acre building lot in the resort development that would ultimately be a site for a retirement home.

On the trip to close the deal in Nassau, I met the three principals of the group, Peter, Ron, and Joe, who were guys in their late thirties and already established operators in Florida real estate. Peter was the promoter with the big ideas, Ron was the accounting guru with a flair for the creative aspects of financial reporting, and Joe was the hands-on construction guy, who also had a pilot's licence. This was particularly helpful, as the company headquarters was in Fort Lauderdale, Florida, about forty miles north of Miami, whereas the San Andros development was about three hundred miles east of the tip of Florida. I went back to Cayman with the assumption that my bosses in Richmond knew what they were doing, and the presumption that the project would be a profitable venture for the bank. Subsequent events would not validate my loyal and somewhat naïve conclusion. I would later find myself right in the middle of the single-most damaging financial loss in the history of the bank. But for now, there were a few more months of business development activities in Cayman before we went on an extended holiday.

Hurricane season in 1973 arrived with a whimper and went out with a whisper. Absolutely nothing happened, and in fact for our entire time in the Caribbean, over a period of five years, we were lucky enough to avoid anything remotely resembling a hurricane. The massive devastation in Cayman that would occur from the impact of Hurricane Ivan in 2004 was a few decades away, and any time there was even a remote likelihood of a hurricane turned out to be just another excuse for a party. By the time the summer was over Ann and I were getting ready for a vacation in South America. The bank had

### THE BOG, THE BAHAMAS, AND BEYOND

arranged for a Bahamian employee to take over the running of the office for a month, while we vacationed in Central and South America on a Pan American Airlines tour that began in San Juan, Costa Rica, and ended in Caracas, Venezuela one month later.

Costa Rica was a neat place to visit. It has long been recognized as the Switzerland of the Americas, because the climate is always Spring-like. The altitude of San Jose compensated for the tropical locale, and with an average temperature of 77 degrees it is easy to slip into a comfortable routine, with lots of daytime hours to be active, and a cool and inspiring night time temperature to venture into the open air atmosphere and enjoy the restaurants and clubs of the capital city. Panama was our next stop, and as it is at sea level, it was hot, humid, and oppressive. During our visit to the Panama Canal we were part of an entourage that included the Latin band Santana, and it just so happened that on our next few stops in South America, Santana were right there with us, performing and touring in their heartland.

There was another reason for a visit to Panama, which had to do with its rather strange link to The Royal Bank of Scotland, my former employer. Joining the Royal Bank was the most significant factor in my life thus far. The bank became in essence the benefactor that gave me the means to step outside my limited comfort zone as a person, and put me in an environment where I could begin to develop personal skills, ambition, presence, and access to the world at large. To paraphrase Sir Winston Churchill, I was a modest man with much to be modest about, when I first entered the door of the branch in the High Street, Falkirk. From that day forward, all I wanted to be was a banker, and with on the job training, education, travel, and social elevation, I began to develop my person and my personality, and the confidence to believe that I could be successful.

Now here I was, in a distant part of the world that for a two year period of time in the late seventeenth century would be the focal point of the Scottish nation's aspiration to establish a Trading Colony in the Isthmus of Panama, then known as Darien, as a counterpart to the London East India Company. All of the capital funds for the venture were raised in Scotland, and in 1698 about 1,200 or so pioneers sailed from the Clyde in Glasgow to the south-western corner of the Gulf of

Mexico. Their mission - to establish a colony that would exploit the natural resources of Darien for trade with the motherland. The next year a second expedition of about 1,300 people sailed to Darien, only to find that heat, fever, and Spanish militants had destroyed most of the colony. The second group experienced the same sad fate as the first, and those that lived to escape the harsh unproductive climate made their way out on foreign ships as best they could. The capital that was lost represented about a quarter of Scotland's liquid assets, and the resultant impoverishment in the country became the focal point of resentment and anger against England, who was seen to be the villain of the piece because of their initial support, then subsequent withdrawal of funding, leaving the Scots to go it alone.

The Act of Union in 1707 joined Scotland and England in the political union of "Great Britain" in part as an attempt to quell political unrest and provide for a financial settlement to Scotland through the payment of the "Equivalent" in the form of coin, tax revenues, and Debentures. A Society of the Subscribers was formed to administer the funds, and make loans to members, and in the process of winding up the Society in 1724 there was a desire to extend the rudimentary banking services into a functioning bank. A Royal Charter incorporating the new Royal Bank of Scotland was duly granted on May 31, 1727. Panama has since risen from the swamps and jungles of the land of Darien, and its most important natural resource is that very neck of land that separates the Gulf of Mexico from the Pacific Ocean, which was engineered to provide access to ships plying their trade between the continents. Ten years later I was back in Panama City on business, and by then had enough command of Spanish to ask a number of locals if they had ever heard of The Darien Scheme, and its connection to my country of Scotland. Not a one knew of this part of their country's history. Two hundred years later over 20,000 men would die of malaria and yellow fever during the construction of the Panama Canal, in a further testament to the unhealthy environment that held sway for such a long time in this part of the world.

The capital of Colombia, Bogota, is a one hour flight to the south and east of Panama, but the city was noticeably different due to the presence of armed soldiers and police on the streets and near the

◂ THE BOG, THE BAHAMAS, AND BEYOND

public buildings. There was a military government in power in the seventies at the same time that the country was ramping up the illegal production of drugs such as cocaine and marijuana for export to the giant consumer to the north, America. The city sits at about seven thousand feet, and even in the seventies had a population of several million. The large number of public buildings and churches made it easy enough to pass a day or two of sightseeing, but we were all happy enough to move on to our next stop in Quito, Ecuador.

It was nice to walk the streets of Quito without the presence of machine guns, and there was such a nice open and fresh vibe to the city. It sits in an Alpine-like setting at about 9,000 feet, and has an accommodating climate - lots of sunshine, yet not too hot. We took a bus out to a rural market town and there was a noticeable air of poverty and need around the small towns and villages that we passed. We have kept a connection of sorts with Ecuador, ever since the early eighties, when we began to sponsor a child through the Christian Children's Fund, and our first and subsequent assigned children have all been from there. Our current child, Diana Lorena Toaquiza, is now fifteen years old, and lives on the altiplana (high plains) in a market town in the southern mountains. We exchange letters on a regular basis, and although it is unlikely that we will ever meet, it is nice to think that my family's photograph rests on a wall of a friend in far away Ecuador.

Our next destination, Lima, is the coastal capital of Peru, and was too big and bustling to have the quaintness that we had seen in Quito. As is true of most of the capital cities in South America, there is a rich heritage of Spanish architecture in the public buildings and churches, and it was in Lima that we visited the glass coffin of the Conquistador, Francisco Pizarro, the leader of the Spanish expeditions to conquer the lands of western South America in the sixteenth century. Just a few years after our visit, archeologists discovered a leaded coffin in the walls of the church, and subsequently determined that these were the true remains of Pizarro. The imposter on display was quietly stripped of his celebrity and consigned to a grave more fitting for a mere mortal.

While we enjoyed our short stay in Lima, the main event was

our trip to the mountain city of Cuzco, and the start of a trip by rail and road through the Urubamba Valley to Machu Picchu. When we arrived by local plane service to Cuzco, we were given cocoa roots by the cabin crew, to chew on as a preventative of altitude sickness. Nobody complained of being ill, so whatever was in the cocoa root worked. Machu Picchu is the "Lost City of the Incas" that has become the icon of the Inca world. It was built around 1450, and abandoned about one hundred years later. Its superb location, perched between two mountain-tops that cannot be seen from the valley below, ensured that the Spanish never discovered this remote city. We had a journey of two or three hours in an old locomotive train that stopped at the villages along the way to let passengers on and off, and provided a commercial opportunity for the locals to sell their wares, mainly cheap souvenirs, through the windows of the train.

When we reached our destination at the foot of the mountain, we transferred to the back of a flat bed truck that had a fence around the perimeter to keep us from falling out on the journey up and down the mountain. The road is a series of switchback curves that allowed us to climb the saddleback between the two mountains of Machu Picchu and Huyana Picchu. The destination unfolds as a fabulous panorama of the mountains around the city, but the city itself is the masterpiece. There are about one hundred and forty stone structures that comprised the community amenities of housing, temples, parks, wells, and irrigation systems, which enabled the residents to live and prosper in a location so remote as to be hidden from the modern world until it was discovered by the American historian, Hiram Bingham, in 1911. At 8,000 feet above sea level, it is actually at a lower elevation than Cuzco, which sits at around 12,000 feet. The hillsides lend themselves to terraced farming, which also makes the surrounding slopes harder for invaders to ascend, as well as protect against land erosion and landslides. The many natural springs around the higher elevations ensure a plentiful supply of fresh water. The city was abandoned in 1572, and it is likely that the inhabitants were affected one way or another by the Spanish conquest of the motherland. The trip back down the mountainside was hair-raising, but we made it back to the valley, and eventually to the hotel in the center of Cuzco. Next day

## THE BOG, THE BAHAMAS, AND BEYOND

we flew back to Lima, and braced ourselves for the next destination, Argentina.

We flew to Buenos Aires across the southern Andes mountains, and the view from the window seat of the plane was fabulous. Snow capped mountains for endless miles, and no sign of habitation, or even the snail tracks of a road system. Somewhere near this flight path was the scene of the infamous crash of a Uruguayan Air Force plane in 1972, when the survivors resorted to cannibalism in order to survive. However, we were safe a mile high in our Pan Am jet, and the journey was untoward. We arrived at the Buenos Aires Hilton to find a political demonstration in the streets, protesting against Yankee imperialism, or some such anti-American vibe. President Juan Peron and his third wife Isabel Peron were back in the Presidential palace, having endured political exile since 1955, and the country was caught up in a wave of emotion. We braved the crowds in the square in front of the palace to see Peron and his Vice President/wife wave to the masses, and made it safely back to the hotel. His second wife, Eva (Evita) Peron, was the one who had captured the public's imagination, and in Argentina she is revered by the people of her country because of her solidarity with the masses, and her compassion for the poor, to whom she dedicated the latter part of her short life of 33 years. We caught up with Eva at her magnificent resting place in La Racoleta Cemetery in Buenos Aires. You know it must be quite a cemetery if it has daily tours.

Buenos Aires seemed to be the most like a European city than the capitals of the other Andean countries that we had visited. The architecture was a pleasing mixture of old colonial and modern buildings, and plenty of green space for the city center residents to enjoy. The absence of native Indian culture was noticeable, and with some 40% of the population of Italian ancestry, the city did have an Italian ambiance. The fashions were contemporary, the décor of the city was Southern European, and the buses and cars seemed to be many variations of the Fiat brand. There is also a significant link to Britain, from whence came engineers backed up by capital raised in the London financial markets to build the national railroad system in the eighteen hundreds. We had dinner in a lovely old city restaurant, and Senor

## THE CAYMAN ISLANDS

Campbell the Maitre d'hôtel was a card carrying member of the Clan Campbell, who wore his name with pride.

Our next flight took us in a north-easterly direction to the Republic of Brazil, and to one of the world's magical cities, Rio do Janeiro. It is hard to find a city more endowed with natural beauty than Rio. For a fabulous panorama of its entirety, just stand on the steps of the monument of Christ the Redeemer and look around at the stunning view. The beaches of Rio separate the bluest of oceans from the surrounding land, in a succession of arcs that form a necklace of gold, and are the playgrounds for the poorest Carioca's to the wealthiest of its residents. We took the hair-raising trip by cable car across to Sugarloaf Mountain, and it is without question the scariest experience that I can remember. There are actually two cable car trips to get there. The first one brings you to the top of Mount Urca, and from there the cable car traverses across the cable lines that are strung between the two mountains, to the 1,300 feet peak of the Sugarloaf. Although only a few minutes of time, there is nothing below but open sea. Travelers are advised to leave their imaginations at home. We stayed at a hotel on the Copacabana, and spent time people watching on the broad sands of the beach. It was a nice change not having to spend all the time on sightseeing, but just to walk the streets, and absorb the sights and sounds of the city. This was the last stay for the group as a whole, although Ann and I had another destination planned for our final week – Caracas, Venezuela.

The Tamanaco Hilton hotel in Caracas is, like everything else in Caracas, built on the side of a mountain. The city seems to weave its way around and among the hills and valleys of the region, at an average elevation of 2,500 feet. Although tropical, the elevation mitigates extremes of temperature, and we found it to be warm enough to sunbathe by the hotel pool in the day, and cool enough for dressier clothes in the evening. I would come to know the city better in later years when we had a significant book of business there, and many corporate and banking clients. We met another Scottish couple around the pool bar, John and Agnes Cunnion, who were both from Glasgow, but had lived in New York for many years. Both John and Agnes passed away recently, and that chance encounter at a bar in a far-away place led to a lifetime of friendship.

## THE BOG, THE BAHAMAS, AND BEYOND

We arrived back in Cayman after our month of travel anxious to pick up our lives in a place that we had come to love in the year or so that we had lived there. The pace of business in the office was hardly a challenge, so Ann and I were able to open at 9am, close for lunch, and lock up for the day between 4pm and 5pm. Once back at Harbour Heights, I would change into my swimming trunks and tee shirt, grab a cold Heineken, and go down to the Clubhouse to play table tennis with Ian Kilpatrick, whose business hours were no more confining than mine. The residents of the condominium tended to assemble around 6.30 pm to have a drink while watching the sun go down. As the sun began to dip into the sea on the horizon we all anticipated seeing a "Green Flash" which is a phenomenon of nature in the Tropics, but is rarely seen. If the atmospherics are right, then as the last piece of the top of the Sun dips into the ocean, it can shine through the meniscus and create a momentary flash of green. I have seen it a handful of times in my life, but have spent many a time looking, and as there is normally a congregation of aspirants with a glass in hand it makes for a pleasant way to end the day. The infrequency of success invariably leads to the rationalization that it is more about socializing than appreciating the science, but when you do see the Green Flash it makes up for all the disappointments.

Weekends were spent on or around the beach. Because many of the apartments were owned as vacation homes by Americans and Canadians, there was always a new face to see around the pool or the beach, and over time we got to know most if not all of the owners. It soon became apparent that for we residents, there was always an opportunity somewhere to socialize. The folks from Louisville would arrive in the form of three or four couples, and the whole week would be dedicated to helping them enjoy their week in the sun. Then it would be the group from Toronto. This was the way of life for most of our time on the island, and we thoroughly enjoyed it. There is something about living on an island, especially one as small as Grand Cayman, where the seascape overpowers the landscape, and the sense of confinement after a while becomes a security blanket, not to be given up easily.

The Caymans are a hugely popular destination for Scuba-divers, who come to dive the reefs and wrecks around the island. Now and then there would be a casualty, although it was invariably a tourist who, after a night on the tiles, would wake up in the morning and decide to try Scuba-diving for the first time. In the early seventies this was easy to do, as there were no provisions for licences, or any other means of demonstrating capability with the equipment. Nowadays it is different, but back then it was simple to dive, after some basic instructions on the way out to the reef. When a diver gets in trouble, and ascends too quickly, there is a chance that nitrogen absorbed by breathing at depth when water pressures are different from the surface can remain in the tissues when the diver surfaces, and cause a painful and often fatal reaction in the body. Bubbles lodged in the joints cause the diver to bend over in pain, and hence the term "bends." A diver with the symptoms needs to be brought into a Hyperbaric chamber, and then "re-compressed" under the watchful eye of a competent professional, who enters the chamber with the patient, and experiences the graduated change in pressure along with the patient. If the diver is caught in time, then a full recovery is the expected outcome of a visit to the chamber. It is not a pleasant experience, but it does reverse the symptoms, with no health repercussions thereafter.

There was no such facility in the Caymans. Even although Miami was but a ninety minute flight away, by the very nature of the illness the changing pressures experienced by flying at altitude would only exacerbate the pain and likely cause the death of the patient. One of our friends, Edna Bissell, was a nurse who worked in the Cayman Clinic, and helped mobilize a fundraising effort on the island to acquire a "Compression Chamber" as it was then known, so that there would be a local response to this all too frequent illness. We all chipped in with money and fund raising efforts and were proud to be able to bring a brand new chamber to the island, which saved countless numbers of lives thereafter. Edna was the designated nursing professional who had to enter the chamber with the diver, and go through the decompression/recompression cycle locked into a metal tube that was about five feet in height and maybe ten feet in length. On the odd moment that I speculated on the pleasures of diving the reefs, and that maybe I should enroll in local diving classes, I thought about that chamber and said to myself, "no thanks, Edna."

### THE BOG, THE BAHAMAS, AND BEYOND

In Easter of 1974 we had a long weekend off the island, in Mexico. A bunch of us decided to charter a plane and head for the Yucatan Peninsula, to visit the Mayan cities of Uxmal and Chicheniza, then finish off with a couple of days on the resort island of Cozumel. The airplane turned out to be a vintage DC9 propeller plane, and the seating plan was sort of like an old time café with booths where you sat opposite your fellow traveler. Perhaps the coziness of the seating was the reason, but in any event we had the most hilarious two hour flight across the Gulf of Mexico, with drinks flying everywhere, and people moving around and switching travel partners in mid flight. It certainly got us off to a good start, and the entire weekend was a positive and happy experience. I should have paid attention to the history of the ruins, but I didn't. I should have shown some kind of acknowledged respect to the wonderful culture of the Mayan civilization, but I didn't. I did, however, have a wonderful time on the beaches of Cozumel with our pals from Cayman, and I think Ann would join me in designating that weekend jaunt as one of those unforgettable times in life, when everything came together in a magical blend of friendship, culture, revelry and leisure.

Our weekly endeavors at the office were once again the pre-eminent focus of our activities, as I was challenged to find decent business opportunities that would meet the objectives that we had established for the local office. Cayman was a small place, with by now no more than fifteen thousand residents, but hard as it is to imagine, there was a governmental structure that was patterned on much larger Crown Colonies, and included the issuance of its own currency, which then as now is set at a value of 1 Cayman Dollar equals 1.25 US Dollars. The growth rates of the local economy were way higher than anything the islands had seen before, driven by the twin engines of tourism and offshore banking/insurance, and this could be felt all over the island. The new bank buildings required construction organizations. The personnel required housing. The disposable income of Caymanians rose significantly as they experienced the bounties from rapid growth of the local economy. The influx of well paid expatriates, with no income taxes, meant increased consumer spending across the board. Car rental agencies suddenly sprung up. Air travel soon swamped the basic facilities at Owen Roberts International Airport, where daily flights replaced once weekly flights. The main harbor at George Town was significantly upgraded, which greatly improved the freight shipping service between Grand Cayman and Miami, as well as Jamaica. The harbor was still not capable of docking cruise ships, but soon Grand Cayman was on the itinerary of the major cruise lines, as they were able to moor at the mouth of the harbor and transport the vacationers by small craft into the heart of George Town.

For all this business activity, it was still hard to find good lending opportunities other than real estate. There was a plethora of condominium and apartment projects created by architects new to the island, indulging the dreams of aspiring local developers, as well as a few American and Canadian investors who invariably came on vacation and "discovered" the island, returning to the mainland with a determination to get some financial support back home for their dream project. Of course, no bank in Eastern Montana or Northern Ohio would readily lend against offshore projects, so they would invariably return to the island with their newly printed plans, and start calling on the local banks to procure the funding. Any prospective investors in Cayman property would invariably find our office, particularly if there was a home connection to Virginia, so we met lots of nice people who would arrive unannounced, looking to borrow funds for their projects, which were "guaranteed" to be successful. I saw lots of plans and spreadsheets, and was happy to give advice about their projects and how to finance them, but regretfully we were just not interested in that kind of business. There were plenty of banks who were, especially the large international banks, so after a while the visitors would head off in the direction that I pointed them in, with a purposeful stride, and the conviction that somewhere on this island was a bank just dying to make a loan to the project that cannot fail.

I was chatting to my neighbor Henry at the pool one day, and he told me of an incident that happened a few days before. He had left his office one morning to walk across to the down-town supermarket, Byrite, for a few odds and ends, and he happened upon a Jamaican employee of his who was standing at the newspaper and magazine rack, reading the papers. The employee was supposed to be in jail for 30 days, having committed some kind of petty crime. Henry asked him what was going on, and had he been released early? It turned out that the local jail let him out every morning at around ten o'clock so that he could walk over to Byrite and read the newspapers, then return to his cell. Unattended! This was normal operating procedure at the jail, and the authorities obviously had figured out that the flight risk was low to non-existent, so why not let the prisoner have the required rest and recreation across the street at the supermarket. It saved the jail from having to provide newspapers for the occasional occupant, and was good for prisoner morale. This is one of these things that could only happen in a small, remote place like Cayman, where everybody knows everybody, and the normal conventions of society do not necessarily apply.

CHAPTER **10**

# Banking Shenanigans

IT WAS AROUND the late summer of 1974 that our business lives were about to change dramatically, with the business failure of our largest client and his Interbank House Group of companies. By now we had a diversified portfolio of loans and deposits on the island, and a larger book of loans and deposits from the balance of our international portfolio, dominated by our Latin American clients. However the pace of business was fairly even and predictable, so that we were never in the office after 5pm, except maybe at month end when we closed the books for the month. In short, life was good and we had lots of time to enjoy our time and place in the sun. Then the roof caved in!

By September of 1974 the Interbank House Group had become a financial and industrial holding company with interests in commercial and mortgage banking, gold trading, an airline, shipping, real estate development, publishing, film making, and even an island museum. Their principal subsidiary was Sterling Bank and Trust. The head office now occupied some 11,000 square feet of lavishly decorated property on the original site, and attractive secretaries in black and silver custom designed pantsuits served a management group of mainly British executives, and clients from all over the world. Our loan exposure at that time was some $1.5 million to their mortgage bank, and term loans of $100,000 and $150,000 each to two shipping companies owned by the bank, secured by ships mortgages over the MV Dominion Pine and the MV Night Train. Both ships were island

### THE BOG, THE BAHAMAS, AND BEYOND

freighters, which brought goods to Cayman from Central America, other Caribbean ports, and of course Miami. For a bank of our size at that time, these loans represented a fairly significant exposure in our international portfolio.

During 1974 the bank had all the outward appearances of a growing and profitable institution, but in fact it was already on a death spiral. With increasing financial commitments to a variety of ventures, including an exclusive real estate project, it was facing a liquidity crisis, as it had been funding all these investments with short term deposits from an increasingly fickle deposit base. Jean Doucet and his family left the Island by Lear Jet on Friday, September 10th. He convened in Montreal with his fellow Shareholders, Accountants, and Lawyers, and the decision was taken to close the bank down and liquidate. On Monday morning we learned through the "grapevine" that the bank had not opened for business, and by 10 o'clock my boss in Richmond was contacted by Doucet, who was now in London, to let us know that the banking group was in voluntary liquidation. Don's news was pretty devastating, and I was concerned about our exposure to losses from our lending business, but by mid morning I had somewhat recovered my poise, helped by the knowledge that Don and Werner were en route to Cayman. While Ann focused on putting together reports and information on the terms of our various loan agreements, I set about establishing priorities for the collection of our loans. They were all secured, and possession of our collateral was as always the primary objective, as it is only by taking legal and financial control of the collateral that a bank is best able to effect an orderly sale or liquidation of the assets. Although our exposure to the mortgage bank was significant, I was comfortable with the quality of our collateral. Our loan proceeds had been on-lent to mainly Caymanian clients, and we had a collateral portfolio of mortgage loans that was one and a half times our loan value, so I knew that we would be in a position to take over the mortgage portfolio and apply the mortgage payments from the entire portfolio against our loan. We would eventually have some fun and games with the company Liquidators, who were trying to keep the mortgage portfolio within the bank's control. However our documentation and legal position was unassailable, and subsequent

## BANKING SHENANIGANS

events enabled us to recover 100% of principal, interest, and expenses. Not only did we take over the local mortgages, but I hired Del Smithers, the Caymanian manager of the portfolio. She knew all of the Caymanian borrowers, and was a huge help in assisting Ann and me with the increased workload of about eighty new customers, all of whom were now required to pay their monthly mortgage payment to Bank of Virginia from now on. A lot of hand holding was required to assure our Caymanian customers that their mortgage payments to us instead of to the old bank would be properly credited against their mortgage balances. The more pressing problem was the location of the two ships.

Within a few days we met with the three Liquidators who were approved by the Court to manage the liquidation of the bank and related companies. It was clear from the outset that they would be adversaries rather than facilitators, as any assets that we took to satisfy our loans reduced the assets that they had to work with in finding enough money to pay depositors. One of the Liquidators was the same English financier and investor, Keith Norman, who was on the Board of Mariculture. During many hours of meetings and negotiations with Keith and his colleagues, we were able to develop a liking and respect for each other that was the basis of our subsequent personal friendship, but at the beginning it was all business, with many a cut and thrust as we tried to outmaneuver each other in the right to control the collateral. It was at our first meeting with Keith and his Co-Liquidators that we were informed that the MV Night Train had left Miami on September 2nd en route to Cayman, loaded with construction materials for the real estate project. This happened to coincide with the development of a tropical storm, which was quickly upgraded to become Hurricane Camille, whose 100 plus miles per hour winds hit Cuba and southern Florida. The storm caused havoc in the shipping lanes, and the Night Train, with its Captain and crew of six Caymanians broke down in the storm, and drifted helplessly towards Cuba. Captain Parsons radioed for help, and by coincidence the SS Richard, owned by Reynolds Aluminum, a major Richmond, Virginia based company, was in the vicinity of the Night Train, on the way to the United States from Jamaica. Although the Captain of the

### THE BOG, THE BAHAMAS, AND BEYOND

SS Richard was willing to help the Night Train he was advised by his head office, with whom he was in radio communication, to refrain from involvement in view of the proximity to Cuba, and the possibility that the SS Richard itself might be compromised by being in or near Cuban waters.

By 8am on September 6th the vessel had drifted to a position approximately 4 miles off the Cuban coast, and was in danger of striking the rocky banks. By 11am a Cuban tug boat had arrived, and offered to put a line out to the Night Train. Captain Parsons had no option but to accept, knowing that without assistance his ship would soon hit the rocks. In accordance with Maritime Law, the Cubans were entitled to a salvage claim, based on the value of the ship and contents that were saved by their actions. She was then towed to the Isle of Pines, a small island off the Cuban Coast, where the ship was boarded by machine gun carrying soldiers, who proceeded to confiscate all the food supplies, and the ships radio. Based on reports later obtained from Captain Parsons and his crew, their stay in Cuba, which was to last 27 days, was a frightening and miserable experience. They were confined to their cabins, given little food, and subjected to taunts and abuse from their guards. Meanwhile, back in Cayman I had been joined by my colleagues from Richmond, and the early days passed in a flurry of activity. At one point we were interrupted in a meeting with the Liquidators, and told that a construction crew from the real estate development had commandeered two bulldozers, and were heading down West Bay Road towards Interbank House intent on revenge for their lack of wages. Never have bankers moved so fast, nor adjourned a meeting with less ceremony. Our lawyers, who also represented Sterling Bank, then decided that their position of conflict was too great, and withdrew from representing Bank of Virginia. In the few days between then and retaining new Counsel, we drew up our own documents, and served hastily prepared and dubious legal notices on our clients and their representatives. Thankfully, none were challenged.

We also located the Dominion Pine in Barranquilla, Colombia, and discovered that the ship had been impounded by the Harbormaster because of non-payment of invoices for paint supplies from a local company on a previous visit. After telephone negotiations with the Harbor Master, hindered by his poor English and my then non-existent Spanish, he agreed to permit the ship to leave, once I had wire transferred $2,000 to cover the invoices and port charges. A few days later the Dominion Pine left Barranquilla with 9,000 bags of cement in her holds, and took in water on a rough return journey to Cayman. Consequently, when I met the ship at dockside in Cayman several days later, and boarded her to take possession under our ship's mortgage, the hold contained what seemed like 9,000 bags of concrete! However, we salvaged what we could, and sold them to a local builder, using the cash to pay the crew's wages. As if to add insult to injury, we learned that the paint supplies invoices were a subterfuge for a bill from a local brothel, which had sustained costs and damages from a previous visit by some of the crew, who had apparently sampled the wares without paying for the privilege. The local Madam was clearly an entrepreneur of sorts, and her method of collecting for the alcohol and human services provided by her hostelry was very effective. There may have been a few pesos that made their way back to the harbormaster of Barranquilla, but we will never know.

By the end of September I had attained a fair degree of knowledge about ships and Maritime Law, and even my friends on the island were calling me "Captain" Hunter. For example, as Mortgagee in Possession on behalf of our bank, I became the official Master of the Dominion Pine when she docked in Cayman. As such, her Captain resigned on my appointment, but I quickly re-hired him as my deputy on board to look after security while at dockside. Under Maritime Law a ship's crew has a lien on the ship for wages. This meant that the first thing I had to do was to make sure that the crew was paid for all their hours since their last pay several weeks before. Each man's hours were checked against the log, and I dutifully doled out some more of the bank's money in order to protect our security. Without cleaning up the wages, we would not have been able to eventually sell the ship. Although the crew had now been reduced to one, namely Captain Ebanks, there was still the odd incident to deal with, now that my responsibilities included a ship lying a few hundred yards off the harbor at George Town. Captain Ebanks arranged for one of the former crew members to sleep on board the ship each night, while he went home. Apparently the seaman invited his pals to come aboard in the evening and fish from the decks, all the while drinking it up and having a great time. Someone spotted lights on the ship going in and out, along with general noise and merriment that carried on the evening breezes to the shore. When tipped off about it, I decided to let it go, and give the former crew some fun. As temporary Master it was my responsibility should anything untoward happen, but I decided to turn a blind eye. After a few nights the novelty must have worn off, or maybe the fish just got wise to the predators above, as the parties soon stopped of their own accord.

The process of selling the Dominion Pine was actually quite orderly, and much different from the experiences that were in store for us with the Night Train. There was no need to "advertise" or otherwise circulate information about the sale of the ship. The Caribbean shipping community has a network of information distribution that is quite incredible, especially considering that this was before the days of the Internet. From Miami to Barranquilla and San Juan to Panama, the drums must have been beating, because I soon was contacted by telephone and telex from all sorts of shipping companies and brokers enquiring about both ships. Since the Dominion Pine was in good condition, and the Night Train was still in Cuba, I focused my energies on finding a viable buyer for the Dominion Pine, and within a few weeks I was able to reach an agreement with a shipping group based in San Juan, Puerto Rico. This turned out to be one of the more uplifting aspects of my many months in the shipping business, as the two gentlemen that I negotiated with were just a pleasure to be around, both in Cayman and in San Juan, where I flew for a day or so at one point in the negotiations. Our loan against the vessel was for $100,000 and we agreed to a sale price of $135,000. The price was partly financed by us, so I had to visit the company's operations in San Juan, and do the usual due diligence on their ability to handle the debt and repay the bank in accordance with the terms of the deal. When I arrived at San Juan I was welcomed by Juan Dominguez and invited to his home for dinner that evening. He had a large family and was a charming and interesting host. His partner Jose Rodriguez was there, and I remember him telling me that he had five passports, and was working on a sixth. He said that it made it easier to do business in many of the ports where they called with freight deliveries and pick-ups. I found it quite amusing, although I did wonder if there was an ulterior motive that was less than honorable. As it turned out, I would enjoy three years of a business relationship with them, while they were paying off the loan, and never had one bit of a problem. They were exemplary clients.

Meanwhile, the Liquidators of the Bank were trying to unravel the complicated structure of the 100 or so operating companies, loosely known as the Interbank House Group. They quickly realized that the resolution of the Night Train matter was best left in our hands as the major creditor, since whatever equity the group had in the vessel was by now diminished, if not non-existent. Later events proved this to be so, since the Liquidators did not realize any funds from the subsequent sale of the ship, all of which went to our bank as the sole secured creditor. However, the path towards repaying the bank from the sale of the ship was a slippery slope, full of twists and turns, as things played out over the course of the next several months. For political reasons, the only telephone contact possible between Cayman and Cuba was to the Swiss Embassy in Havana, through a US telephone circuit, thus enabling all calls to be monitored by the CIA. Accordingly, negotiations with the Cuban authorities for the release of the ship and crew were conducted in rather difficult circumstances. However, the Cubans made their position quite clear. Bank of Virginia, as owners in possession of the MV Night train by virtue of their ship's mortgage, were required to post a $100,000 bond with Lloyds of London, covering the salvage claim by the Cuban Government. The exact amount of the salvage award was later established at $45,000 and this sum was ultimately paid by Lloyds to representatives of the Cuban Government in November, 1976.

But before all that, we needed to get control of the ship back in Caymanian waters, and so we had to get the Cubans their Lloyds Bond, which took several days to negotiate. In the process, I also discovered that the official Receiver of Ships in Cayman was not the Harbormaster, as he had no radio equipment! Instead, that responsibility was held

◄ THE BOG, THE BAHAMAS, AND BEYOND

by Delworth Ebanks, the owner and operator of an Exxon petrol station near the harbor. Delworth's station was always a center of social activity, as he sold peas and rice - a local delicacy, and cold beer in addition to 89 octane gasoline. I had been told by the Swiss Embassy on September 25th that the ship would be leaving Cuba any day, and I spent many a night at the petrol station while Delworth worked his radio, trying to reach the Night Train. This wasn't quite as dull as it sounds, since a crowd of locals gathered at Delworths around nine o'clock each night for snacks, drinks, and Reggae music. Finally, on the evening of October 3rd, while Ann and I were having dinner at the house of our lawyer, Doug Calder, we checked in with Delworth for an update, and he had just had radio contact with the ship. We headed down to the petrol station, leaving two nervous wives in charge of a briefcase with $4,000 in cash, being the amount of the towage fees which we had committed to pay the Cuban tugboat master. Sure enough, we spoke briefly by radio with Captain Parsons, who told us he would arrive in Cayman early the next morning.

At the crack of dawn I looked out of my bedroom window and there, in the distance, was the outline of the Night Train and the Cuban tug. Soon I was down at the dockside to prepare for the formalities involved in taking possession of the vessel. Because the ship had no means of power, it was not possible to bring her in to the harbor, and so she was "hove to" about one mile offshore. By mid morning the news had spread that the "Night Train" had arrived from Cuba, in tow by a Cuban tugboat, and soon the harbor was crowded with locals, anxious for a front seat at the day's events. Meanwhile, Doug and I were in the offices of the Harbormaster, along with Government officials from Immigration, Customs, and (believe it or not) Mosquito Research. The Cuban tugboat captain and his political officer met us in the office in order to complete the formalities of handing over the vessel, including payment of the towage charges of $4,000. To my surprise, they refused to accept payment in U.S. dollars, insisting that it be paid in Canadian dollars. This was quite in keeping with the diplomatic atmosphere of the time in Cuba and US relations, but we had no option but to try and get them their money and see them off the island. I had to call around some of my banker friends until I could

◄ 142

## BANKING SHENANIGANS

find one whose vault wasn't time locked, and then arrange to exchange the dollars for Canadian currency. The fact that the exchange rate meant that the Cubans were actually receiving the equivalent of a lesser amount of US Dollars was not important to them. It was a matter of principal, and it cost the Cubans about $400. By mid-day all was completed, the Cubans had sailed away, and we were ready to embark on the small boat which would take us across to the Night Train. To the cheers of the crowd the boarding party set off, and after a short but uncomfortable journey in increasingly choppy seas, we reached the Night Train.

Boarding in the choppy sea was a problem, but finally we made it and were greeted by a grateful Captain Parsons and his six man crew. Unfortunately for my rather sensitive stomach, the Government Officials had priority, and so went about their business of ship inspection, spraying for mosquito's, checking passports and papers etc. Finally, it was our turn to present our documents, take control of the vessel, relieve the Captain of his command, and legally take possession of the ship. However, this ceremony was temporarily delayed while I threw up over the rails, having succumbed to the constant pitch and roll of the vessel. Once I recovered my composure, our Lawyer read out the legal notice of possession, and I became Master of the ship. Strictly speaking the Notice of Possession should be mailed to the mast, but this was 1974, and even the Night Train had a steel mast. My first official act as Master was to re-hire Captain Parsons, along with a couple of the crew members, to maintain watch over the ship. We soon returned to the dockside, and made arrangements with the Harbormaster for safe haven just outside the harbor. Wednesday saw a return to more typical Cayman weather of blue skies and calm seas, and the beginning of my experiences as a de-facto ship-owner. First of all, I had to pay the crew wages. At the same time, we began the process of obtaining legal ownership of the vessel, which would give us the right to sell her. Early on in the proceedings we had dispatched a Sterling Bank employee to London, to make sure all of the insurance papers were in order. It seemed like all I did was spend the Bank's money in these early days trying to preserve good title to the ship. Once the insurance negotiations were over, it was time to deal with

## THE BOG, THE BAHAMAS, AND BEYOND

the cargo. With the break in the weather, we contracted for the transfer of the cargo to another ship, which was then unloaded at dockside. The cargo consisted of several containers of steel beams and lumber, one automobile, furniture, and miscellaneous commercial goods. By law, each cargo owner was required to post a bond for their share of the salvage claim, and most of the owners preferred to walk away rather than take on this commitment. I was then faced with selling the cargo as best I could, which I managed to do over the course of several weeks.

After a few days, life in the shipping business began to take on some aspects of a routine, with my daily talk with Captain Parsons (onshore!) and ongoing dealings with cargo, crew and Counsel. Soon we began to get calls, telexes, and visits from people interested in buying the ship, most of whom flew into the island from South America. Among the potential buyers was a Miami businessman whom I shall call "David" and his Colombian partner "Juan." David was a charming fellow, and Juan did not say much - just hid behind his sunglasses and chewed gum. One way or another we finally came to terms on a sale of the Night Train. David would buy the ship for $75,000 to be paid at closing. He returned to Miami with Juan, and we set up a closing to occur in Richmond in January 1975.

The Cayman Islands lie to the south of Cuba, and to the north of Jamaica. The prevailing winds tend to come from the south-east for most of the year, but winter brings an occasional north-wester, when the winds spring from the Gulf of Mexico and gather speed on their journey south to the Central Caribbean. The harbor in Grand Cayman faces the west, and so is particularly vulnerable. Sure enough, on November 10 we received word of the likelihood of a storm hitting Cayman from the north-west, with an estimated arrival date of November 15. Captain Parsons duly recommended that we arrange to move the Night Train to safe anchorage in the North Sound, the large expanse of shallow water guarded by a coral reef some 10 miles round the coastline from the harbor. I contacted Lloyds to request permission to have the ship towed, and received a telex response on November 11 requiring that the towing be done by a Lloyds approved tug. One phone call to the Harbormaster confirmed there was no such vessel

## BANKING SHENANIGANS

in the Cayman Islands. We finally located one in Kingston, Jamaica, some 280 miles to the south. Meanwhile, the Cayman weather was beginning to reflect the approaching storm, as the seas were more active, and the clouds rolled in. With the help of Stanley Ebanks, my shipping agent and by now good friend, I contacted the owners of the tug, and discovered that the earliest landfall in Cayman would be November 16. I telexed back to Lloyds to explain the situation, and of my concern that the Night Train would be totally exposed to the approaching north-wester. Not only that, she was anchored one mile from a populated waterfront area, and I was concerned about the liability should the ship be driven on to the shore. After several hours delay I was advised by Lloyds that the Night Train could only be moved by an approved tug, and that if she was moved by any other vessel then the insurance would be invalid. We continued our long distance dialogue as the day progressed, and the exchange of telexes had all the elements of a poker game. Unfortunately I lost, as Lloyds refused to back down.

The heart of the storm was now two days out, and I remember sitting in the bar of the "Lobster Pot" with Ann, and thinking that if I didn't get the Night Train out of the Harbor, she would more than likely end up on top of the pub. On the ground floor of the Lobster Pot was Bob Soto's Dive Shop, and I went down to talk to Bob about the situation. He volunteered the use of a dive boat to use as a tug, with the unlikely name of the MV Lollipop. The Lollipop was actually a WW2 landing craft altered to suit the diving business. I now had an "unapproved" tug, but nevertheless a tug, and at Bob's recommendation I paid a call on a retired Caymanian sea captain (and local worthy) Captain Roy McTaggart, to ask if he would tow the Night Train into the North Sound. He agreed that it had to be done, but that it was not without risk. The entry point through the reefs into the North Sound was only sixteen feet wide. Next morning, with the winds picking up, Captain McTaggart took the MV Lollipop with the Night Train in tow round the West Bay peninsula and through the channel into the Sound. The whole operation took four hours, and provided about one week's worth of headlines in the local paper. To this day, I still find it hard to believe that Captain McTaggart was able to get both vessels, one of which had no power, through a 16 foot wide channel in rough seas. With the Night Train safe, I telexed Lloyds, who condescended to resume insurance coverage. As expected, the full force of the northwester hit the next day, and Ann and I were able to celebrate our small victory in where else but the bar of the Lobster Pot.

With the Night Train no longer in danger, I returned to the business of negotiating with David on the sale of the ship. The deal was struck on an "as is, where is" basis, meaning that David would buy the vessel in her current condition, and be responsible for all repairs to the vessel in order to make her seaworthy again. We arranged to meet in Richmond, and so a few weeks later I met David at head office so that we could close the sale. At closing David produced a Pan Am Airways bag, from which he pulled out enough bundles of cash to cover the sale price of $75,000. With the help of a teller from the branch, we completed the exchange of cash for title to the ship. Not satisfied with buying just the Night Train, David then pointed to his Pan Am bag and said that he had enough additional cash with him to buy the Dominion Pine. I had to disappoint him, since I had already reached agreement with the Puerto Rican group for a satisfactory sales price, so David left with title to the Night Train and at least $100,000 in cash still packed in his Pan Am bag. Back in Cayman, I began to tidy up all of the many details arising out of my time in the shipping business. The Dominion Pine was picked up by her new owners, and left port en route to San Juan. After a few visits, and the installation of a new crankshaft, David had the Night Train in decent enough shape to leave Cayman for her new life as a sugar carrier. Based upon subsequent events, the sugar business never did materialize, and the Night Train was to become one of the most infamous ships in the history of Caribbean drug traffic, of which more later.

One of the more unusual financing deals that I developed was our business with the turtle farm in Cayman, operating under the name of Mariculture Ltd., and their particular species was the Green Sea Turtle, or to give it the proper name "Chelonia Mydas." This species of sea turtle is indigenous to many of the tropical areas of the world, and their value as a source of food and protein for the early seafarers of the Caribbean is well documented. The Cayman operation was the first of its kind anywhere to attempt the rearing of Green Sea Turtles, from incubation until their commercially viable age of about three years, and about one hundred pounds in weight. One of the interesting things about Chelonia Mydas is that ninety five per cent of the turtle has commercial value, and the other five per cent can be chopped up and mixed with the feedstuff for the live breeding stock. The shells are used in the jewelry business, the meat can be cooked as a stew with many variations thereof, and the underbelly is used to make soup.

The farm was located along the rocky north-west point of the island and had a small natural beach that was an important part of the plant. Turtles lay their eggs in many of the remote beach areas of the western Caribbean. When they are ready to lay, they swim ashore to a sandy beach and use the front flippers to push the sand away to create a large hole. Then the turtle rests astride the hole and drops the ping pong ball size eggs into the sand. The mother pushes the sand back into the hole, where they are left to incubate, and eventually the baby turtles emerge from the sand, usually in the evening, where, helped by the slope of the beach and the lights from the night sky, they make their way into the ebbing water. In the wild, the number of baby turtles who make it to maturity is miniscule, about one out of a clutch of about one hundred eggs. Most of the capitulation by the baby turtles is to predators in those early hours in the sea, being much favored by birds, crabs, and all sorts of marine life. However, the two months or so of incubation under the sand is also a time of exposure to land based predators, and often the entire clutch of eggs will be ravaged by animals from peccaries to dogs, depending on the location of the beach.

The low survival rate of Green Sea Turtles in the wild was the basis on which Mariculture was able to negotiate with countries in Central America for the right to gather thousands of turtle eggs from their beaches. The gathered eggs would be placed in Styrofoam boxes and flown to Grand Cayman, and their destination in the sand of the Mariculture beach. The company was able to make the case that the survival rates would be much higher in a farmed environment, as they would hatch all the eggs in the plant, then in due course release a

### THE BOG, THE BAHAMAS, AND BEYOND

specific amount of maturing turtles into the sea, that would be several weeks old and capable of sustaining life. This seemed to be a win-win situation, for the turtles that survived and the sponsoring countries, and ensured a valuable source of product for the company. The hatchlings destined for rearing were placed in large tanks of water, and subject to normal fish processing techniques to ensure healthy and protein enriched growth. Once commercially viable, the turtles were slaughtered and the parts separated for refinement into the finished product, and shipped to their customers.

The company needed working capital financing to get them through the breeding cycle, and on to the markets they had opened up in the United States and Japan. In the course of negotiating the loan I met with most of the US based directors, which would become important a year or so later when the company's business plan was destroyed by international legislation that put Chelonia Mydas on the endangered species list. This legislation effectively prevented the company from shipping their produce anywhere in the world, and despite protestations through official diplomatic channels, their market was essentially taken away from them. They were never able to get enough governmental support to make their case, even though it added to the net re-productive population of the species. The Cayman Islands Government just had no clout with the NGO's in Washington DC, and so their only market was taken away almost before it opened up. In the end, the individual directors paid off our loan personally, and Mariculture was sold to the Government. The farm survives to this day, but is mainly a tourist attraction, and no longer supports the one hundred or so employees that made it, for a time, the largest employer on the island. The Green Sea Turtles in the wild continue to lay their eggs in clutches of one hundred, sometimes a few more, sometimes a few less, but predictably an average of one hundred. This is the evolutionary inspired number that the producing turtles are hard wired to produce to ensure survival of the species, and perhaps a more fitting destiny than swimming in circles for three years.

In February of 1975 Don came down from Richmond with the news that there was a position waiting for me at the head office in

## BANKING SHENANIGANS

Richmond, as a Vice President of Bank of Virginia International. The plan was to close our Cayman office and move our offshore business back to the Bahamian bank, which was now 100% owned after buying out Lady Sassoon's minority stake. As it was not viable to move us back to Nassau, in view of the work permit situation, the job in Richmond would be practical experience that would enable us to eventually move to London, in order to open a Representative office of the bank. This was all a lot to take in, as we were so happy in Cayman, and would have been quite happy to spend a few more years offshore. On the other hand, from a career perspective, the experience and responsibilities of my new job in Richmond would be fulfilling, and there was an end game in the London position that seemed quite exciting.

Within a couple of months we were celebrating a farewell dinner at the Grand Old House restaurant with our closest friends from our time on the island. These three years (and the two before) had been a wonderful experience for Ann and me, with memories that have endured as I write this four decades or so after the fact. To have lived on a tropical island is an experience that with the passage of time reaps a greater harvest in the memories and evocations that enrich our quiet moments. When you are young, you daydream about the future, but the reflections in later life are about things that really happened. There is a more certain happiness in these contemplations, which more than compensate for regrets of any roads not taken. Our life in the Caribbean, a mere five years of our personal history, was a definitive period of our lives, and we left the islands without knowing what the future might now hold, but happy and secure that we could handle it together.

CHAPTER **11**

# Beyond

IN APRIL OF 1975 I was transferred to Richmond, Virginia, to the head office of the bank. This meant closing the Cayman office, transferring the book of business to our Bahamas affiliate, and leaving the Bank owned condominium on the beach. Not an easy transition! We swapped a home on the beach for a home in the suburbs, and prepared ourselves for life in the real world.

In the time between the mid seventies until early 1982, I was a Vice President of the bank, with responsibilities that involved a lot of international travel. In fact, our transfer to Virginia was supposed to inculcate me into the Bank of Virginia organization, and prepare me for a move to London in order to open the bank's first European office. I actually entered the USA on an L1 Visa, which is a transfer of a foreign national employee outside the USA into the country, and is designed for a fairly short term duration. This also allowed Ann to enter as a resident, but did not permit her to work. Our residency visa was good for one year, and I immediately began work on the feasibility study for the London office, with a couple of trips to scout out the situation and do the proper research on what would be the best business model for the London Representative Office. However, after my analysis of the opportunity, I realized that it was actually not a very smart idea for a bank of our size, and limitations, to open in London. We would be setting ourselves up for an expensive profile, but without a real opportunity to do much in the way of one-on -one customer business. We would be no more than a small bank lost in the crowd, without any strong credentials that would lead to a profitable book of business. I duly submitted my report to management, with the realization that the personal implications for Ann and me were fairly clear. No job in London might lead to no job in Richmond. As it turned out, I was offered a position in the International Division which enabled us to convert to a Green Card, that is, permanent residency, so we settled down to live the life for a while and see how it might work out.

However, I continued to have responsibility for our offshore banking offices, and for the ongoing liquidation of our Cayman portfolio. In the Fall of 1975 I was sent a copy of an article in the Miami Herald, which reported that David had been arrested on a sailboat in the Florida Keys, which was loaded with marijuana. Ann and I had been out for dinner with David and his wife in Miami the month before, and he was as friendly as ever, regaling us with tales of his experiences as a ship's captain. Several months went by, and then out of the blue an article appeared in the Richmond Times Dispatch on the seizure by the US Drug Enforcement Agency (DEA) of the MV Night Train off the coast of Virginia. At that time, the $64 million worth of marijuana was the largest ever catch by the DEA. The article mentioned that the DEA was seeking information on the ownership of the vessel. Our Richmond Counsel was able to give them information without exposing us to publicity, which was our main concern. Fortunately the crew had thrown the ship's log overboard when the DEA showed up, so Bank of Virginia's connection and my name as Master of the ship never did become public knowledge. In late 1976 an article appeared in the Miami Herald reporting that David had been murdered. It appears that he answered his doorbell one evening and was greeted by a hail of bullets from an automatic weapon. There were no clues as to the assailant, and as far as I know there never was an arrest. Since my network of contacts in Miami and Cayman was pretty good, I was able to piece together the connection between these two series of events. When David was arrested, he probably turned State's evidence, which led to the eventual seizure of the Night Train. This was obviously not well received by his Colombian partner, and from that point on he was a marked man. This is all supposition on my part, but is not hard to accept given the sequence of events.

## THE BOG, THE BAHAMAS, AND BEYOND

The MV Night Train was eventually sold at public auction by the Drug Enforcement Agency. The buyer was none other than the original owner in Florida, who had first sold the ship to the Sterling Bank group. Since he had accepted payment for the ship in Certificates of Deposit of Sterling Bank, which was subsequently liquidated with no recovery to creditors, he at least had the satisfaction of regaining possession at a knock down price of a few thousand dollars. Viewed retrospectively, my whole experience in the shipping business was an interesting, character building adventure that I would never have missed. Any banker who has worked in commercial lending long enough will accumulate a few war stories, but I had mine at the start of my career, and learned enough from the experience to stay away from ship loans forever after.

Meanwhile, back on the home front, Ann and I were trying to make the best of our new situation, and even though we were thrilled with our new house in a wooded sub-division in the West End of Richmond, it was a long way from Seven Mile Beach. It was so much easier a move for me, as I had a career to build, and my work in the International Division was interesting, and fulfilling. For Ann it was a difficult time, as she was not allowed a permit to work, and even though the wives of my co-workers were welcoming, and became her good friends, it was still a lonely time for her. It was especially hard when I was overseas on business, sometimes for two weeks at a time. I was the first 'foreigner' hired by the bank from overseas, so I was a bit of a novelty around the building.

I did the rather politically incorrect thing of flying the Cayman Islands flag, which incorporates the "Union Jack," from a tree in our front yard on Independence Day, 1976, which just happened to be the 200 year anniversary of this most patriotic of American holidays. However, I got my come-uppance that night when someone stole it - either a patriotic American, or a fellow Brit with a touch of homesickness.

The first bar in Richmond that became our "local" was Rose Marie's, located in a small strip shopping center close to our home in the West End. It was a "redneck" bar, meaning that the clientele were mostly working class men from the modest homes in and around the area. A few of us, all Brits, had adopted the bar as our pub of choice, and had many a good night sparring with the locals on cultural differences, and drinking with them to the similarities. One Friday night a man showed up at the bar and announced that he had a horse for sale. Sure enough, there was a large horse at the edge of the car park, tied up to a fence that separated the bar from the Pizza Hut next door. Some guy in the bar decided that this was an offer he could not refuse, so he struck a deal with the seller, left the bar, mounted the horse, and disappeared along Patterson Avenue. I have a feeling that his conversation that night with his daughter went a lot better than the conversation with his wife.

This bar was also the one time place of employment for a character who became known as "the man with the plan, from Powhatan". Powhatan is a rural district to the south-west of Richmond. John, the owner and operator of the Bar, had hired the guy to sweep out and clean the bar every morning. Now it happens that the telephone for the bar was on the inside wall at the back of the building, and there was a public telephone on the wall just outside the front door to the bar. Just inside the front door was a glass refrigerated cabinet, where John kept six packs of beer and sodas that his patrons would sometimes buy on the way out. John began to notice a problem with his stock, with the inventory in the cabinet always less than that indicated by the level of sales. It turns out that the man with the plan, as he swept out the entrance area to the bar, would dial the bar's phone number from the wall, thus requiring John to go to the back of the premises to answer. Then the man with the plan would step in to the bar, grab a six pack or two from the cabinet, and quickly put them in the trunk of his car, which was parked right outside. Once the shift was over, the man would drive back home to Powhatan, having successfully executed the plan!

With a population of about five million people, Virginia had an equivalent size population to Scotland, and there were several good sized independent banks that had their head offices in Richmond, the state capital. This was a city of about half a million people, yet had a small town feel about it. Situated in the central region of the state, it lies about 100 miles east of the Atlantic beaches and 100 miles

### THE BOG, THE BAHAMAS, AND BEYOND

south of the nation's capital, Washington DC. There are four distinct seasons, but summer usually comes early, and Fall (Autumn) late, so that summer is long, and usually hot. The temperature often hovers around ninety degrees Fahrenheit for weeks on end, and humidity makes for a double whammy that chases the inhabitants into the nearest air-conditioned space. The city was established at the fall point of the James River, which marked the limit of sea going vessels into the interior from the river's mouth at the Chesapeake Bay. Virginia was at the forefront of the political developments that led to the Revolutionary War with the UK, and to independence in 1776. Some of the most famous names in American history are sons of the "Old Dominion" such as George Washington, James Madison, Patrick Henry, and Thomas Jefferson. Not only did Virginia play a leading role in the independence movement, the capital city of Richmond became the capital of the Confederacy during the Civil War, or "The War between the States" as it is known by the politically correct. Virginia is the most northerly of the southern states, and strategically placed so that the military actions between the Northern and Southern armies would eventually play out on her fair and pleasant land.

With history as a life-long passion, it is strange that I never did develop much of an interest in the history of what has been my home state for almost forty years. My home library tells the tale. There is not much in the way of Virginian historical tomes, unlike my Scotland section, which never seems to disappoint me, and runs the gamut from Billy Connelly to Fiona Watson, plus everything written by John Prebble that was ever published. Still, there have been odd moments when I have experienced a personal connection to the history of this great state, and one in particular comes to mind. My long time banking colleague W.H. Martin III, or "Marty" as he is known to everyone except the printer of his business cards, lives on a forty acre spread in the neighboring village of Mechanicsville, Virginia. The size of his acreage, which has been in the family for generations, is not happenstance. This particular size of acreage for a "farming" property is common all across the country, and is a consequence of the various attempts by local, regional, and national governments to codify the system of land grants to new citizens willing to farm the plentiful and bountiful lands of America. Three centuries ago, forty acres just happened to be about the right size to enable a farmer to work the soil and provide for his family, and no doubt somewhere in the distant past of Marty's family there was a particular Mr. Martin who stepped forward to claim his land right for himself and his progeny. On one of my visits to Marty on his home turf, he gave me a perfectly formed piece of iron "shot" that he had found on his property, fired from a Civil War canon during the Battle of Cold Harbor, which took place just a few miles away, in 1864. When I hold the piece of metal in my hands I wonder who shot this round, and what were the circumstances.

My work in the International Division was really interesting, in large part because of the management team in the Division, of which I was a junior member. My boss Don Just, to put it mildly, was brilliant, and I mean that not only in the academic sense, but also in terms of his overall personality. I think of him as I saw him then; tall, good looking, educated, highly motivated, hilarious, intellectual, energetic – there is no way to put him together in such a mundane way as this description and capture the essence of this remarkable person. He and I were the same age, but Don had a conventional college and MBA education, and enough chutzpah in the interview process that he joined the bank and went straight into a management role. He would ultimately leave the bank in mid career to run a local Ad Agency that he transformed into a nationally ranked marketing firm. He sold it to a London agency, then became owner and operator of a hotel in the Outer Banks of North Carolina. After starting and then selling another Ad Agency, he is now a Professor of Management and Marketing Studies at Virginia Commonwealth University. In later years I had two of his graduate students as renters in my apartments, and they were in awe of him. Along with Don there was Werner Versch, who was the senior loan approval (Credit) guy, a business development officer John Ferguson, our "numbers" guy Steve Smith, and our Operations guru from Brooklyn, New York, Paul Bartal. Werner was a brusque Bavarian with a heart of gold, and Steve was a quiet and somewhat serious Accountant, who tended to see a glass as being half empty rather than half full. We used to kid him on about being negative, and I remember asking him in the cafeteria one day to go ahead and say something positive for a change. He quickly replied "I am positive that we are not going to make our profit goal next month". That was as good as it gets from Steve. It was a complete shock for all of us when he died from a heart attack a few months later. His wife found him in the morning on the living room floor, and he must have keeled over after he rose from his chair. We also spent a lot of time with Werner and Angie, along with their two kids, (wee) Werner and Karen. That small group of colleagues and their families were our lifeline in the first year or two in Virginia, and only with the passage of time were we able to build other groups of friendships. Our neighbors on either side, Tommy and Debbie Eubank, and David and Lora Coleman, became lifelong friends, and of course once I started playing football it opened up the entire community of fellow Brits and Europeans, and eventually, Americans.

In the summer of 1976 we received Immigration approval for our Permanent Residency Permits, known more colloquially as "Green Cards." This was a major event for Ann, as she was now able to work. In no time at all she joined a department of local Government, the State Crime Commission, in a down-town office building. She got to commute again, have lunches with colleagues, and generally participate in the welcoming fold of the workplace that she so greatly missed when she was confined to life in the suburbs. This had been a lonely time for Ann, so her ability to get out to work every day was a huge improvement in her daily life. It was fun for a few months being able to commute together, but then that came to an end when the bank opened their new corporate headquarters in the suburbs, and I dropped Ann at the commuter bus stop each morning, and picked her up in the evening. Still, our life in Virginia was taking on a familiar structure, and although not that much interested in the celebration of two hundred years of American independence, we were living up to the promise of permanent residency implicit in the ownership of a Green Card.

This was a time when smaller regional banks like Bank of Virginia were becoming involved in international banking, because it was exempted from the restrictive branch banking laws that made it difficult to expand even in the home State, and all but impossible to expand across State lines. The state regulations did not apply to foreign branches or subsidiaries, so we were able to open for business in the Bahamas and the Cayman Islands, but not necessarily in another Virginia city. The way that we built our "book" of business was to establish lending limits for various countries, mostly in Latin America, that had the need to borrow dollars. This was in essence an allocation of creditworthiness that gave us the ability to make loans in those countries up to the country "limit". We quickly developed relationships with governmental, banking, and even corporate borrowers in the primary Latin American countries such as Mexico, Venezuela, Brazil and Argentina, then with lesser countries such as Costa Rica, Nicaragua, Colombia, Ecuador, and Chile. Eventually we opened a Representative office in Mexico City, which initially was headed up by a Richmond colleague, and later by our first Mexican employee, Ramon Diez-Canedo. Ramon and his wife Jacaranda became friends with us over the years, and with high level contacts in the Mexican government he was a key resource for our bank during the hard times that later befell his country. .

My role in the group was to negotiate credit lines from international banks so that we could borrow in the Eurodollar market and fund the growth in our loan portfolio. This took me to New York on a quarterly basis, and to Europe at least once a year. I was on the most important learning curve in my career, and I much preferred the responsibilities of international business to the parochial mantra of branch banking. I was also lucky to have been in close contact with the Chairman of the Board, a six foot five former CIA operative called Frederick Deane Jr., or "Rick" to everyone in the bank. I first met him in Nassau when I was sent to the airport to pick him up on a visit to our bank that culminated in our acquisition. We got along famously from the outset, and when we moved to Cayman, Rick his wife Dorothy and their children came for a vacation. I am sure Rick had a hand in our eventual move to Richmond, and he always went out of his way to make sure that Ann and I were settling in to our life in Virginia. I remember the first time I visited his office on the sixth floor, which was fairly ostentatious, as befits a leading banker in the capital of the state. Rick asked me what I thought of his (large) office,

◄ THE BOG, THE BAHAMAS, AND BEYOND

and I told him that it seemed a bit much. He laughed, even though I was serious, and he told that story for ever after. He just liked the idea of having a young serious Scots banker on board, and would forever tell people that I was the only thing worthwhile that they bought when they acquired the Bank of Nassau.

One day Don asked me to meet with him and the President of the Bank for breakfast, to talk about a special assignment. This involved the real estate development company based in Fort Lauderdale, Florida, known as San Andros, that was developing, with our financial support, several thousand acres of land at the north end of Andros Island, in the Bahamas. In 1973 I had travelled to Nassau from Cayman to attend the loan closing, and all I had to do then was stick the corporate seal on the document, sign it on behalf of our bank, and fly back to Cayman. In the ensuing three years the company sub-divided the land into quarter acres lots, refurbished the hotel, and improved the runway of their own airport, which would facilitate direct flights from Fort Lauderdale on the company plane. Our bank had committed to a multi-million dollar development loan to enable them to make the capital improvements to the project, and fund the sales and marketing of the Lots to their prospective buyers. By 1976 the company had used up all of the loan funds, but the thousands of sales contracts that they had negotiated and assigned to us as collateral were of doubtful quality, and our bank was having serious concerns about the ability of the company to successfully develop the property, and pay off our loan.

For a few months I spent two days a week in the Florida office, meeting with the principals, their finance and accounting staff, and generally monitoring the progress of the company. It was clear from the get go that there was a big disconnect between what the principals were telling the bank, and what was actually happening on the ground. The sales were being generated through a network of real estate brokers in the Midwest and Canada, and were sold on the basis of about $100 down payment and $100 a month for each Lot in the subdivision. These were non-recourse contracts, meaning the buyers could walk away at any time from the deal without being responsible for the unpaid loan balance. Joe Murphy, a plumber from Cincinnati, was typical of the profile of the average customer, and I met Joe and his fiancée when we shared the company plane over to the island.

Joe was a fairly typical buyer - young, financially immature, and anxious to make a trip to the island to see the piece of land in the Caribbean that he and his beloved were buying, and on which they would one day build their retirement dream house. The trip over was less than two hours, flying over fabulous green and blue waters, so clear that you could actually see the outline of large fish, probably shark, from the window of the plane. Once on the island we checked in at the hotel for the overnight stay, then jumped on a jeep to drive the ten minutes or so to the actual Lot that Joe had purchased. The sales guy had a hard time identifying the marker for the Lot, which just seemed to be in the middle of an extensive area of undeveloped land, but he eventually found something, then paced off about one hundred yards into the bush, to identify the property line. This was the future retirement home site of Joe Murphy, and I have to say that to my surprise, they were both delighted, and had me taking photographs of the happy couple standing on the sandy track that would one day be a road, and the swampy looking bush that would one day be a home. Joe eventually stopped paying for the Lot and walked away from the deal after three or four months, and he was typical. By then, buyers remorse kicks in, and there is something else to spend their money on. They got a free trip over to the island, free accommodation for one night, and more than a few glasses of Rum Punch courtesy of the company. Meanwhile our bank had financed all of that activity, and even the $100 down was kept by the selling broker as commission. It was not hard to see that the same Lots were being sold over and over again to buyers who had little incentive to stay the course, and that the bank was funding the production of low quality receivables, or "paper" as these contracts were known as in the industry.

Meanwhile, there was a growing staff of young sales and marketing types in Fort Lauderdale who were having the time of their lives working for the three principals, having marketing parties for brokers, and parading their clients back and forward to the island. The cocktail hour in the office normally began around 3pm, and drinks were served in the President's office to whichever group of staff and customers happened to be around. He had a pet boa constrictor (or python) in a large glass case in his office, and on a Wednesday afternoon he would invite everyone in to see the weekly feeding. He would produce a couple of mice that were delivered each week by a local pet store, and release them into the case. They would bet on which mouse went down first, how long it would take, and so on. Ann was able to come down with me a couple of times, but I was glad to get this assignment over, and return to a "normal" job at my office in Richmond. The Bank eventually pulled the plug on the company, and took a huge hit to our profits that year. Even the company contribution to the profit sharing pool was shelved, thereby causing much unhappiness among the general staff of the Bank, and a bit of a hit to the reputation of the guys in International, who were attributed with the blame. As the deal with the three partners in Florida had originated with the Bank's President, he was the fall guy within the organization, and was fired around the time that the company announced the losses from the loans that were charged off.

On a trip to the Far East in 1977 I had lunch as a guest of The Hong Kong and Shanghai Banking Corporation at their old head office on Hong Kong Island. It has since been replaced by an imposing architectural icon of a building, but it was then the heart of this unique British Colonial banking organization. The bank was founded in 1865, inspired by Thomas Sutherland, the then head of the P&O Steam Navigation Company. The prospectus announced that the bank would be locally based, but operate on "Sound Scottish banking principles." It operated that way for over a hundred years, until the acquisition of the London based Midland Bank in 1990 required that the head office of the combined organization be based in London.

My host for the elaborate lunch at the bank turned out to be a fellow Scot, Douglas Carr, who had responded to the call to "Go East, young man" in the early nineteen fifties. In looks, speech, and demeanor, he epitomized the expatriate banker who loves living somewhere exotic, but can't shake the need to dress and act as if he lived in Edinburgh. This may be a bit harsh on Mr. Carr, since I spent all of two hours in his company, but there is a stereotype of the expat banker out there, and Douglas was up there with the best of them. One of his first purchases on arriving was a fifties era motor cycle that he parked outside his apartment, ready for his commute to work. Each morning he would sit astride the "pillion" seat, and proceed to kick start the engine. This was a process where the outcome was pretty certain, but the time involved and the number of kick starts before ignition was indeterminate. After several days of this early morning routine, he noticed that a group of locals would gather at the far end of the apartment block, and there would be much noise and chatter, with many sets of Chinese eyes locked on Douglas and his motor cycle. Then, when his kick start sequence ended in ignition, there would be a huge cheer from the group, and some more noise and chatter before the group dissipated. It turns out that they were betting on the number of times he would have to kick the pedal prior to the engine starting, thus reinforcing another stereotype, the proclivity of Chinese people at all walks of life to gamble on the strange and mundane attributions of chance. When in Hong Kong I stayed at the Peninsula, one of the world's great hotels, and was duly picked up at the airport in a dark green Rolls Royce which they send to pick up guests. After the tortuous journey I had to get there, I told myself to sit back and enjoy the experience, as it would only happen once. It did.

The weekend in Hong Kong was also memorable for another reason, which had everything to do with what was happening on the other side of the world, in Richmond, Virginia. I called Ann to see how she was doing and she told me that she had been to the doctor, and he confirmed that she was pregnant. I was in my room at the Peninsula, all alone, pondering what was about to happen in our lives, and who our little baby would be, and become.

Two years or so later, my then boss of the International Division, Julian Banton, was also out in the Far East for a conference, and had a lay-over in Hong Kong. I set him up with Douglas Carr for a lunch at the bank, and a dash of local culture. Everything went well until the Port wines and cheese plates were served by the young Chinese waiter. In faltering English he motioned to Julian concerning the Camembert Cheese, and when Julian nodded his head, the waiter proceeded to cut off the rind of the camembert, its most valued quality, leaving Julian with the now undressed wedge of cheese. Douglas was mortified, and

◂ THE BOG, THE BAHAMAS, AND BEYOND

could only mumble apologetically the word "savages!" while shaking his head in disgust at the retreating form of the young waiter.

While visiting a client bank in South Korea, I was asked by my counterpart at the bank if we would be agreeable to receiving one of their employees on an internship for a few weeks in the coming summer. This is a fairly typical way in which banks help each other out, so I quickly agreed. Our Intern was a Mr. Hong Kee Bok, although in South Korea the surname comes first, so his Anglified name was Kee Bok Hong. We had two weeks of his time, and then he was scheduled for another internship with a bank in California. We quickly found out that Kee Bok had very little command of the English language. He smiled a lot, and nodded his head, but I don't think there was a lot of comprehension. I had worked out a schedule for him to go to different departments of the bank, but we soon had feedback that keeping him occupied for a whole day was hard work. Anyway, we managed to get through the two weeks by everyone in the department taking turns to spend time with him, and being bankers, we arranged a golf outing for his last official day. A few of my colleagues joined Kee Bok and me at a local course, and there we were on the first tee ready to begin. When it was Kee Bok's turn, he barely connected with the ball and it trundled off to the left. He immediately raised his hand and shouted "ah ha, Mulligan!" thereby demonstrating a fairly acute knowledge of idiomatic English, and the amateur golfer tradition of having a free second tee shot (known as a "Mulligan") on the first hole, if needed. We later wondered how much he understood of what we said, when what we said was not particularly sociable.

Although my day to day activities no longer involved working on our offshore real estate situations, I was occasionally brought back to help out or add past knowledge to the "work out" of our problem loans in the Bahamas. In late 1977 I had a call from one of my colleagues, Amos Dickinson, who ran the bank's Real Estate Division, to see if I would go with him on a trip to the island of Norman's Cay, which is one of the islands in the Exuma's, south of the island of New Providence. Amos is actually a nickname, as his real name is John. However, growing up in the rural Eastern Shore of Virginia in the nineteen fifties, and having a brother named Andy, he was odds on to pick up that particular nickname, as one of the most popular shows on television at the time was the "Amos and Andy Show" of a black family in rural America. We even saw that show on the BBC, although it was the late fifties by the time it made it across the Atlantic. As Amos Dickinson is white, his nickname shows that comedy does sometime transcend prejudice, even back then, when there was a visible and potent division between the races in the South generally, and in rural Virginia where Amos was brought up.

The Florida office of San Andros had formed a separate subsidiary company with a view to developing several tracts of land that they had acquired on the island. This property was included in the company's real estate assets that were part of our collateral, so the bank had a financial interest in the viability of the Norman's Cay project, as well as the main one on Andros. Amos and I flew down to Fort Lauderdale, and then on to Norman's Cay in the company plane. Norman's Cay is only about five miles long, and is fairly narrow, but at the north end the land curves round and back parallel to the island in a sort of a hook shaped peninsula. Before landing we circled the island from low altitude and it was absolutely beautiful, about as pretty a Caribbean island as you can imagine. The runway began at the southern tip, and was in walking distance of the only hotel.

We did not know it at the time but we visited the island when it had already been chosen by one of the Colombian Drug Cartel, Carlos Lehder, as a base for their cocaine distribution in the USA. Several of the residents on the island were in process of selling up their properties and moving back to the States. There was no Immigration Department at the airport office when we landed, although we were coming from a foreign country. There was some local chatter about a businessman from Colombia buying up all the homes on the island, and making it clear that newcomers were not welcome. We got back to Richmond with a few convictions about Norman's Cay. It was a beautiful island paradise – that could not be denied; it was so small that it could only be viable for development for the ultra affluent market; and it had no real value as a possible source of repayment for the bank, as our right to get legal control was so convoluted that it was just not worth it. Well, we got to the correct answer, although for all

◂ THE BOG, THE BAHAMAS, AND BEYOND

the wrong reasons. Within a few months there were reports that the island had been closed to visitors, and that people approaching on yachts and power boats had been threatened by gunfire, and turned away. The Nassau newspapers covered the story, but it never gained wider traction as newsworthy, and not much was heard of Norman's Cay for some time. A year or so later Amos went back to the island on the company plane for one last attempt to ascertain if there was any value in the undeveloped Lots, and this time they had to abort their landing as they were shot at on their approach to the runway. Whatever was happening on the island was not good, and from then on our corporate interest in that particular property waned.

Carlos Lehder was arrested by the US Drug Enforcement Agency in 1982, and was convicted on drug distribution and related crimes, for which he was sentenced to life in prison plus 135 years. He had transformed Norman's Cay into the main trans-shipment point for the movement of cocaine from Colombia into the United States. However, that was not the end of the story. In Nassau, there was a public outcry the following year when NBC Television in New York broke a story on the Carlos Lehder influence in the Bahamas, reporting that Bahamian officials were on the payroll of Colombian drug lords. The long time Prime Minister of the Bahamas, Sir Lyndon Pindling, was among the politicians implicated, and the subsequent local political pressure and the additional diplomatic pressure from the United States led to the appointment of a Commission of Inquiry in the Bahamas. The Report's revelations of widespread official corruption forever tarnished the reputation of Prime Minister Pindling, and almost brought down the Government.

Lehder is believed to have agreed to testify on behalf of the United States in the subsequent trial of President Noriega of Panama, who was convicted in the U.S District Court in Miami of racketeering and related charges. It has been reported that in the Fall of 1995 several protected witnesses at the US Correctional facility in Mesa Arizona said that Lehder was whisked away in the night, and no one has heard of him since. Conspiracy theories abound in this case, speculating that he is a free man again for his services to the Central Intelligence Agency in helping convict Noriega. If so, he will live rather well, as he is reported to have earned two billion (with a "b") dollars from his base in Norman's Cay, most of which was never recovered.

The trip to the Bahamas with Amos also provided an excuse to add in a trip to Cayman, so Ann made arrangements to travel down separately and then we met in Miami for the Cayman Airways flight to George Town. It was lovely to be back in that special place, and see many of our friends from our recent past. We were invited to a cocktail party at the home of one of the island's local entrepreneurs, Steve Ebanks, and many members of the expatriate community were present. One of our friends introduced us to a visitor from Scotland, and it turned out that the man was from my home town of Falkirk. When he told me that he lived on Cromwell Road, I asked him if by any chance his house number was twenty five. When he surprised me by confirming that it was, I told him that I used to deliver his newspaper, and, at the right time of the season would "pinch" the apples from the tree in his back garden! The Crawford house at 25 Cromwell Road was the last delivery on my route, and perfect for a quick getaway on my bike. He took it well.

There was another surprise in store for us at that party. We were re-introduced to the former President of the bank in Nassau, whom we had last met on our honeymoon in Arran. Not only had he managed to bury his past indiscretions as a banker in Nassau, he had just been recruited by the Cayman Islands Government to be their new Inspector of Banks. This meant that he had responsibility, among other things, for the granting of bank charters to applicants wishing to own and operate banking operations in one of the world's premiere tax havens. While our cocktail conversation was pleasant enough, I knew that I was going to have to think about this situation, and what if anything I should do about it.

Back in Virginia, I met with our legal counsel, who felt that we were obliged to report on this development to our regulatory body, The Federal Reserve Bank of Richmond. They in turn passed along the information to the Bank of England, who apparently was originally responsible for hiring this former banker to take up the post in the government of a member of the Commonwealth. Several months later we were advised by the Bank of England that the investigation had not uncovered any irregularities, and so they stood behind the new Inspector of Banks in his appointment to this highly influential government post. However, that was not the last of it. A year or so later he was discharged from his position and prosecuted by the Cayman Government for financial irregularities. He spent time in jail, and this presumably brought an end to his career in offshore banking. And so the year of 1977 was brought to a close, with the impending birth of our baby Shona, on January 7, 1978.

The pregnancy went well, but Shona decided five weeks ahead of time that she needed to be out and about, so off we went to the hospital late on a Friday evening. I was told to go back home as nothing was going to happen for a while. Next morning I was back at the hospital about twenty minutes ahead of delivery, and ready for my appointment with what turned out to be a four pounds seven ounce baby daughter. Shona was premature, actually by about six weeks, so there was a fair amount of nervous tension around the delivery room. We were scared and excited all at the one time. It is amazing to think back to how small she was when she was quickly presented to her mother, and then retrieved for rapid insertion into the Incubator. Within a few days she was released in the security blanket that was her Mum and Dad, and if we did our job well then our daughter will always feel that sense of security and comfort that is perhaps the earliest of senses to be acquired, the love of a parent. I have an abiding memory of those early weeks with a tiny and vulnerable baby girl, when my boss Don came round to the house (as he often did) to hang out. He was well over six feet tall, with large and cultured hands, and he would hold Shona in the palm of his hand while nurturing her with a soft and measured Midwest accent from his home State of Wisconsin.

Shona's arrival actually brought the headcount at home to four, as we had acquired my brother Jack in the household. He arrived in 1977 for a three month stay, and decided that he would like to remain in the USA for a bit longer. We had no problems with that, but after we talked about it we developed a plan that seemed to make sense, given that Jack did not have a work permit. We told him that if he enrolled in Junior College we would be happy to pay for his education, so he was able to get into a local college with courses in Hotel

Management, which was his chosen field of study, and hopefully career path. We bought him a Honda Moped motor-cycle, and he was able to commute to the college as well as get around in our section of town. Eventually we sold the Honda and bought him a used car, a Ford Falcon, which had a relatively short life in our driveway, replaced by an old Volkswagon Beetle bought from friends in the neighborhood.

I would say that the most traumatic moment of our lives together with Jack was when he came home one night and, after Ann had gone off to bed, told me that he was gay. He knew that was the way it was when he was in Scotland, but didn't know how to deal with it at home, and it may account for his desire to come to Virginia, and deal with his sexuality without the compromise of Mum, Dad, and the rest of our sisters. Anyway, I remember shaking his hand and telling him it was OK, and it would not make any difference to our relationship as brothers. It never did, and over the subsequent years, once Jack had gone back to Scotland, he was able to deal with his sexuality with the family so that it was never an issue or concern for his siblings. As for Mum, it was just something she knew but didn't talk about, and that is just a function of coming from a different generation.

Jack's life as a student in America came to rather an abrupt end after he had been with us for about 18 months. He managed to get a paid internship at a local hotel in downtown Richmond, so had saved some money. He decided that he would go back to Scotland over the Christmas holidays, and return for the start of term in mid January. His travel visa for the USA had expired, so while he was home he went through to the US Consulate in Edinburgh to get it renewed as a student visa. The Consul decided that Jack was not eligible for a visa, as he had plenty of alternative study choices right here in the UK, so his application was denied. We were left with lots of memories of Jack's time with us, mostly good, and kept his clothes for a while in case he managed to get back. It was not to be.

It was in the early summer of 1978 that I began to conscientiously run a few miles every day, whereas up until then I had always ran just to keep fit for soccer. That year there was an announcement in the local paper that there would be a marathon race, to be held through the streets of Richmond, in September. There was some talk among

◄ THE BOG, THE BAHAMAS, AND BEYOND

the lads in the German Sports Club soccer team about entering enmasse, but nothing came of it, so I put together a training schedule for myself, bought my first pair of Nike running shoes, and got on with it. The schedule covered a three month period leading up to the race, and I increased my weekly mileage so that by the week before the race I was comfortable running fifteen to eighteen miles a day, with one day a week off. I eventually settled into a running pace of eight minutes per mile, and by race day I knew I could handle an eighteen mile run, so the final eight miles would be the great unknown. To keep my marriage intact, I incorporated my daily runs in my commute to and from work. The headquarter building of what at the time was known as Bank of Virginia Company was a brand new office building and complex near an intersection with the main highway, Interstate 64, that was about 12 miles west of the town center. It was about five miles along a few country roads from our home in the West End, and in the basement there was a gymnasium and shower facilities, so it was really easy to incorporate my running into my daily activities, although it was tricky dealing with the need to have clean clothes and shoes in the office ready for use. The race was a huge civic success, and has been run every year since. There were about five thousand entrants of all shapes and sizes, as there was a five miler incorporated into the main race. I surprised myself my holding my eight minute per mile pace for the entire event, and my certificate attests to a three hour twenty eight minute run. Although I have run on a regular basis ever since, I only did the one marathon, and had no ambition to do it again. Somewhere in my late fifties my pace went from eight minutes to nine minutes a mile, but I continue to run for fun as well as exercise, and have never felt it to be a grind.

Our trip home to Scotland in the summer of 1978 was the first time that we had taken Shona on a long journey, and for her it would be the first of so many trips overseas on so many occasions. Our families were desperate to see her, and the welcoming crowd at Glasgow Airport was testament to the love and caring of our family and friends in Scotland. Our trip was also memorable for the playing of the World Cup (Football) in Argentina. Scotland had qualified for the final series of matches and there was great excitement across the land for the chance of glory in this, the world's premier sporting event. Because of our failure to beat Iran, and a loss to Peru, Scotland entered the final qualifying game against The Netherlands needing to win by a three goal margin just to get to a penalty shoot-out, or a four goal margin to go through automatically. In a game of tremendous excitement, Scotland were soon a couple of goals up, and very much in contention to pick up more goals and achieve the unimaginable. Well, as has been so often the case in the sports history of our beloved country, we got close enough to feel that we somehow snatched defeat from the jaws of victory. The Netherland side managed to keep it close and we eventually won by 3 to 2, but not enough to move on in the competition. We did have the singular honor of scoring the best goal in the competition, a fabulous effort by Archie Gemmell after a mazy dribble around three or four Argentinean defenders, followed by a rocket of an angled shot into the net. We watched the game at 9 Alexander Avenue on a color television set that had only recently reached the suburbs of Falkirk.

I came back to America with a backload of work projects in the busy and exciting world of international banking at Bank of Virginia. My original boss and mentor Don had moved on and up in the company, and was now running our Northern Virginia retail banking operations. His replacement, Julian Banton, was rapidly becoming a friend as well as a boss, and I think for the first time Ann and I began to think of Virginia as at least a proxy for home, with the realization that we were assimilating in our own way to the reality of life in suburban America. We were far removed from our family and friends, and without the glamour and spice of living in the tropics that we had for the first five years of our life together.

CHAPTER **12**

# The Spanish Connection

IN THE EARLY part of 1979 our bank was approached to see if we had an interest in discussing a possible investment of new capital of around $20 million, by a Spanish business and banking group. This came at a time when our stock price had been below book value for some time, and here was a possibility of attracting capital at a higher price than the market value. After the usual sparring and preliminary negotiating, an agreement was reached whereby the Spanish group would subscribe to a new issue of common stock through a private placement, and thereby own about sixteen per cent of the common stock of Bank of Virginia Company. At a certain point in the proceedings I accompanied our Chairman, Rick Deane on a trip to Spain to meet with our new investors. Time being of the essence, and my travel companion being the Chairman, we travelled by Concorde from Washington to London, then on to Madrid. The financial terms had been agreed, but it was still subject to final discussions on Board of Director appointments, and the trip was also a chance for Rick to develop a personal relationship with Senor Juan March Delgado, the head of the March family, whose holding company would be making the investment in our bank. The Concorde flight was pretty special, and a first for both of us. I managed to fly Concorde again a year or so later, but the first experience was exciting if not particularly memorable. The take-off is so much steeper than the regular climb of a large airplane, and the cruising altitude of around 57,000 feet put us high enough to see a distinctly deeper shade of blue in the sky than normal. The flight across the Atlantic took three hours and twenty minutes, at a cruising speed of around 1,350 mph, and twice the speed of conventional aircraft. This was early in the life cycle of Concorde, and it came to a rather inglorious end after the crash near Paris in 2000 when all 100 passengers and the crew of nine perished, as well as four people on the ground.

The March Group is one of the wealthiest families in Spain, and we were a guest of Juan March Delgado, the head of the family and the older of the two grandsons of the founder, Juan March Ordinas, who died in 1962 after amassing a huge fortune. He was the seventh richest man in the world by the end of the Second World War, as reported in the New Yorker magazine article by John Brooks that was published in the May 21, 1979 issue, with a second article in the following week. I remember that particular magazine article so vividly, because it hit the press the same week that we were in Spain to meet with Juan March. On arrival in Madrid, Rick received a phone call from our lawyer in Richmond to let him know that there was an article in the New Yorker that was not favorable towards the March patriarch, Juan March Ordinas, and that this was causing our Board of Directors to question the impending financial relationship between our bank and the March Group. When Rick told me of the call, I immediately volunteered to go out into the streets and find a copy of the magazine, as most of the reputable U.S. publications were available from street vendors throughout the city. Sure enough, I got my hands on a copy, and brought it back for Rick to read. It was much ado about nothing. It would be no different than an article about the original Rockefeller fortune, or the Kennedy family wealth. The fact is that many of the great family fortunes throughout America and Europe were accumulated by nefarious means, whether it was the legal shenanigans of the Rockefellers, or the smuggling of alcohol from the Bahamas by the Kennedys. The article, and its subsequent follow up in the next issue, was a marvelous piece of reporting by a highly respected journalist, but the passage of time had, as always, tempered the common view, and the reputation of the current March family in Spain was beyond reproach. From the son of the founder, to his sons and daughter, the family had matriculated to a level of Spanish society that included

### THE BOG, THE BAHAMAS, AND BEYOND

King Juan Carlos as a friend, and Rick was able to deal with the concerns of the Board back in Virginia with a few phone calls.

While Rick digested the March family history only enough to enable him to deal with what turned out to be a slight impediment to the progress of the $20 million investment in his bank, I was engaged with the story. The article actually began with the scene of the greatest financial coup of the many that were engineered by Juan March, which occurred after he had been dead about eight years, in 1970. The International Court of Justice in The Hague, Netherlands, rendered a verdict in the case concerning the Barcelona Traction, Light and Power Company, Ltd., which had originally been brought before the Court in 1958, when Juan March Ordinas was already rich, famous, and powerful. This was a long way from his humble beginnings in the interior of the island of Majorca on October 4, 1880. His father, a farm laborer, had late in life managed to become a pig farmer, and had encouraged his son's aptitude for numbers by sending him to the Franciscan school on the outskirts of the island capital of Palma. The next record of him is as a twenty one year old pig dealer, buyer of land, and a financier of contraband. Many sailors from the Balearic Islands dealt in contraband, particularly tobacco, which was purchased in Morocco, shipped to the islands, and stored in caves prior to its distribution to the Iberian mainland. To a native of Majorca, smuggling was fair game. He took it to another level, however, when he used the profits from his investments in land to acquire an Algerian tobacco factory. He then acquired a fleet of launches, faster than those of the Spanish government, and soon he was making enough illegal profits to make significant legal investments in real estate and hydro-electric power in Majorca.

The twenty year governing reign of King Alfonso XIII of Spain, ending with the forming of a civilian Directorate in 1923, was the time when Juan March made his first fortune, powered by tobacco smuggling, but also with the help of other types of contraband demanded by the wealthier classes in Spain. He also gained fame and notoriety for outsmarting the Spanish Government over the shipping of shoes from North Africa into the Spanish mainland. Production of leather shoe products in Spain was protected by the Government, so imports were restricted. Juan March bought entire shiploads of shoes in Algeria, Tunisia, and Morocco, and then separated the right shoes from the left shoes, to be shipped on separate vessels. Once landed in Spain, he would match the right shoes with the left shoes, and go on to take his profits. Eventually, one of his boats was apprehended by the Spanish government, and the merchandise, consisting of several thousand unmarketable shoes, was confiscated by Spanish Customs and Excise. When the merchandise was auctioned off in the normal process applied to confiscated goods, Juan March had an agent buy the entire shipment for a nominal amount, there being no other bidders. Once the left shoes were matched up with the right shoes, his booty was intact, and ready for distribution on the black market.

In 1911 he managed to get the Government in Spain to grant him a monopoly on tobacco sales in the entire Spanish North African zone, apart from the two ports of Ceuta and Melilla, which he later acquired in 1927. Even with the trading monopoly he continued to smuggle tobacco into the homeland, cheating not only the Government but his own officially sanctioned company. With the onset of World War One he negotiated an agreement with the British Admiralty whereby the British promised to use its influence to get the French to authorize the export of tobacco from Algiers, and in exchange March promised to provide information and intelligence on Mediterranean ship movements to the Allies. By the time the First World War had ended, Juan March had consolidated his fortunes among a diversified portfolio of business interests that was but a platform for the fabulous wealth he would create in the second half of his life.

Not that it was all plain sailing. When King Alfonso yielded the reins of government to the Primo de Rivera Directorate in 1923, Juan March was forced into exile, and then later welcomed back to the national stage in the period leading up to the establishment of the Spanish Republic in 1931. Once again a Spanish Government would castigate Juan March, and in fact sent him to prison in 1932, but inevitably he bounced back and was able to pursue his private business interests unobstructed. By 1935 Juan March was pre-occupied with the Nationalist coalition that launched the Spanish Civil War, and when General Franco emerged as the leader of the movement, it is believed

◀ THE BOG, THE BAHAMAS, AND BEYOND

that he was financed by Juan March. The plane that was sent to the Canary Islands to pick up the General, and bring him to Morocco to take command of the Nationalist Army, was provided by a typically March inspired maneuver involving a British plane that was procured for him by his London merchant banking firm of Kleinwort's. When the Republican surrender on April Fools Day 1939 recognized the inevitability of a Franco dictatorship, Juan March was once again in a powerful position to expand his wealth and influence as a result of backing the right horse in the stakes for the Spanish nation.

The Second World War was a strange time for the Iberian Peninsula, given that the rest of Europe was consumed by the war, and the few nations like Spain that desisted involvement were left to ponder their fate while Great Britain and Germany played the latest version of the great game. It was to the advantage of Juan March that Franco emerged from the post war geo-political landscape as a bulwark against the rise of Communism, and so what was good for Spain was good for Senor March. General Franco established a policy to try and restore to Spanish ownership many of the leading business enterprises in Spain that were under the control of foreign investors and owners. Who else but Juan March would emerge as a beneficiary of government policy, and set in motion a calculated play to appropriate ownership of Barcelona Traction, Light and Power Company Ltd., suppliers of about 20% of electric power in Spain.

Barcelona Traction was actually a foreign holding company, which was chartered in Canada in 1911, and its primary operations were in Catalonia, where it produced about 80% of the Province's electricity. It had been controlled by Belgian investors since about 1925 and the Spanish operations were conducted by separate but wholly owned Spanish companies. With the onset of the Spanish Civil War, the company was prohibited from exchanging local currency for Pounds Sterling with which to pay interest on their Sterling Bonds, and so technically the company had been operating since then in default of its Bond obligations. This situation continued throughout the Second World War, and by the end of 1947 there had been eleven years of missed interest payments, yet the company was flourishing and financially sound. This was the Achille's heel that Juan March spotted, and decided to exploit. It became his chief pre-occupation from then until his death twenty one years later. March had begun buying up the Bonds in 1944, and eventually owned almost the entire issue. In 1948 he petitioned a provincial court in Catalonia for a bankruptcy order, which was granted, much to the dismay of the Shareholders, who learned of the bankruptcy after the fact. Bondholders do not own the company, and it is the shareholders who are entitled to the company's assets, except in a situation of bankruptcy. By 1949 it was March's nominees who were running the company, and by 1952 he had contrived to have the company's assets put up for auction in Spain so that only a Spanish company could buy them. He bid the minimum price of $280,000 and was given control of a business that was generating the equivalent of $5 million a year in profits.

He spent the rest of his life defending his ownership of the business, as the legal maneuverings culminated in the case being brought before the International Court of Justice at The Hague, in the Netherlands. He spent more and more of his time in Geneva, and was part of the regular clientele of a beer garden, where he played dominoes most afternoons, constantly chewing cigars. Back in Spain, the Juan March Foundation, which he had established in 1955, was building its reputation in philanthropy, with grants and awards in the arts, the natural sciences, and the social sciences. The Foundation became even stronger after his death, and now has an international reputation. It was a car accident outside Madrid that led to his death in 1962 at the age of 81, and a further eight years would pass before the Court rendered its decision, which secured his rights to ownership of the Spanish operations of Barcelona Traction. Today the company operates as a wholly owned business of the March Group, and Juan March Ordinas lies in his stately mausoleum in Majorca, not far from the headquarters of Banca March, which he founded in 1926. As a testament to the financial prudence in the bloodline of the March family, the bank was recently (2010) graded number one in Europe for the soundness of its capital base and asset structure.

We had arranged to meet Juan March and his associates at the headquarters of the Juan March Foundation, which is also a museum and art gallery. Juan operates from here when he is in Madrid, and his

### THE BOG, THE BAHAMAS, AND BEYOND

brother Carlos runs the banking side of the business, from the principal office in Madrid, although the bank is actually headquartered in Palma, Majorca. After introductions and small talk, we were driven to our dinner engagement in a private room at the Jockey Club in the city center. In addition to the chauffeur driven cars there was an extra vehicle with a number of other men, who were the visibly armed security detail. This was a necessary requirement of the March family, as their position as wealthy and influential citizens made them a potential ransom target. We found them to be utterly likeable and charming people, and this was true over the many subsequent years of our relationship. They all spoke excellent English, as is normal in the business world in Spain, and indeed throughout Europe. During our dinner conversation we learned that the next day we would fly to Majorca, to spend the weekend at the family home on the south-east corner of the island. That first meeting between Juan and Rick went well, and was the start of an enduring friendship.

The one hour flight to Palma was on the company Lear Jet, and was an easy trip across mainland Spain and over to Majorca. From the airport a fleet of cars was waiting to take us to the family estate, which was a couple of hour's journey to the far corner of the island. As we entered the gates of the estate we could see the residence in the distance, and as we drew closer the shape of the building became clear - a fifteenth century castle surrounded by courtyards and outbuildings. This was the family home, and Don Juan made us most welcome. The guest rooms were magnificent, and by the time I returned to my room after a welcoming glass of champagne, a maid had already unpacked my suitcase and hung my clothes.

The evening meal was served in the medieval dining room, and the décor and ambiance made for a convivial dinner party. Rick is a commanding presence in any situation, and he was in his element with Juan. It was clear that both wanted to make the relationship work right from the start. I teamed up with my counterpart, Leopoldo Caravantes, who ran the International Division of Banca March, and for many years to come he and I would be good friends and colleagues. Next day we all met after breakfast for a walk along the beach. The estate has about seven miles of beachfront, completely unspoiled, and

## THE SPANISH CONNECTION

as we strolled along the high tide line there was a team of security guards who kept up with us as we moved along the shore, with rifles slung over their backs. It made me think of our time living in Cayman, on another seven miles of glorious beach, and how free and easy it was for locals and holidaymakers to move around with impunity.

Within a few weeks the deal was signed and the new capital was subscribed. Juan and his advisor Alfredo Lafita were elected to our board, and served as directors until 1992, when their shares were sold in a private placement, and the funds were sent back to Spain to be deployed elsewhere in the March Group. It had been a profitable investment for them, but by then the personal aspect of the relationship was no longer there. It was never the same after Rick retired, and then died suddenly a few months after his last day at the bank. Rick was a tough, smart, and dynamic personality, whose influence and reputation at the national level was larger in many respects than the organization that he led. From our first meeting in Nassau he seemed to like the idea of having a young Scotsman working for his bank, and that was the start of a long and wonderful relationship. Once when he and I arrived late in Paris one night, my sister Connie and husband Sam were waiting for us when we arrived to check in at the Ritz. For some reason our reservations had been messed up, and the hotel check-in Manager had little sympathy for two troubled travelers. Thank goodness we had Con and Sam with us, as they both worked in the hotel business, and made it clear in forty mile an hour French that this was not acceptable. After loud voices, flailing hands, and Gallic shrugs, good sense prevailed and they magically found us a couple of rooms. He and I travelled together overseas a number of times, mostly in Europe, and I have nothing but fond memories of Rick, and the times we had away from the bank, on the road together. I think in retrospect that the deal with Banca March was a salutary moment in his long banking career, and challenged a mantra of parochialism that was always present in the corporate culture of our company. His bank had stepped up in the world.

The responsibilities of parenthood had led to somewhat less of a social life than before, but we somehow managed to juggle our several groups of friends so that we kept up with them all. The boundaries were fairly predictable. Close business colleagues and their wives and families. Neighbors from our cul-de-sac and the larger sub-division, Raintree, where we lived. The foreign contingent represented by my football playing pals and their wives and significant others. That was about it. But it was more than enough on which to build a home, and that is what we contrived to do. I became comfortable with the responsibility of fatherhood, as I was able to grow into it over time, whereas Ann was thrown in at the deep end. She learnt the craft of motherhood so quickly, and her relationship with her wee baby was lovely to see and to know.

It was during our trip to Scotland in the summer of 1979 that Ann's father Archie died. He had checked in to the Southern General Hospital for a bleeding ulcer, and had undergone surgery. A group of family members had assembled at the hospital for a regular visit, and Ann's Mum had gone in first to see him, while we waited. Suddenly we heard a commotion along the corridor, and rushed up to Ann's Mum, who was visibly distressed with the knowledge that her Archie had had a heart attack. There was no rush to the operating table, as he had died suddenly and without hope of recovery. This was such a huge shock, and only the innocence of her eighteen months of age sheltered Shona from the distress and sadness that we all felt. What had began as a wonderful family holiday had ended in tragedy. Archie was cremated in nearby Craigton, and the family was changed forever. Ann's Mum was a wonderful wife and mother, and the love and care that she no longer could express to her Archie was not lost, but simply redirected to the rest of her family. That winter she travelled to Richmond so that she could spend a few months with us, and that became the first of an annual trip that she made so that she could spend time with Ann and Shona, and in due course, her future grandchild Cassie.

One of the nice things that happened during Mum's stay that winter was being able to tell her that Ann was pregnant, and expecting a baby in October. Because Ann had not carried to full term the first time, her doctor wanted to make sure that she be given every chance to go the distance this time, so we reluctantly dropped our usual travel plan for Scotland that summer, and stayed in Richmond. By now

## THE SPANISH CONNECTION

Shona had began to absorb words, conversation, and chatter, and generally exhibit the ability to communicate. She felt the excitement of the imminent birth of a baby sister or brother and then on October 29 along came Cassie Elizabeth Hunter, her and forever best friend.

CHAPTER **13**

# Family Times

AS TIME WENT by we developed an ever widening circle of friends, so that by the time Cassie came along our lives were fairly predictable, but never dull. Cassie was a couple of pounds and a few ounces heavier at birth than Shona, so we had none of the "preemie baby" issues that we had with her sister. Ann's Mum arrived in December and was a huge help to Ann as she dealt with the competing attentions of two daughters. We had to wait until the following summer to show her off to the Hunter's in Scotland, but unfortunately our annual holiday was again interrupted by death, this time of my Dad, on June 2$^{nd}$ 1981. He had struggled for years with ill health, and eventually his heart gave out just a few days after he saw his new grand-child. He died in my arms, after falling in his bedroom. Our family doctor answered her phone at two in the morning and immediately drove to our house to see him, but there was nothing to do but write the death certificate and give me some advice about what to do next. The National Health Service in the UK has lots of critics, as it is the international standard for Government provided Health Care, and it seems you either love it or you hate it, depending on your circumstances. What I can say through experience is that my Dad received the best of treatment and care from the time he had a heart attack at aged 45 right up until his death at 60. I write this having lived longer than Dad, and never having experienced the many health problems that he endured throughout his life. Those who know me can attest to my dedication to physical exercise, and all I can say is that you at least need to give yourself a chance at a longer life by keeping fit, even if the genes may not match the ambition. As a product of my parents, I have at least a fifty-fifty chance of inheriting the longevity genes of my Mum, which is my best hope.

The vacation time that year was bittersweet, and our wee baby Cassie was unaware of all that was going on around her. She seemed to thrive in the company of her extended family, and was always looked after and comforted by her older sister Shona. Both girls grew up very much a part of the lives of our Scottish families, and given the globe-trotting nature of the Hunter's, have been able to experience many strange and exotic places together just to see uncles, aunties, and cousins.

This was the year that a group of us from the German Sports Club broke away to form a new soccer team, the Pink Panthers, and over thirty years later the club is still going strong. For us older alumni, the connection is purely social, and the annual "Pink Drink" at the Penny Lane Pub has been a Christmas tradition since the first year. Back then we were a bunch of young, mostly foreign soccer fanatics, who played the game pretty well. The names of the original Pink Panthers are a casting list for the show that became the rest of our lives. Chris Potter, who came over as a slender nineteen year old from Birmingham, England. Alan Day, a lanky midfielder from Liverpool who had a PhD and was clearly the brains of the team. Richard Adams, the Godfather of our daughter Cassie, who hails from a small village near Cambridge, England. Klaus Illig, born in Germany, raised in Canada, and otherwise known as "Kaiser." Tony Randjelovic, who came from Yugoslavia but now comes from Serbia, thanks to the reorganization of that part of Europe after President Tito died. Bob Pollitt, born in Baltimore by chance and raised in Bolton, Lancashire, who was the uncontested social leader of our group. Bob "Chopper" Harrison, from Bedfordshire, England, whose nickname describes his soccer skill. Jack Lawton, also from Bolton, who conceived of the club along with Chris Potter, and gave it the name as a put down to the competing "Richmond Lions" team. Peter Martin, our first goalie, and one of the many employees of Philip Morris Tobacco Company who did not smoke. John Small, of Hull, England, who recently retired after a singing career in the local pubs and clubs of Richmond. Bryan

### ◄ THE BOG, THE BAHAMAS, AND BEYOND

"Mucker" Clarke, who led the team from behind. We also allowed the odd American into the squad. Roy "Cyril" Harding, who became a tough tackling full back in no time. Randy "Scissorhands" Bryant was our long-time goalkeeper, and Dave "Tricky American" Dunivan boosted the IQ averages for the squad. Just a few years ahead of us in age and experience was our social mentor, Terry O'Neill, owner of the Penny Lane Pub, and an icon in the Richmond area. Terry's pub has been a downtown fixture since the late sixties, and is the place where we can always find each other.

Our first home at 10310 Pebblebrook Place was the scene of so many happy memories. We would eventually trade up to a beautiful new contemporary style home in a nearby part of the county, but those early years with our two young daughters were special. They both attended nursery school from an early age, mostly at River Road Baptist Church. Many of the churches in Richmond run a nursery school for the local community and are non-denominational rather than parochial. It is quite usual for Presbyterian families to use a Catholic Church facility, and vice versa. Our girls were well prepared for entry to the local public school system, and would eventually attend public Elementary, Middle, and High School in Henrico County, before University. Both of our girls are outgoing by nature and were very much involved in the academic and vocational structure of the various schools that they attended. They both played girl's soccer in organized leagues for many years, and Cassie stuck with it through High School and was a talented left winger, although she is right footed. Just like her dad. Shona was more into the social aspects of her team, and somewhere between child and teenager she shed the soccer boots and found a better fit with dancing shoes at Miss Mary's Dance School near our home. She did score one goal in her soccer career, and it was quite appropriate that the ball reluctantly trundled across the goal line, to the surprise of Shona, her team-mates, and the parents on the touch-line.

In the early years of our life in Virginia we usually spent Friday evenings in the company of our friends. From around 5pm till 7pm cocktails would be served in the garden when our neighbors on either side, the Eubank's and the Coleman's, brought their deck chairs and their young kids to hang out before bed-time. Then, Chris and

Barbara Potter would show up with liquid re-inforcements, and then help us get the girls ready for bed so that we could spend the evening watching a show on TV or just talking about "stuff." These were good times, and the basis of lifelong relationships. We are Godparents to Natalie and Jon Potter who, like our kids, really enjoy their connectedness to the UK.

My work at the bank was enjoyable and fulfilling. Once again I was so lucky to work for a superb business professional, and Julian Banton would eventually become President and CEO of a major bank in Alabama. By now our international group numbered about thirty or so employees, and our foreign loan portfolio was primarily in Latin America and Europe. I was appointed head of the International Division of the bank in 1982, with a new title of Senior Vice President, when Julian moved up the corporate ladder. This was my first position of divisional responsibility for the day to day running of the business of international banking. However, I had but a few short months to get accustomed to being the boss when the world changed, with the default by the Government of Mexico on its sovereign debt to the international banking community. Suddenly the body corporate of our organization was looking to me for information and answers to some fairly basic questions such as "how are we going to get paid back?" and "what does this mean for the rest of our portfolio in Latin America?" Suddenly I was back in the loan collection business, although now we were one of hundreds of creditors, and so this was a very different dynamic from my previous experience in one-on-one negotiations with defaulting clients. At the same time, the exposure to potential loan losses was now such a big number, as in essence every loan we had in Mexico was now at risk - of a total of about sixty million dollars.

With the benefit of time and distance there are so many things that we can look back upon, and easily rationalize the onset of the Latin American Debt crisis, and its many causes and repercussions. The American banks in particular were willing lenders, and the Latin American countries in general were willing borrowers. While it is true that many of the loans were for much needed infrastructure and industrialization of their economies, the lending also enabled many of the Latin countries to fund unrealistic currency policies, particularly

◄ THE BOG, THE BAHAMAS, AND BEYOND

in Mexico and Venezuela. The worldwide recession of the seventies and eighties, the increase in the price of oil, and the high interest rate policy of the U.S. Government, seemed to coalesce in a perfect storm, and the Finance Minister of Mexico was the unfortunate weather forecaster with the job of telling us all to take cover.

Within a few weeks the contagion had spread throughout Latin America, and the banking industry had to learn how to deal with this mind boggling event and its consequences, most of which were unpleasant. In our particular case we had the majority of our exposure in the form of loans to the Government Sector, or to Banks that were Government owned or controlled. But, as a fairly small player in the scheme of things, we had little control over the outcome. The large Money Center banks had the political clout and the biggest stick to wield in negotiations. Regional banks like us quickly aligned ourselves with Citibank and Bank of America and the like, so the negotiations and compromises on how much of the debt would be repaid, and on what basis, was organized and delegated to a smaller but much more influential committee assembled from the financial community. At the same time, many of our loans were to smaller private banks and corporations, so in these situations we had to conduct our own negotiations with our customers, and whatever arrangements we made had to conform to the policy of the various Central Banks. Over the subsequent months I was a regular visitor to Latin America, and was lucky to have Ramon in our Mexico Rep Office, so that we could split the travel duties and travel to our clients in Central and South America.

Our situation in Chile, for example, was typical of our experience. In 1973, General Augusto Pinochet, helped by the CIA, took over the communist government of Chile headed by Dr. Salvador Allende, and ushered in a new era of dictatorship and human rights abuse. He would lead his country for seventeen turbulent years until transferring power to a democratically elected president in 1990. I visited Chile while Pinochet was still in power, to meet with a couple of the Chilean Banks that owed us about five million dollars. I was able to structure a transaction that provided for repayment of our loans in full, albeit over a stretched out period of time. A couple of years later we sold our loans to a New York investment bank, as part of a corporate strategy to reduce our exposure to Latin America. The discounts that we experienced in selling these loans, and indeed pretty much all of our Latin American loan portfolio, were in retrospect a high price to pay, especially since the Latin American countries that we lent to did not repudiate any debt, and indeed continued to service their loans on re-negotiated terms that were common at that time. With hindsight, we could have kept the loans on the books and saved about $25 million of unnecessary loan charge offs. Chile has since renounced the extremism of left and right, and has had many years of democratic government that has led to much heralded economic and political stability in the last two decades.

As is the case with all financial bubbles, when they burst there is a period of time when things are at their lowest, and the repercussions are most severe. Then there is a period of recovery, which often takes a few years, and then it becomes apparent that there is a new successor paradigm at work, that looks like business as usual, but with the application of lessons learned. So, as bankers, we took our collective lumps in the form of significant loan losses, and many of the smaller players like Bank of Virginia exited the business. The larger banks stayed in, and over the years have for the most part developed successful and profitable niches in overseas markets, with a more disciplined approach to risk. There have been many gyrations in the financial markets since the eighties, with a few notable calamities, but nothing as consequential as the bubble that burst in 2008 in our own domestic market, requiring massive intervention by the U.S. Government in the financial markets to avert not just a recession but a depression. I was a long time retired from banking when that happened, but was not surprised when it did. Bankers spend other people's money. If it was their own, the occasional meltdowns would probably never happen.

It was about this time in our lives when our past experiences of living in the Bahamas intersected with our current life in Richmond, and provided one of these pleasant interludes in our family story that resonates with each of us individually, as well as collectively. Simply put, we bought a vacation home in the Bahamas, and for a few years when the girls were young, it became our family getaway place.

### THE BOG, THE BAHAMAS, AND BEYOND

I received a phone call from a lawyer in Richmond, David Greenberg, who had got my name through bank channels as someone who knew about the Bahamas. It turned out that he and three of his legal buddies owned a cottage on one of the Bahama Islands, Spanish Wells, and were now interested in selling it. They had bought it for a song, and no longer had any real interest in visiting on a regular basis. It even had a name, "The Barristers" as a testament to the occupation of the owners. David wanted my advice on how to go about the sale, and when we met at his law offices we quickly developed a level of trust. He said they were looking to get $15,000 which was about what they paid, in the hope that they could get a quick sale and be done with it. I told David I would get back to him in a day or so. After work that day, I went for a drink at Penny Lane Pub with my pal Werner Versch, of our International Division. Werner was a Bavarian by birth and upbringing, and had moved to the New York area when he was about sixteen, to stay with his older sister. He learned to speak English watching movies and TV, and although he had a good command of the language and could function without any problems in the business world, there was no disguising his Bavarian accent. Along the way he got through High School, then college, and a Masters Degree in Business. No question, Werner was smart, and an all around great friend over many years. He handled problem loans, and was known in the bank as "the work-out Kraut". I told Werner of my meeting with David Greenberg, and Werner's first thought was "let's buy it!" This coincided with my first thought, so we quickly moved on to next steps. Now we had to raise $15,000, which would have been easy enough for us to borrow, but it was hardly worth the effort going through loan applications. So, we took the easy way out, visited our banking office, and each withdrew $7,500 on our credit cards.

Next day I called David and told him I had sold the cottage, and also bought it! He was delighted, and we took care of all the documentation through our bank lawyer in Nassau over the following few weeks. Werner and I formed a partnership the easy way, by shaking hands, and pretty soon we were the proud owners of a white wooden cottage with blue trim windows and a garden with coconut and lime trees, on the main street of Spanish Wells, opposite a public beach of white sand and ocean blue. I promptly made plans for our family of four to spend a week's vacation at the cottage later in the year, which was pretty adventurous considering we had bought the place sight unseen. Before that trip however, I was due back in Nassau on a business matter for the bank, so I made plans to fly over to the island, check out the cottage, and then fly back to Nassau. Both Werner and I were Directors of Bank of Virginia (Bahamas) Ltd., and were used to making quarterly trips to Nassau for the Board meetings. We chartered a small plane for a one day trip over to Spanish Wells, and flew back to Nassau in time for dinner on Paradise Island. The flight over was uneventful, and we were able to see the cottage and meet with our inherited caretaker, Margaret Pinder. She promised to have the place ready for our trip in November.

The flight back was in a small four - seater plane with just me and a very young looking pilot up front, and Werner in the back. We took off from North Eleuthera directly into the afternoon sun, and as the pilot was revving up for the start, he casually mentioned that he had left his sunglasses at the airport. So, we roared off down the runway and up into the air. At perhaps two or three hundred feet up, the door to my right opened up and all of a sudden I was looking down from a great height, trying to pull the door closed. No way it would close, so the pilot said he would bank and return to the airport. I immediately started shouting "bank left, bank left" as a bank to the right would toss me out into the Bermuda Triangle. Even this pilot wasn't that stupid, so he cruised around a left hand turn and landed safely. He sashayed over to the office building to pick up his sunglasses, made sure the passenger door was properly locked on the way back, and off we went headfirst into the blazing sun again. "No problem, man!"

The island of Spanish Wells has such a unique place in the story of the Bahamas, which I was familiar with from when we lived in Nassau. It is located just off the north-west tip of the larger island of Eleuthera, and so the journey from the airport in North Eleuthera required a taxi to the dock, and then a water taxi across the half a mile of water to the island. The taxi driver parked his car, cranked up his small boat, and completed the journey to the island. From the dockside in Spanish Wells it was a couple of hundred yard's walk to the cottage, which had

### THE BOG, THE BAHAMAS, AND BEYOND

a front garden overlooking the ocean, and a back garden overlooking the narrow straits that separated Spanish Wells from Russell Island. In those days Russell Island was officially uninhabited, but in fact was home to many Haitian families who were in the Bahamas illegally, but were condoned by the locals as long as they were off Spanish Wells and on Russell Island by 5 o'clock each night. They provided a cheap pool of labor for the islanders. If you have a sense that there might be a lack of political correctness about these parts, that is probably a bit understated. Let's just say that the vast majority of the local population in Spanish Wells are white Bahamian, in a country that is predominantly black.

The indigenous people who originally lived throughout the Bahama Islands are known to us as the Arawaks and the Lucayans, and they were exterminated by the Spanish Conquistadores, through genocide and diseases from which they had no immunity. The island became a last stop for Spanish galleons returning home from the America's, where they could refill their water supplies from wells that were created for this purpose, thanks to the abundant water table below the surface of the island. All it took, apparently, was a two foot hole dug into the sand to get to the water table. The Spaniards called it St. George's Cay, and for one of their most famous explorers, Juan Ponce de Leon, his search for the Fountain of Youth in and around Florida and the Caribbean would be fruitless, save for the water fountains at Spanish Wells on the way home. It was first populated by the Eleutheran Adventurers, a group of Puritans who fled England for a new land free of political or religious persecution. They picked up advance members of their sect in Bermuda, and headed west in search of paradise. They shipwrecked off Eleuthera in 1647, and were eventually helped by their Puritan brothers in Massachusetts Colony to move to the easily defended small island of Spanish Wells, where they decided to settle. In gratitude to their brothers in Massachusetts, in 1650 they bequeathed the financially failing Harvard College in Boston with one of its largest gifts, which saved the university from closure. One hundred or so years later, another group of settlers landed here, only this time from the United States. These loyalists to the British Crown had left America during the Revolutionary Wars, seeking a place on the continent that was still pro - British. The islanders became farmers and eventually fisherman, and so the importation of slaves into Nassau for agricultural plantations never really affected them. When the slave population of the Bahamas eventually became free citizens of their own country, Spanish Wells became a white outpost in an otherwise majority black country. Other "out" islands in the Bahamas had significant numbers of white citizens, but Spanish Wells was the only one to be fully Caucasian. The white Bahamians in their own country are known as "Conchy Joes" and even in today's population of about 300,000 Bahamian citizens, some 45,000 or so are estimated to be "white". They generally are quite comfortable with their heritage and status, but continue to support the Free National Movement political party, which is a nominal opposition party to the established power base of the black majority, the Progressive Liberal Party. Although lobster fishing has been the commercial mainstay of Spanish Wells for decades, there was a period of time in the seventies and eighties when it was, like its sister island of Norman's Cay in the Exuma's, a trans-shipment point for drugs being shipped from South America to North America.

Around Thanksgiving time in 1983 we left Richmond for a week in Spanish Wells. After our three airplane journeys, then the taxi to the dock, Ann and I and our two girls were perched in the Boston Whaler water taxi, taking in the beautiful scenery and excited about our vacation. As we entered the straits to the docking area, we saw that there was an old DC3 prop plane lying in the shallows just off the entrance to the small harbor. The taxi driver told us that it was a drug drop that had gone wrong a few months ago, and the smugglers were never apprehended. Given the rather small area of land for them to hide on, it is local knowledge that they were sheltered by their island clients, and shipped off to safety in due course. You would think that the authorities would want to rid this eyesore from the gateway to the island, but it lay there for several years before it was finally taken apart by the government. I sense that Spanish Wells was proud of its smuggling status, regardless of the reputation of the product.

The cottage, although wooden, was structurally sound, and lay at the narrow eastern end of the island, close to the docks, the supermarket, a bar, and the island mortuary. Obviously the concept of zoning was not readily apparent in the Spanish Wells Planning Department. The garden was as advertised, well laid out with abundant tropical vegetation, although the location right on the main street (at that point of the island it was the only street) meant that it doubled as a race-track for the local teens on their motor scooters. Yet again in my life I was surrounded by hostile Lambretta's and Vespa's, although this time the presence of my young children required that we be really cautious any time we left the front door of the cottage. The only real problem with the place was the cockroaches, and even though Ann and I were well used to the Bahamian variety after our years in Nassau apartments, it was still a bit of a challenge for Ann, and of course my two very girly girls of two years and five years of age. We managed to arrange for a couple of bunk beds to be installed, and so with Ann and me upstairs in one bedroom, and the girls bunked downstairs in the other bedroom, it was quite cozy. We spent the week on the beach, and generally relaxing in and around the cottage. There was always something going on in the harbor area, and we had a memorable family holiday, even although Cassie walked into a mass of sand burrs and we spent ages painfully extricating them from the soles of her bare feet. The return journey once again required us to fly on a propeller driven small plane from North Eleuthera to Miami, but the weather was clear and we had a safe and enjoyable journey across the Devil's Triangle, and then on to Richmond. We went to Spanish Wells as a family unit another two times during the time that we had it, and loved the sea, sun, and sand. There was not much else.

Over the course of the following four years we had folks from Richmond rent the place from time to time. After a few of years, there was less and less chance for family trips, what with competing school related events, and in 1986 Werner and I decided to sell the place. It was easy enough to do. I told Margaret to ask around and sure enough there was a young couple on the island from New York, who were setting up a photograph studio, and looking for a home. I went down one more time, reached an agreement, and sold it for twice what we paid. Now I look back and wonder why we just didn't keep it. That's when I tell myself to look forward.

## FAMILY TIMES

Back in Richmond, my business life was consumed with the Latin American debt crisis, as I had to keep on top of all that was going on across the continent so that I could represent the bank in either direct or indirect negotiations on the repayment, or more often than not restructuring, of our loan portfolio. One of our private sector loans in Mexico was to a Brandy Distillery in the State of Aguascalientes, which literally means "hot water," attesting to the many hot springs found in that part of the country. I met up with Ramon at our Mexico City office, then we flew to the town, which is in West/Central Mexico, and at that time it had a population of about half a million people. We were met by the owner of the company, a rather grand old Mexican gentleman, and driven to his hacienda in the nearby countryside, where we stayed overnight as his guest. That evening we went into town with our host and a number of his family members/employees to the local Dog-Fighting ring, not to watch dogs fighting but instead to watch Cock-Fighting, a local passion. I was dressed in my favorite cream colored business suit that I had bought on a previous visit to Hong Kong, which I thought would be appropriate for the somewhat tropical environment of western Mexico, and soon realized that I was overdressed for the event, the locale, and the locals. Our party of about a dozen or so took our superior seats with an excellent view of the events, and after our host made a big show out of buying raffle tickets for all of us, we settled down to watch the "entertainment." As a spectacle, it was pretty disgusting, but this was a situation where I put my personal feelings to the side and did my best to enter into the spirit of things. Having been to a couple of bull fights in Latin America I expected it to be a rather tame affair, but I have to say the cocks were in it to win it, and used their sharpened spurs as pretty effective weapons. Finally, there was a big to do in the center of the ring, when the Maestro drew the winning ticket for the raffle, and lo and behold my number was called out. I was directed down into the center of the ring, and given a wad of Mexican pesos, which had a value of around one hundred dollars, and so was a pretty healthy sum in those days. The presentation was a bit surreal, as here was this sharply dressed gringo picking up what was probably a monthly wage packet for the locals. I could not think quickly enough of a way to unburden myself of this windfall,

### THE BOG, THE BAHAMAS, AND BEYOND

so I made my way back to my seat with my head down in unappreciated contrition. This was also the trip where I tasted a couple of the local delicacies for the first, and last, time. A Tepisquincla (my hazy recollected spelling) is a breed of dog in Mexico that is very small and has no hair. It is eaten as a special treat, but I can't imagine why. Then I had Armadillo, and was equally unimpressed. It was a relief to get back to Mexico City and the spicy Enchiladas.

Summertime saw us back in Scotland for a month of rest and recreation, and it turned out to be little of the former and much of the latter. We had a super family holiday in the Island of Mull, in a rented house at Carradale overlooking our honeymoon island of Arran, which we shared with Grandma Hunter and a revolving door of Hunters, Winfield's, and Saim's. This was typical of so many of our family holidays as the kids grew up. We went to Scotland as a base each summer, and then joined up with Connie and her family in France, usually with Grandma Hunter in tow, and everyone else in the family coming in and moving out depending where they were coming from or going to. In later years we would use Lorna's overseas location as a base, and just by following Lorna around the world we were able to visit Bermuda, Crete, Sicily, Texas, and more recently Gibraltar. These were all wonderful family holidays, and kept the cousins connected over their formative years.

In January 1984 I was returning from an overseas trip, and had connected to the Richmond flight from Miami. Company policy was to travel coach class, except for journeys involving international travel, so I was seated in the first class section, at the front of the plane. We landed in a thunderstorm, and because of construction work at Richmond airport we had to de-plane outside, then make our way to the terminal door to access the building. The rain was bucketing down, so Eastern Airlines had arranged for umbrellas to be available at the bottom of the stairs. I lined up second to leave, with another male passenger from the First Class section ahead of me. Once he was down the steps and opened his umbrella, I quickly de-planed, got my umbrella, and took off running towards the door. I overtook the other guy on the way, and as I reached the door to the terminal there was a thunderous crash and a bolt of lightning that was scary. Twenty yards or so behind me, the other passenger was struck dead by the lightning, although at the time I did not know it as I was through the door and into the terminal. I read about it in the newspaper in the morning, and called Eastern Airlines to ask about it, which is when I learned that it was my fellow First Class passenger who had been killed. He was a father of two, not much older than me. I suppose I was in the right place at the wrong time. I ran, and he walked, and for him everything changed, and for me nothing changed. There is just no way to rationalize it, and I gave up a long time ago.

Whereas the Hunter side of the family had lots of cousin relationships, there was only one immediate family member in Glasgow, Ann's sister Agnes, who had married her school boyfriend Billy (Brown). Her first child, Alison, was born in 1986 and Lindsay completed the family in 1989. As close as Ann and Agnes are as sisters, it is no surprise that our girls have been close to Alison and Lindsay. On countless occasions we have disembarked at Glasgow Airport and taken the short taxi ride to Barrhead, to unload our suitcases and begin our summer holidays. There are so many wonderful memories that stem from these many years of travel, where both sides of the family played such an important part in making our family of four, living far away in time, distance and culture, always feel so connected to our roots, and in instilling a love for Scotland and its people in the hearts of our two girls.

In the summer of 1985 I was sent by the Bank to the University of Virginia, in Charlottesville, to experience a six week immersion in the academics of business, known as The Executive Program. There were about one hundred or so participants from all over the country, and another twenty or so from overseas. In many ways, this was my university education, squeezed into six long and challenging weeks at the Business School, taught by Professors in the gamut of business practices such as Accounting, Economics, Computer Science, Finance, and Marketing. I was lucky to be given this opportunity, and recognized that this was one of the ways that the organization recognizes someone on the "fast track" for promotion in the not too distant future. From a family perspective it was hard to be away for such a sustained period of time, although I was able to get the odd day back in

### THE BOG, THE BAHAMAS, AND BEYOND

Richmond, which after all was only about an hour's drive away. Shona was seven and Cassie was only four, so they were young enough to miss their Daddy, and it was also hard for Ann to be without my parental support in the most active and family oriented time of the year.

At the final weekend of the course there was a "graduation" ceremony of sorts, to which families were invited, so Ann brought the girls along to the Saturday afternoon reception and barbecue. Shona was old enough to know that university was a place you went to after leaving school, and the visit must have registered with her as from then on she only ever talked about going to UVA when she left High School. To her credit she graduated high in her Class and her application was accepted. She went on take double majors in English and Social Studies, graduating in the Class of 2000. Cassie was accepted by James Madison University, in Harrisonburg, Virginia, where she majored in Finance, and graduated in the Class of 2003. Our girls were educationally streets ahead of their Mum and Dad, thereby repeating a familial, and indeed societal, trait.

Events in the larger world in the mid-eighties were proving to be no less fascinating than those we had seen in the sixties and seventies. For every sea change in business or culture that opened up new opportunities such as the Internet, and Live Aid concerts, there were paradigm shifts in global politics. While we can look back at the rise to power of Mr. Gorbachev in the USSR as a portent of the fall of Communism that was to come, so too can we see the increasing footprint of the militant Islamic group, the Palestine Liberation Army (PLO), in the hijackings and bombings of transportation targets, mostly airplanes, but also the cruise ship "Achille Lauro." When airline security was stepped up the terrorists chose easier targets, and engaged in mass shooting of passengers on the ground in Rome and Vienna. The PLO was the aperitif ahead of the more potent power of Al Queda, which would rise to prominence and infamy in years to come.

Just as the USA was in national mourning in 1986 over the explosion and complete destruction of the Space Shuttle Challenger there came word of a nuclear accident in Chernobyl in the Ukraine, that created a moving cloud of radioactive contamination over a large part of western Soviet Union and Europe. This resulted in the mandatory evacuation and resettlement of more than 350,000 people from the most severely contaminated areas of Belarus, Russia, and Ukraine. The last report from a Russian publication, *Chernobyl*, in 2004 suggested that almost one million excess deaths from cancer had occurred as a consequence of this nuclear accident.

We would normally be heading back to Scotland again for our summer holiday, but this was the year that we sold our "starter" home in Pebblebrook Place and moved "up-market" into a brand new contemporary house in George's Bluff, about a couple of miles away. We contracted with a friend and neighbor Mike Pierce, who introduced us to his architect, and between us we came up with the design of a house that would meet our needs and fulfill our aspirations. The projected completion date was July 15, and we did not plan a trip to Scotland that year, but instead got ready to welcome some of our family from overseas into our new home. It was especially nice to have Agnes and Billy come over from Scotland with Alison, who was just two years old, and be part of this new and exciting time in our lives. Mike turned over the keys of the house just a couple of days before they all arrived, and apart from a rogue gas barbecue tank that went on fire on the (wooden) deck at the back of our house, all went well.

I was invited to a management group meeting at the bank, where our Chairman announced that we were about to acquire a bank in Maryland - Union Trust. From now on our footprint as an organization would surround and include Washington DC. For technical reasons to do with the combination of the respective company stocks, the transaction was described as a merger, but in reality it was very much a take-over, as we were the larger bank, and it was clear from the outset that the new organization would be run from Richmond. As the then head of the International Division, I assumed that I would run the combined international organizations, but I soon found myself a victim of company politics, and moving to a new job in the bank, quite different from my responsibilities for international banking. When the horse trading was going on among the top executives of both banks on how the new organization would emerge, it turned out that their President was gung ho on his international group, and having lost most of the early rounds of card play when they divided

◄ THE BOG, THE BAHAMAS, AND BEYOND

up the bank, he took a stand on retaining responsibility for international banking in Baltimore, a much larger city than Richmond. I was soon invited for a career discussion with my boss, Mac McDonald, who laid out for me the reasons why I would no longer run the Division. Instead, they moved my colleague John Vogel from head of the National Division to a "Special Projects" position, which enabled a lateral move for me from head of International to head of National Banking. I was so comfortable with my role in the organization, and knew that deals like this are made all the time in merger situations, so I was quite happy to go with the flow, and grasp this new and different opportunity within the bank.

My colleague John Vogel, who gave up his regular job so that I could move over to run his division, was a good friend. We are about the same age, and our career track at the bank was pretty consistent. We both made Senior Vice President at the same time, and later would make Executive Vice President at the same time. While John and I were friends, we were completely different personality types. John is a Type "A" personality, has a voice that carries the day in group conversation, and he operates in a field of high energy in everything he does. To quote my bank buddy Dave Brantley, "Vogel is like a well struck tee shot in a tile bathroom!" John was representative in a way of the many really good friends that I had at the bank, most of whom served with me for over twenty years. The gold lapel pin that I was eventually given on my 25 year anniversary was appreciated. I had been absorbed by the company through acquisition, so it is not as if I chose to work there, but in the way of things it all worked out so well. Like John, I was a company man, and would not have had it any other way.

The National Banking Division was the part of the bank that dealt with large nation-wide organizations that did business in Virginia but were headquartered outside of our natural market. In fact, our customers were all over the map within the continental USA, so now my job no longer required international travel, and I am glad to say we had no customers in Alaska, and sorry to say that we also had no customers in Hawaii. I enjoyed some aspects of my new role, which was much more integrated into our branch banking system than our international group, and the group of mostly younger bankers, predominantly male as was the case in these days, were easy to be around and anxious to work with their new leader. These were also the times when banks were becoming focused on organizational improvement, and it was no surprise when the bank engaged outside consultants to somehow unlock the secrets of the organization, and teach us how to transform our businesses. It seemed that we just rolled from one group of "experts" to another, each having a new and better way to improve our financial performance, but inevitably ending their engagement with the recommendation to cut staff and re-organize in some different fashion. This was my first experience with "downsizing" and for the first time I had to make choices about who should go and who should stay. We had a young Irishman on staff, John Hunter (no relation) and as the new man in the group he was the first to go. He was such a nice guy that as I was finishing up our meeting, having told him the bad news, he told me that this must have been difficult for me, and not to worry. John later moved to a competitor bank in Northern Virginia, with a new wife and a new job, and I hear about him from time to time through mutual friends. Not all my involvements in hiring and firing were as pleasant, right down to the time when it was the turn of my boss to give the news to me. But that would come much later, and in circumstances that were quite different than the warm and friendly tone of my meeting with young John.

I quickly found out that Corporate Banking was a chance not so much to learn new skills but to apply some basic skills in a different way. The analysis and understanding of the risk elements that pertain to lending money to foreign governments has much to do with macro-economic factors, such as national and international debt levels, exchange rate policies and the balance of trade, and in the case of Third World countries (or Emerging Markets) the overall degree of political risk that is assumed when lending money across geographic and political boundaries. Lending to corporations within the continental United States however, removes many of these risk characteristics, and replaces them with risk elements that have much more to do with the ability of a single borrower to have the resources to repay the loan within the time frame and on the terms upon which the loan was made. The variables that collectively represent

◀ THE BOG, THE BAHAMAS, AND BEYOND

the quantifiable risk to the bank of losing money by lending to a given company are often described as the four C's of Credit – character, capacity, capital, and collateral. While this paradigm is typically applied when making loans to individuals, it is also applied to corporations, who after all do have a distinct legal personality. Character relates to the financial responsibility of the borrower - is there a history of past borrowing activity that was consistently handled properly, so therefore there is no reason to expect that it will be any different in the future. Capacity refers to the likelihood that the business will be able to generate revenues from their chosen business activities with which to fund the repayment of the loan. Capital refers to the aggregation of resources within the organization that show that the business has the financial resources to repay the debt, and Collateral is the assets of the business that are used to secure the loan, so that in the event of a problem the bank has something tangible that can be sold to liquidate the debt.

I think I made the most of my chance to be in the mainstream of the organization. It was really like running a sales organization, and what we were selling was money in the form of loans, and services in the form of cash management. Now and then we would gather for a couple of days or so in some handy location not far from Richmond, where we could meet on planning and strategy stuff during the day, and then relax at the hotel in the evening. I look back on it and think to myself, what a waste of time, and yet at that time it was just the way things were done. I remember hosting a sales conference, and opened the meeting with a parody of the words of the Chinese philosopher Lao Tzu, by announcing that "a journey of a thousand miles begins with a cold beer!" and promptly displayed bottles of Budweiser to the surprised group of young men and women bankers, for consumption later.

When I made the move from International to National I did however keep one account relationship, which was a multi-million dollar Loan Facility for a Hungarian born Doctor who owned and operated his own hospital in the Northern Virginia suburbs just outside Washington D.C. This amazing man, who was in his late seventies when I dealt with him, had attended medical school in Warsaw,

Poland, and was trapped there by the Nazi occupation. He arrived in America after the war armed with his medical degree, only to find that it was not recognized by the American Medical Association, so he had to start Med School all over again. He used his earnings as a doctor to invest in commercial property, and by the time I knew him he was the largest individual owner of office buildings leased to the United States Government. His wealth was somewhere around half a billion dollars (in 1986) and he amassed this fortune in real estate all the while practicing medicine as a surgeon. His investment strategy involved financing his mortgage debts in foreign currencies, and then writing sophisticated option contracts in the Foreign Exchange Markets to hedge his exposures, while leaving room for upside movement in currency prices with which to take profits. He dealt with my pal Werner in the early days of our international banking group, and when Werner left the bank to go into business on his own I took over the relationship. His stuff was so complicated that I had to prepare the accounting entries every time his loans matured, and were rolled over, as there was no one else in the bank that knew how to do it. As time went on he gradually reduced his involvement in foreign currencies, and eventually sold his hospital when he finally retired. Still, it was a fascinating experience to know someone like that, and to see how he went about creating financial value from currency speculation.

Although most of our lending was fairly straightforward and unexciting, occasionally we saw deals that were unusual, and also fun to work with. We financed a pioneer company in the Global Positioning Satellite business, when the science was fairly new, and the commercial marketplace had not yet spotted the opportunity, apart from one small company in Washington DC that was a customer of our bank. Their prototype GPS product was marketed to long distance trucking companies as a means of keeping track of their drivers and equipment, using satellite resources of the U.S. military. It turns out that the military were really interested in GPS because of its potential value in advanced warfare, and so hosted our customer's technology on military satellites. We financed the first application of their technology on a French rocket that was fired from their launching station on Devil's Island in South America. They were able to secure insurance

### THE BOG, THE BAHAMAS, AND BEYOND

that would pay out in the event that the launch was unsuccessful, and so we as a bank were assigned the proceeds of the insurance policy before we made our loan. On the other hand, if the launch was successful, then there would be businesses and governments lining up to gain access to their GPS capability, so the financial prospects of the company would be much improved, and there should be enough new found financial muscle to handle repayment of our loan. Well, as it happened, the launch was a bust, and we did in fact get paid out from the insurance proceeds. The GPS business is now huge (think of Google Earth) and along the way our small customer in Washington sold their technology early in the game, and the owners never really made the big bucks.

In the summer of 1987 we were back in Scotland, and did some touring up north. By now the girls were old enough to appreciate the scenery and to listen politely to one more history lesson from their Dad as we travelled through the Highlands of our beautiful country. We even took a boat trip on Loch Ness, and our guide told us about the recent exploration of the bottom of the loch by an American group who hoped to film Nessie. It turned out to be a million dollar waste of money on their part, and I felt better then about the fifty pounds or so that I had to pay for our boat trip, which seemed about forty pounds on the high side. Back in Falkirk, and then Glasgow, our girls were much more enamored with the recent movie "Dirty Dancing" that they had seen prior to the trip, and were able to impress their cousins with their attempts to imitate the moves. While all this was going on that summer, the population of the world hit five billion people, which was a much more impressive statistic than that which greeted me at the office one October morning. Wall Street, in the form of the Dow Jones Industrial Average, dropped almost 23% in concert with major market falls around the world. It turned out to be one of these periodic shake ups that the markets go through from time to time, with no single cause of the crash, but rather a combination of events and circumstances that trigger a change in the psychology of investors. Within two years it was back to where it was before, and so began another market cycle that would run till once more investors would tip the scales of greed and fear with a weighty batch of sell orders.

## FAMILY TIMES

Around this time in our lives, Shona made the transition to Middle School and left her sister behind at Maybeury Elementary. Both girls were far enough along the learning curve to show lots of academic and scholastic talent, as well as being very social. The class size was around 25 or so, compared to the 40 kids that Ann and I shared our school days with. They were used to standing up in front of the class and speaking or presenting, and they were much more confident students than we had been. From the early days of Kindergarten, kids are encouraged to participate in "show and tell" by bringing a special object to school and talking about it in front of the class. Our experiences were much more collective than individual, and it clearly makes a difference when kids are exposed at an early age to the responsibility of speaking in public.

With our regular jaunts across the Atlantic each year, and periodic trips that required air travel, any international incident, be it terror related or accidental, was always something that played on the mind. In the year (1988) that saw a change in the law to allow pubs to open twenty four hours a day, with much cause for celebration in Scotland, there were two "national disasters" that happened in our small country that had international repercussions. That summer, while we were home, the Piper Alpha Oil Rig in the North Sea exploded due to a processing malfunction, and 166 oil workers on the rig died a horrible death in the conflagration that followed. Another two men sent to rescue survivors also lost their lives that day. The rig, operated by Occidental Petroleum, was never reactivated into service. Because of the British Petroleum refinery in Grangemouth, next to Falkirk, there had always been a large number of local men and women employed in the oil business, and several of the fatalities were local to our area. That same year ended with the bombing of Pan Am flight 103 over Lockerbie, and the loss of 270 lives, 11 of whom were residents of this small town in the Scottish Borders. As I write this some twenty plus years later, this incident is still in the headlines, due to the overthrow of the Kaddafi government in Libya, where the plot was conceived, as a response to President Reagan's decision to bomb Tripoli in 1987. The terror bombing of a night club frequented by U.S. soldiers in West Berlin was believed to have been sanctioned by Kaddafi, and the

◄ THE BOG, THE BAHAMAS, AND BEYOND

American bombing of Kaddafi's compound in Tripoli was Reagan's unilateral response. Such is the way of things in international diplomacy, where the tactics and strategy of international relations often comes down to a "he shot/we shot" mentality.

In the Fall of 1988 I was pulled out of my regular responsibilities for a couple of weeks to take a colleague of mine, Sandy Teu, on a tour of our main banking contacts in Europe. I had many years of history with our European banking correspondents, and now that this was part of Sandy's department, he wanted to meet our customers. Our trip would begin in London, then take us to Paris, Amsterdam, Frankfurt, Zurich, Milan, and back home. Sandy and I were great friends, and still see each other on a regular basis. He ran our Bond trading department, our investment portfolio, and foreign exchange trading. In the banking world, traders are a breed apart. They do not concern themselves with mere deposit taking and lending. Theirs is the transactional world, where deals are done on the phone, for millions of dollars at a time, and profit is gained through small fractions of a percent on a large volume of transactions. The assumption is that if you make a trade that earns a buck, someone else in another trading floor is losing a buck, and the joys of a trader are both financial and gutteral. There are certain truisms that pertain to a trading floor in any bank anywhere. The men are loud and invariably obnoxious, by design. The women, although fewer in number, are aggressive, and the Pods (workspaces) are invariably demarcated with pizza boxes and high energy soft drinks. In any trading floor anywhere you will see a row of clocks set to the local time of the main world financial centers. Because I was a mainstream banker who just happened to be on good terms with the trading room, I was accorded the honor of a Falkirk clock lined up on the wall between Dubai and Geneva. This was a rare accolade from a trader to a banker, and a source of mystery to one bank examiner, who thought that there must be a currency exposure somewhere on the books to warrant the attention to Scotland. The other thing about trading rooms is that everyone has a nickname. Sandy was, and still is, known as the Lizard, which played to his reputation as someone slick, quick, and hard to pin down. He even had a patented handshake where he tucked his right thumb into the palm of his hand when proffering his hand, as if it were the front end of a snake. Try it, it's not a good feeling.

So, Sandy and I duly headed for London to begin our trip. After a couple of days of meetings, liquid lunches, more meetings, and drinks/dinner as befitted a couple of American bankers in Europe, I wasn't feeling too good as we headed to Heathrow for our flight to Paris. When Sandy asked me how I was, I said I felt rather dull, so from now on he should call me Derek Dull. We had a few laughs along the way, playing off my new persona, and by the time we got to Zurich I was feeling good again. When Sandy enquired after my health that morning, I told him I felt vibrant, so he should call me Victor Vibrant. In mid morning we had a half hour break between appointments, so we stopped at a street café in the Paradeplatz for a coffee. I went inside to order, and while I was waiting I was approached by a Middle-Eastern man who asked me if I was Mr. Dull. I mumbled something about being Victor Vibrant, and made my way back to the table for a good laugh with the Lizard. Sometimes truth is stranger than fiction.

In 1989 Ann gave in to the building pressure to quit smoking, which by now was becoming much more of a societal issue than before, as well as a hot topic round the dinner table in our house. Shona and Cassie would come home from school with the propaganda about how smoking is so bad for your health, even secondary smoke, and poor Ann finally decided that she should stop this habit that she knew was bad, but that gave her pleasure for so many years. She quit cold turkey, and will tell you today that it was the hardest thing she ever did, and also how much she would love to light one up again. Ann was a social smoker, and if she did light up on her own it was to fill an odd moment of the day, with a cup of tea, and a chance for some happy contemplation before the school bus delivered our girls back to her. Once the door opened and the girls came in full of joy and conversation, Ann was there for them, ready to react to the events of the day, and respond to their needs. She had known for some time that she would need to someday face the challenge of giving up cigarettes, and I think she had to identify with a cause that was so strong that she knew she had to comply, and the girls provided it.

Now and then the postman would deliver a bulky airmail letter

◄ THE BOG, THE BAHAMAS, AND BEYOND

from South Africa, and I would open it up with a smile already on my face, in contemplation of the laughs to come in reading the latest epistle from my pal Ian Laurie in South Africa. By now Ian had remarried, and his first wife Janette was back in the Falkirk area, with their two children, Joelle and Jason. Ann and I would often meet up with Janette and the kids during our annual holidays, so that Shona and Cassie also felt a closeness with Ian's first family. A few years later Janette died from the terrible disease of cancer, although by then Joelle and Jason were in the work-force and were somehow able to get through this tragic period in their lives.

Ian lived with his wife Rosie on a sixteen acre parcel of land that they had bought in Natal Province, and they would eventually build a beautiful home there as they raised their three children, Taryn, Natalie, and Tom. The children were into their early teens when Ian and Rosie decided to move to London, over a real concern about crime and lack of personal security in their beautiful country. The system of Apartheid would eventually fall, after Prime Minister De Klerk promised political freedom for the black and colored South Africans, yet failed to deliver better lives for the vast majority of the population. The years leading up to the fall of the Minority Government and the rise to power of Nelson Mandela were difficult times for the country, and even after Mandela's accession there was a real breakdown in law and order. There were two occasions when Ian was driving the kid's home from school and was almost hijacked by hoodlums trying to run his car off the road. Ian and Rosie reluctantly closed up the house, and bought five single tickets for the plane journey to London.

The silver lining for us was the ability to see Ian, Rosie, and all the kids on a regular basis during our annual trips to Scotland. All five of Ian's children are linked to our girls through the magic of Facebook, and the blood of their fathers, thanks to a ritual performed in the back hall of our house at 9 Alexander Avenue when we were children. We became blood brothers with the help of a sharp knife and the encouragement of my sister Betty and Ian's sister Kathryn, who also ended up bleeding, but blooded, by the time the ceremony was over.

In 1989 the first cracks appeared in the Berlin Wall, and by the end of the year the Wall was down and the world changed forever. The

Communist Government of East Germany collapsed, and the path towards a fully integrated East and West Germany was now inevitable. This was a time when television news was being delivered 24 hours a day, thanks to the innovation of Ted Turner in Atlanta, with his CNN channel that revolutionized popular culture. The change in the political and social order in all the countries of the Eastern Bloc, once the Soviet Union imploded, was quickly becoming reality, as country after country rejected the mantra of Communism and instead looked to their own particular brand of democracy.

We were all living in interesting times, to paraphrase an old Chinese saying, and the Internet was well on the way to transforming not just popular culture but indeed every aspect of our lives. In the Fall (Autumn) of 1990 I was part of a group of managers from different parts of the bank to visit M.I.T (Massachusetts Institute of Technology) in Boston for a two day working session on technology and banking. On a coffee break I was asked by a colleague of mine, David Hunt, if I fancied a move to a different part of the bank, to run the Trust and Investment business of the organization. This is the part of the bank that handles all of the fiduciary services that the bank provides, where the bank takes on a special responsibility to manage the financial assets of its wealthy customers. The Trust Company is the legal owner of their assets, and has specific instructions on how these assets should be managed, and who the beneficiaries of the estate are who will receive distributions from the assets under management. While many of the customers are widows and orphans, the Trust Company also provides asset management services for existing customers, in the knowledge that one day the accounts will be wrapped into the estate of the client, and protected for the benefit of the beneficiaries. In many organizations, and ours was no different, this business was viewed as something you have to have in order to serve your customers, but was rarely perceived as a line of business that could provide much in the way of profitability to the bank. There was a feeling in the bank that it was time for the Trust Company to step up, and I was given the chance to take over from the former President of Signet Trust Company.

In many ways the Trust business was similar to the Securities business that I had first dabbled in when I worked in the New Bond Street office of the Royal Bank of Scotland in 1965. Then later, when I went to Nassau, my first title was actually Trust Officer, as much of the offshore investment business that we did was set up in offshore trusts, to avoid taxation at the domicile of the client, usually a high tax jurisdiction such as the UK or the United States. It did not take me long to decide that this was a move that would be good for me, so I bade farewell to my friends in the National Division and got out of the lending business and into the world of stocks and bonds again.

Signet Trust Company had two main operating centers, one in Richmond, and the other in Baltimore, Maryland, in the offices of the former Union Trust Company, which was now part of the Signet Bank organization. There were about 120 employees in the combined group when I took over, and for the first year it was primarily a case of consolidating our activities to avoid duplication of effort and cost. By the end of the first year we were down to about 100 employees, and were ready to contribute profitability in our second year as a consolidated Trust Company. I was also part of a team from across the company to look at how we could combine all the various investment activities conducted by the bank in different departments, and create a single sales force of investment professionals. Like most banks, we had Trust people offering asset management services, a Discount Broker offering investment products, an Insurance Company offering insurance/investment products, and a Capital Markets group offering Certificate of Deposit and Government/Municipal Bond Investments. All of these groups tried to sell their products to the same base of bank deposit customers, so it was not just confusing for the customer but also for the organization. We were the first of the larger regional banks to combine all of those activities under one management and delivery structure, and my responsibilities expanded when I was given the job, which added a sales force of about 120 brokers who covered the branches throughout Virginia, Washington DC and Maryland.

While I had plenty to do, and a lot more people to do it with, our bank was increasingly subject to painful consulting assignments, when yet another group of "experts" would show up, with a mission to create the next great banking organization out of the tangled web of "unproductive" personnel that constituted our human resources. This was a movement that was epidemic in banking in the late eighties and early nineties, and our organization was no different than most. We just had to buckle down and pay tribute to the latest fad in business organization and methods that were brought to us by the consulting guru's of New York, carrying out their mission to free the organization of all the barriers to excellence, most of which were apparently of our own making. The sure outcome of most of these initiatives was another round of organizational change, with lots of firings and occasional hirings. Every time it happened there were casualties among the ranks, from all levels of staff and management, and it definitely instilled a sense of insecurity among all of us, including the management group. Each consulting episode that reached its conclusion with continued employment was considered a victory. A victory in battle, but not necessarily in war.

The approach of Summer meant that once again we would head across the Atlantic, and in this case the Summer of 1990 found us leaving the sanctuary of Scotland for a week or so of holidays with our French family, Connie and Sam, Axelle, Virginia, and Remi. By now the Saim family were quite settled in the Vendee Province, and they lived in a rural community but only a few miles from the regional market town of La Roche-Sur-Yon. The Vendee has a reputation in France as one of the more Catholic, and conservative, areas of the country, and back in 1815 when Napoleon escaped from Elba and enjoyed 100 days of freedom before his recapture, the people of the Vendee refused to recognize him, thereby bucking a national trend, and proclaimed their loyalty to King Louis XVIII. Life in the Vendee is no less controversial than it was in those days, although the issues are not life threatening, having more to do with such as the opening of a new road that would scar the pristine landscape of a sixteenth century monastery. Personally, I am with the monastery on this one, and I have a feeling, based on many years of visiting the Vendee, that the local Canon who represents the Church of Rome might prevail over the bureaucrat from Paris.

The Fall (or Autumn) of 1990 turned out to be memorable for another overseas trip, only this time it was for a "boondoggle" in the

## THE BOG, THE BAHAMAS, AND BEYOND

lovely island of Bermuda. Ann and I were invited by a major client, Federated Investors, based in Pittsburgh, to join a host of their other clients for a business meeting in Bermuda, with lots of time available between "work" sessions for relaxation and recreation. It was a fabulous long weekend. We arranged for Shona's schoolteacher to stay at our home and look after Shona and Cassie, so that Ann and I could travel happily in the knowledge that our girls were in good hands, and in fact were thrilled about having "Miss Seacrist" to look after them. We were also able to see my sister Lorna and her boyfriend Ron, who met in Bermuda while he was stationed at the US Naval Base. In fact, one year later we returned to Bermuda for their wedding, and although there were no expense accounts to pay the freight for that holiday, it was a wonderful time together in an island that we have visited many times, and were never disappointed.

CHAPTER **14**

# The Blue Nile

IAN SCOTT IS a well known Falkirk "Bairn" because of his reputation as an historian in our town, and at the national level for his many contributions to the Saltire Society in Edinburgh, which is the leading institution dedicated to Scottish history and culture. Ian is a long time friend of my sister Rena from their days together in the original Falkirk Folk Club back in the Nineteen Fifties. He retired a few years ago from teaching at Forth Valley College, and then went on to write the definitive history of our town in "The Life and Times of Falkirk". He is a great source of knowledge about our town and the surrounding area. It was from reading Ian's book that I learned about a local man, James Bruce of Kinnaird, who became famous as an explorer in Africa and discovered the source of the Blue Nile in Abyssinia (now Ethiopia). The story of his travels and exploration in eastern Africa was published in London in 1790 as "Travels to Discover the Source of the Nile" and achieved the dubious alliance of critical acclaim and contemporary incredulity. This combination was guaranteed to make his book a commercial success. He was a Falkirk Bairn who was larger than life, and has my vote as the most interesting son of our town.

James Bruce of Kinnaird was born in 1730 on the family estate on the outskirts of Falkirk. His ancestry included the famous Scots noble families of Hay and Bruce, so he entered life as a member of the privileged class. This entitled him to deference from the working classes, and membership in the upper classes of society should he make the normal progression through education at the best Public (i.e. Private)

## THE BOG, THE BAHAMAS, AND BEYOND

Schools, which he duly did. He spent his formative years in England so that he would not be exposed to the cause of Jacobinism, which sought to restore a Catholic Monarchy. The Battle of Culloden in 1746 put paid to the Catholic Stuarts' pretensions to the throne of Scotland and England, and in 1747 young James Bruce was repatriated to the family home of Kinnaird House. He entered the University of Edinburgh to study Law, but by 1748 he was forced to end his formal education because of ill health. It is unclear what was actually wrong with him, but this six foot four inch tall young man suffered from wheezing, shortness of breath, and was generally in a weak physical condition.

For the next five years he would hunt and shoot on the extensive Kinnaird estate, read the bible, and study foreign languages. He gradually filled out, and with his physical recovery he developed an ambition to go overseas, to India, where (Sir) Robert Clive was paving the way of colonization on behalf of the Empire. The path of progress lay once more with the road to London, so off he went to a familiar place, with the expectation of travel and adventure. For the next several years Bruce travelled throughout Europe, until the death of his father in 1758. It was in winding up his father's estate and settling with his half-brother, David, that he assumed ownership of the coal seams on Kinnaird land that had historically provided a modest income to the family. With the increasing use of coal to fuel the foundries of Falkirk, he was able to contract for the supply of coal to Carron Company, whose foundry was built on Kinnaird land acquired from the Bruce family. He found himself to be predictably wealthy for the rest of his life, and in a position to fulfill his aspiration for exploration and adventure.

As a Man of Letters, and a peer among the upper classes of London society, he was able to move around the corridors of power and influence. He put together a recommendation for a military plan to capture Ferrol, the important Spanish port in Galicia in the north-west of Spain, which gained him access to Sir William Pitt, the Secretary of State and soon to be Prime Minister. Pitt was impressed by Bruce, but unwilling to sponsor a new initiative against Spain. It was France that had the attention of Secretary Pitt. Disappointed, Bruce returned to

# THE BLUE NILE

Kinnaird to attend to the affairs of his estate, only to be summoned by Pitt, who was re-thinking the military possibilities of Ferrol in the context of an invasion of neighboring France. Once again these plans would be shelved, but in the process he was introduced to the great Statesman Lord Halifax, with whom he conversed at length on military and diplomatic affairs in and around North Africa and the Middle East. Bruce was fluent in Arabic, and would go on to master thirteen foreign languages. Lord Halifax offered Bruce the Consulship of Algiers, with a diplomatic mission to enable British trading ships to have free passage along the Barbary Coast of North Africa. This was the time of the Barbary Pirates, and it was no easy matter to achieve the aims of diplomacy with armed despots who had sovereign power. However, Bruce would later maintain that his assignment in Algiers on behalf of Lord Halifax and the King was to use his post as a platform from which he could undertake exploration of the art treasures in the hundreds of sites throughout the Middle East that required classification. It was in these conversations with Halifax that the discovery of the source of the Nile was identified as an objective of great national importance to the expanding British Empire.

As it turned out, his two years in Algiers were spent almost entirely on the diplomatic effort, due to the activities of the ruling Dey, the Governor of Algiers, and his penchant for plunder and duplicity. Bruce was succeeded in 1765 by a new Consul, and immediately embarked on a mission of travel and exploration in Algeria and Libya. He was shipwrecked off Benghazi, and had to swim ashore to safety. Only his mastery of Arabic saved him from a likely death. He was able to continue his travels, and in the process of observing and recording numerous sites of antiquity in the service of his country he kept his eye on the larger goal – discovery of the source of the Nile.

His arrival in Alexandria in June 1768 presaged his formal attempt to discover the source of the Nile, which he believed to be in the highlands of Ethiopia. It was another two years before he made it to the then capital of Gondar, during which he contracted malaria but managed to recover. In October 1770 he set off on the trek towards the mountainous region around Lake Tana, whose streams led off to eventually form the great river. The final march was on November 14,

### THE BOG, THE BAHAMAS, AND BEYOND

and having reached the lake, he picked up a half coconut shell, filled it from the spring, and drank a toast to King George the Third, and, among others to Catherine, Empress of Russia, who was busy fighting the Turks, thereby pleasing the Greeks. This additional salutation was to acknowledge the assistance of his Greek companion and servant, Strates, who lived in Ethiopia, and who apparently knew much about the location of the source. Bruce traveled back with his party to Gondar before heading north and west in order to pick up the river again at Sennar, known there as the Blue Nile, and then to its confluence with another river at present day Khartoum. Bruce does not dwell too much on the existence of a separate river source, today's White Nile, with the Blue Nile that he explored. This is understandable, since he must have been devastated to find that there had to be an undiscovered source of the other river. However, it turns out that on average the Blue Nile contributes about eighty percent of the volume in the true Nile, as most of the waters of the White Nile disperse in the swamps of Southern Sudan. We know this from modern science. Bruce could only ponder.

Regardless of the dispute among historians over the provenance of the matter, no one can deny the accomplishments of this charismatic and resourceful adventurer. Quite aside from the business of exploration, he was a large man with a large appetite for life, and by all accounts not averse to sexual relations with women along the way. He seems to imply having had a love affair over an extended period of time with Esther, the wife of the real ruler of Ethiopia, Ras Mikael Sehul. He made his way back to London over a period of three years, but his stories of his travels and discoveries were treated with disdain, notwithstanding the rapturous reception he received in the other capitals of Europe. He retired to his home in Kinnaird, and it would be sixteen more years before his landmark publication that salvaged his reputation.

The author Miles Bredin in his biography "The Pale Abyssinian" had this to say about my favorite Falkirk Bairn - "In his heyday he was considered charming and handsome as well as extraordinarily large. He was six feet four and immensely strong. Women everywhere adored him, from the harems of North Africa to the Salons of Paris and the court of the Abyssinian Emperor. Men too, loved him, but only a certain kind of man. In them he inspired an almost fanatical loyalty. He could ride like an Arab, shoot partridge from the saddle at gallop, and faced danger with icy calm........above all, a magnificent man." His body lies in an enclosed crypt in Larbert Old Church cemetery, on the outskirts of Falkirk, with a metal obelisk standing testament to the life of this exceptional man. He brings life to the motto of the Burgh of Falkirk: "Better meddle wi' the De'il (Devil) than the Bairns o' Falkirk."

My readings and research several years ago as I absorbed all that I could about my local hero also stimulated an interest and fascination with the country of Ethiopia. There just seems to be a lot to this beautiful country that occupies most of the Horn of Africa. A highland complex of mountains and plateaus are separated by the Great Rift Valley, and surrounded by lowlands along the periphery. The lack of natural features and definition around the edges are the likely reason that the borders have been established over the centuries more by treaty than by design, whose subsequent basis and interpretation have created regional disputes with the neighboring countries of Somalia and Eritrea. It is a place that I have long wanted to visit.

Until then, I must enjoy the reading of the tale rather than the prospect of the journey, which is how I stumbled across Emperor Menelik the Second, who ruled as Emperor from 1889 until 1913. This odd character in the history of Ethiopia emerged from the tribal hinterlands to lead his country to victory in a war against the colonial power of Italy, which established his military reputation. His subsequent rule did much to raise the profile of his country, as he was fascinated by modernity, to which he was exposed by the courtship of other European powers following his defeat of Italy. He founded the Bank of Abyssinia, established the first postal system, built railways, introduced the telephone and telegraph, and of course the first automobiles. During the early part of his reign he heard about the (modern) method of executing criminals by using the electric chair. He promptly ordered three to be delivered to his palace in Addis Ababa, in order to better regulate this fairly common outcome of his justice system. Only when they were delivered and did not work was he apprised of the need for electricity. It would be many years before

## THE BOG, THE BAHAMAS, AND BEYOND

he was finally able to bring electric power to his country, and in the meantime he used one of the chairs as a throne. In later years the Emperor Haile Selassie would emerge with a world-wide reputation as leader of his country, but the Emperor Melenik is my Ethiopian Man for all Seasons.

This may seem an odd time to move from a story of a relatively small and unimportant backwater of Africa to the relationship between the two world superpowers, the United States and the Soviet Union, but in 1991 we were all suddenly caught up in the incredible changes that were happening in Eastern Europe. The onset of a new world order that discarded the Cold War for a new period of rapprochement between America and Russia held so much promise for an end to the Nuclear Arms race, and a more open society that might operate on a "western" economic and societal paradigm. Time has shown that the Russian way is, well, Russian, and their concept of democracy is not necessarily the same as that of the West. Elsewhere, there were lots of things going on to stimulate anyone interested in current affairs, not the least of which was the occupation of Kuwait by Iraq, led by Saddam Hussein. There was an unequivocal response from the Republican government of the United States and its allies, with the launch of Operation Desert Storm. This was when the media as a proxy for the fourth estate came of age, when cameramen from Cable News Network landed on the beaches at the vanguard with the American forces, and we were all armchair spectators to a war in the comfort of our living rooms, courtesy of CNN. Inevitably, Saddam and his army were chased all the way back into Iraq, but then President Bush (the first), instead of following Saddam to Baghdad, withdrew the troops, and allowed him to remain in power. Before long he was embroiled in a long and costly war with his immediate neighbor, Iran. It was this strategic decision by President Bush to let him off the hook that created the circumstances that led to the second "Bush" war with Iraq, but that would be ten years in the future, and after the terrorist attacks of 9/11.

This also was a time in our lives as a family that we were captivated by the emergence of a truly superstar sports hero, Michael Jordan, as we watched him become the greatest basketball player of all time.

In my case, I can quite happily watch just about any sport, except maybe frog racing, although even then if it was a Saturday afternoon in between two premier league matches, then I might be persuaded. For some reason Michael Jordan became Ann's hero, and as she was caught up in the emotion and adulation, we were all sucked in, and watching Michael became very much part of our TV time entertainment over a period of several years. He was an awesome athlete, but he could also communicate so well. He has a particularly distinctive cadence to his voice that makes him really pleasant to listen to, and he is charismatic in a sport that tends to produce heroes who are long on talent but short on persona. Shona and Cassie would watch the games with us when the Chicago Bulls were in the play-offs, and Michael was in prime time frame of mind. He played one game against the New York Knicks when he had the flu and a temperature way over 100, and had to be helped to the bench each time-out, having made unbelievable shots to keep his team alive and eventually victorious.

While on a business trip overseas in April of 1992 I got word that Rick Deane had died suddenly in Florida, at the age of 65, and I was not able to make it back in time to attend the funeral. He had a huge influence on me in my career at the bank, and Ann and I were truly saddened by his death. He had already retired as Chairman of the Board of Signet Banking Corporation, which was the latest iteration of the original Bank of Virginia that he had joined in 1953, as Assistant to the President of the Bank, Mr. Tom Boushall. I met Mr. Boushall on a few occasions over the years, and it was he who had started the original Bank of Virginia back in 1923, as a bank dedicated to serve consumers. The old corner office building at 8$^{th}$ and Main Streets in Richmond was built as a head office during the depths of the Great Depression, in the nineteen thirties, and was the first office building in Virginia to have air conditioning, which at the time was described as "manufacturing its own weather".

The growth of the bank for the first fifty years or so was in good old fashioned consumer banking - taking deposits from regular people and making consumer loans and loans to small businesses. In the nineteen sixties there were winds of change blowing through the national marketplace, as banks all across the country suddenly

◄ THE BOG, THE BAHAMAS, AND BEYOND

discovered the states next door, and began to plot how to expand their business across state lines. There were plenty of legal impediments to interstate banking, but they would gradually be replaced by a more permissive and accommodating regulatory climate that was negotiated by bank lobbying firms across the country, responding to their clients hunger to expand markets. It was this push by banks to open up new markets that would eventually lead many of the more aggressive regional banks into the international arena, and the acquisition of The Bank of Nassau in 1970 was a direct result of this strategy by the Bank of Virginia.

It is the nature of banking in the United States that in any given year dozens of small banks are acquired by larger banks. This reduces the absolute number of banks in the country, only to be replaced by new start up banks hoping once again to benefit from community support for their services, but always with the ulterior motive of building up their local business portfolio then selling out to a large bank for a profit on their investment. This may be perceived as a cynical view of a time tested paradigm, but I lived in that world for a long time, and have no doubt that this is the driving force behind the continuing formation of new banks, providing what are increasingly recognized as generic services of taking deposits and making loans. Many of my former colleagues from our bank can now be found in management positions in a number of community banks in and around Central Virginia that did not exist ten years ago.

Our photo albums for the early nineties bring back some great memories. It was such a special time for Shona and Cassie, as they both developed from lovable children to young ladies, and provided so many milestones for us along the way that are typical of what so many other families experience, and yet are so personally significant. No matter how simple or routine it sounds, graduating from High School and gaining acceptance to college is a big deal within the family unit in the United States, much more so than we can remember from our own transition from school into the work-place in Scotland.

Our trips to Scotland enabled us to keep up with an evolving family situation back home, as Ann's sister Agnes had her second daughter

Lindsay, a sister to Alison. We didn't go to the Highlands that year, but I do remember a day trip to Helensburgh to visit Hill House, the former home of a Scottish businessman that was designed by the artist Charles Rennie McIntosh in 1902, and is generally considered his masterpiece, incorporating as it does external architectural with internal design features and art in his "Glasgow" style that was in the van of the Art Nouveau Movement. We stopped in London that year to stay with our friends, Keith and Claire Norman, in Bayswater. Keith and I were able to reminisce about our experiences in Cayman, when we were adversaries in the winding up of Sterling Bank and its related businesses, and somehow in the process became good friends.

In July 1994 we flew to Bermuda for what would be a lovely vacation with my sister Lorna, her then husband Ron, and her unborn child, who at that time was resting comfortably in the womb, blissfully unaware that her name would be Shelby, while her mother tried to stay cool in an apartment wanting of air conditioning. As always, there is never a bad time to be had in Bermuda. It has a lovely climate, rarely too hot or too cold, and mostly somewhere in between for most of the year. Ron was able to get us passes for the U.S. Naval Base, which just happened to have the most beautiful beach you could wish for, available only to the members of the United States Forces and their families and guests. They even supplied snorkeling equipment, and sailing boats. It was no surprise when we later saw an investigative report on U.S. television on the practice of senior US Naval commanders to use the base for regular vacations with their families. It caused such an outcry that the base was eventually closed, so I am glad that we were able to slip in under the radar, so to speak.

CHAPTER **15**

# Our World Changes

IT WAS IN the mid-nineties that Ann and I decided to go through the US naturalization process, to obtain citizenship in our adopted country. We arrived here twenty years before, not by choice but by circumstance, and as the possession of our "Green Cards" verifying our permanent residency status had worked rather well for most of our time here, we did not feel any great compunction to become US citizens. Both our girls had dual citizenship and never really thought of Ann and I as "Americans," probably because we always thought of ourselves as British. However, I became aware of certain tax disadvantages that apply to Green Card holders in a scenario where one of the parents dies, particularly if the deceased parent has title to most of the financial assets of the household. The surviving spouse who does not have US citizenship is not entitled to the marital deduction of the first $600,000 of the estate, and then when that surviving spouse later dies, the entire estate is exposed to the full range of inheritance taxes and death duties. By now I had built up a net worth that in large part was vested in shares and stock options of my long time employer, Signet Bank, and also a related company, Capital One, which had spun off from Signet Bank, and had significantly increased its share price since it became independent. A career in banking is not exactly a high risk situation, unless you happen to be a teller in a tough part of town, so I had no reason to fear for my imminent demise because of a dangerous work environment. However, I did fly all the time, often to rather strange and unusual airports, and also on occasion in small private planes, where the risk is statistically higher. So, not to have changed our status would have been rather a selfish decision, as our girls could easily have lost half of their inheritance, had the worst happened, especially when Ann and I sometimes travelled together. Anyway, we filled in the forms and went about the paper process for naturalization, which took a few months.

I also wrote to the British Embassy in Washington to advise them of our situation, and asked for confirmation that our British Citizenship would not be affected in any way. I had a nice letter back to say that the only way that we could lose our UK citizenship was if we voluntarily renounced it, and under no circumstance would the United Kingdom renounce us! Thus comforted, we finally travelled to the US Immigration office in Norfolk, Virginia, took a simple general knowledge test about the United States of America (sample – "who was the first President of the United States?") and were soon on the schedule to take the oath of allegiance. This took place in the Federal Courts Building in Richmond, in September 1995, where we and about two hundred other foreign born applicants made all sorts of promises to the Government, in exchange for a gold embossed certificate, and the right to get a new passport. We acquired US citizenship just for tax reasons, rather than personal choice, but it was the right thing to do for our girls, and we have no regrets.

We kicked off the year 1995 with a Burns Supper celebration, which we held in our house, and invited our friends and neighbors who were part of our occasional "Dinner Club" group. There were six couples, and I put together a program that required participation by everyone in reciting some of the mellifluous work of Scotland's national poet. The accents were not quite a match for the beauty and grace of Burn's narrative, but Tony Lovette did enough to earn the prize. He subsequently purchased a kilt in the Fraser tartan, which his name entitles him to wear, Lovette being derived from the Lovats of the Fraser Clan in north-east Scotland. His wife Debbie's rendition was not up to Tony's standard, even after practicing with our daughter Cassie, whose Glasgow accent is impeccable.

In the summer of 1995 our bank acquired a family of mutual funds from a company in New York, and for a while I was involved in the

◄ THE BOG, THE BAHAMAS, AND BEYOND

acquisition process. During the course of the negotiations I developed a rapport with the company president, Michael Freedman, and it is a friendship that has endured, although Mike's tenure as a bank employee only lasted a few months. No sooner had we completed the acquisition than the responsibility for managing the acquisition was moved to our Retail Banking Group, who were experimenting with the whole concept of direct marketing of bank products, and wanted to integrate the mutual funds into their "national" distribution chain. Mike resigned in exasperation at being told how to sell mutual funds by a group of financial analysts not long out of college. This entire strategy that our bank had embraced was no more than loosely targeted marketing, and its credibility as a core competence (some would say, incompetence) was finally debunked when our bank was acquired by a much larger institution, and the management and their regiment of analysts were quickly disbanded.

It was in London in the mid sixties that I first became exposed to the investment world, with my assignment to the Securities Department of the Royal Bank of Scotland in New Bond Street London. It was this specialty skill set that enabled me to transfer to the Chief Office in Glasgow, and ultimately to qualify for a job in the Bahamas. When I eventually moved from the entry level management position in the Bank of Virginia to an executive role, it was to be the President of the Trust and Investment Company of Bank of Virginia. In this position, I became once more involved on a daily basis with the world of the Stock Exchange, and the management of investment portfolios for the three thousand or so Trust accounts of our customers.

I always thought of the investment world in banking as a sort of parallel universe. It didn't really have anything to do with banking *per se*, but was a natural extension of the bank's role as a financial intermediary on behalf of our customers. Once you got past the basic banking services of checking accounts, savings and deposit accounts, and various types of loan products, the next logical place to focus our financial expertise was on that part of the customer's wallet that dealt with all that was left over from their bank accounts, and that was their pension and investment accounts. Our role as Trustee is to be the fiduciary of record for our clients, and to make all the investment and related decisions regarding the trust assets, such as stocks, bonds, money market funds, and real estate. We had responsibility for the appropriate investment of the client's assets that met the fiduciary test of suitability and safety for the client. Although I was Chairman of the Investment Committee, which oversaw the management of all Trust and Investment Accounts, we had professional investment management specialists on staff who actually came up with the decisions on what to buy and sell for the client accounts.

Perhaps because of my periodic brushes with the investment world throughout my career, I have always had a deep personal interest in the stock markets. Not from the perspective of a trader, but more from the compulsion to know what was going on in financial markets, as it is so intimately tied to the general business and banking world that I grew up in. Even in my early studies for the Institute of Bankers exams, I found the investment courses more enjoyable, or perhaps tolerable, than the others, such as Accounting, Law, and Economics. Whenever I had an occasion to talk to groups of people about investments, which has happened many times over my career, I often make the point that successful investing happens when information and psychology come together. It is not enough to know something about a particular company, or stock, or product that may have an effect on the price of a given stock. It is also vital that the information is used to implement a strategy for buying or selling that takes into account the larger context of variables that are at work in the ups and downs of the stock market. I would often use a story about the Battle of Waterloo in 1815 to illustrate the point.

The Rothschild family is one of the fabled financial dynasties of the last two hundred and fifty years. From their beginnings as Jewish merchants in Frankfurt, Germany, they spread throughout Europe by putting together a network of trading companies, all connected to Frankfurt, and focused on growing the wealth and influence of the Rothschild's in the markets of their neighboring countries. The five sons of Mayer Rothschild were his emissaries, and everything they did was in pursuit of the family fortune, rather than their individual reward. Nathan Rothschild, based in London, was to have a dramatic effect on the already established stock and bond markets

## THE BOG, THE BAHAMAS, AND BEYOND

by his actions around the time of the Battle of Waterloo, which saw France and the United Kingdom face off in a battle for the supremacy of Europe.

The Rothschild's had built up a network of couriers that enabled them to communicate with each other on the various business and financial events that took place throughout Europe, in many cases ahead of the natural news dissemination process. Remember, this was when having good communications technology was by owning the fastest horse. All of London was waiting with bated breath for news of the battle. In the Stock Exchange the eyes were turned on Nathan Rothschild, with most traders waiting to see if he bought or sold British Government Bonds, and assuming that if he started to sell then the news from Waterloo must be bad. One day Nathan Rothschild took up his position at the already famous "Rothschild Pillar" and with discreet nods to his agents, had them sell British Government Bonds. The word spread that Rothschild was selling, and the market assumed that Waterloo had been lost, with terrible repercussions for the British Government, now thought to become the poor man of Europe. The result was a dumping of Government Bonds, which brought the price lower and lower as sellers vastly outnumbered buyers. At a certain point in the day Nathan gave another discreet signal to his agents, who immediately began buying British Government Bonds at the bargain basement prices. It is thought that Nathan Rothschild made a profit of twenty times his investment in this caper.

The point I always make is that the information is important, but it is the way you use it that can sometimes make the difference in the outcome of the investment. This scenario for the dramatic financial coup by Nathan Rothschild has been generally acknowledged as accurate by financial historians over the years, although a recent history of the House of Rothschild by the established Oxford Don, Niall Ferguson, takes issue with the legend, and believes that the gains from Nathan Rothschild's Waterloo investment strategy were much more modest. He may be right, but I still prefer the original, even if it is a myth.

The story of the Rothschild's is from a financial world much less sophisticated than the one in which we live in today. If you had to analyze the story in business terms that are taught in every college course on Finance today, you would still see similarities, and be able to identify strategic and tactical moves like those that enabled the success of the Rothschild's. The banking business today, in all its manifestations, still generates winners and losers, all seemingly engaged in the single discipline of the business of money, yet with differing degrees of success and failure. I was fortunate enough to experience firsthand what turned out to be a revolution in the credit card business in the United States, and my bank, in its former iteration as the Bank of Virginia, was in the thick of it.

The credit card business in the United States is a major part of the money business, and in its simplest terms is a business that facilitates payment for goods and services between buyers and sellers, and provides a financing option to the holder of the card. It is that simple. One of the most significant events in the development of the industry took place in a rather unforgettable hotel in Richmond, Virginia, when representatives of a group of banks agreed to collaborate in the founding of Master Charge (now Master Card) as a way to streamline and facilitate the growth of the credit card as a payment mechanism for individuals, and a collection mechanism for shopkeepers and vendors. As the credit card became ubiquitous with the growing consumer society in America, Master Card was one of a handful of huge national and international players who dominated the industry. Within our bank, the Credit Card Division grew in leaps and bounds, and was a valuable contributor to company profits. Granted, there were times in the business cycle when charged off loan balances cut deeply into profits, only to be supplanted with even higher levels of profitability on each successive upswing in the business cycle. This was a roller coaster that eventually required the organization to consider the value of either retaining our position in the industry, or exiting a business that had such volatile characteristics.

While our bank was pondering this strategic dilemma we happened upon a couple of guys who were consulting to financial businesses, and who were conveniently based in Northern Virginia, only a couple of hours drive away from Richmond. Richard Fairbanks

## THE BOG, THE BAHAMAS, AND BEYOND

and his partner Nigel Morris spent several weeks immersed in the credit card operations of our bank, and their mission was to recommend whether or not we should continue to stay in or perhaps sell our business to some other financial firm that might be more comfortable with the temperamental profits and losses that seemed to come with the territory. During their analysis of the business, they became fixated on the nature of the customer base, and how it might respond to various types of differentiated marketing solicitations. Because of the availability of individual credit reports on potential customers they found that they were able to create different loan terms to different customers that took into account the respective credit worthiness of each customer, and how likely they were to default in their payments over time. In the conventional credit card industry, every customer received the same credit card terms as everyone else. What Richard and Nigel realized was that those customers with a higher risk profile, and therefore a higher likelihood of default, should pay a higher rate of interest on their borrowings. Conversely, customers with a better risk profile can justify receiving a lower rate on their account, and would gravitate to the credit card provider who offered them more attractive terms. They also found that by structuring specific offers to a given group of cardholders they could analyze the performance of the portfolio over time, and develop fairly good insights as to how various card portfolios would perform as regards future delinquencies and charged off balances. In summary, they believed that the credit card business had many of the characteristics of the insurance business, where all pricing and product terms were based on the unique individual, rather than the conventional approach of one size fits all.

Within a few months Richard and Nigel had joined the bank, and were installed in the credit card group with the mandate to re-engineer our entire business practices, and build and grow the portfolio using "Information Based Marketing Strategies." The head of the Credit Card Division at the time, David Hunt, was responsible for hiring these two guys and it must go down as one of the best hiring decisions in US corporate history. What they did was truly remarkable, and within a few years our Bank Card Division had become the largest and most consistent provider of company profits, and had industry wide recognition as a change agent in a highly competitive industry.

The Bank Card Division had become such an important part of the earnings of Signet Banking Corporation that we began to look for ways to leverage its incredible success. As banks in general have a higher investment rating than stand alone credit card companies, and therefore a lower multiple of stock price to earnings, there was the recognition that as long as our credit card business was part of a regional banking organization, then the stock price of the bank would not recognize the implicit value of that business. The outcome of these deliberations, instigated by Richard and Nigel and agreed to somewhat reluctantly by our management, was the decision to spin off the credit card business into a separate company, and shareholders of Signet Banking Corporation were given shares of the new organization, which they now owned in addition to their original holding of bank shares.

In February 1995 the new company, Capital One Financial Corporation, began trading as a separate company on the New York Stock Exchange, and one share of COF opened for trading at $19 per share. Richard was now Chairman of the Board of a major stand alone financial organization, and Nigel was President. They both became mega-wealthy overnight, but there's no question that they deserved it. Nigel is a fellow British citizen, from Wales, and retired from the company a few years ago to live the good life with his young family, while Richard continues to lead Capital One in the transformation of the company into a leading financial services organization. It has since re-organized as a banking business, and today is the sixth largest US bank (by deposits.)

We had an enjoyable vacation with our friends the Adolf's when we went to Freeport in the Bahamas for Spring break. Cassie and her pal Robin had talked the parents into the trip to recognize their scholastic achievements (?) so we joined the weekly Richmond junket from the Richmond Airport, and had a great time. We have a photo of Cassie and Robin with O.J. Simpson, who was under contract to the Casino as a hospitality host. This was several months after he became the "news story of the decade" in 1995 when he was charged and subsequently acquitted of the murder of his wife. The iconic argument from the Defense Counsel that "if the glove don't fit, you must acquit" is now part of celebrity trial folk-lore in America. It is hard to imagine a similar scene in a major criminal trial in the High Courts of the United Kingdom, with a be-wigged Barrister adorned with a lesser wig appealing to the higher authority, a Judge whose wig is always a more complete appendage than the mere petitioner, thereby conferring status. It is odd situations like that which always prompt my cultural tendency to compare the country of my life with the country of my birth, and I keep a mental record of wins/losses, ready to pull them out in any situation where the conversation turns to the pluses and minuses, or sometimes just the differences, between the respective societies.

It was my first time in Freeport since the mid seventies, when I went down there to close a loan we made to another (American) professional footballer – "Gerry" who played for the Washington Redskins. When I got back to Richmond I followed up with a letter to him, and also reminded him of his promise to let us have season tickets. Sure enough, they arrived in the mail, and I saw some fantastic games over the course of the season, accompanied by different members of staff of the bank, who rotated the rights to the other tickets. Within a few months Gerry had converted the apartment building that we financed into a time sharing facility (this was a relatively new concept in the mid seventies), and from being a fully rented building with consistent monthly cash flow, it turned into a barely used vacation spot that had little in common with the photographs in the brochure that was provided to potential time sharers. After several months of an absentee landlord and a declining population of visitors, the property soon became a trashy rundown apartment building, and we ended up foreclosing on the property. During the time that Gerry was opposing our collection efforts he hired yet another lawyer, but this time from the shady side of the street. Suddenly the bank received a letter from his lawyer accusing the bank of making the loan just to get the season tickets, and that by inducing his client to acquire the building with our loan funds and giving us valuable season tickets we were in violation of US Banking

# OUR WORLD CHANGES

Laws, and subject to all sorts of penalties, including imprisonment of any individuals found guilty of this practice. Naturally I was a bit concerned, but fortunately our lawyers came from the sunny side of the street, and were more than a match for my accuser. Since we had made the loan through our Bahamian bank, which is not a US bank (even though it was owned by one) then the US laws did not apply, and his assertions were without substance. However, I have to admit that it was purely by luck that we made the loan through our offshore bank, and it was a rough few months of living with this over my head while the attorneys fought it out. Within the bank, it was not a problem. The Chairman was solidly in my camp, and my colleagues had a laugh at my circumstances.

There were a few more players who added skill and personality to the squad by the mid-nineties: Jimmy "Left Foot" Gill - say no more! Paul "Mash" Marsh - the only Pink Panther to have broken two legs on the same day (not his). Mark Bell - defender of the faith. Graham Peers - safe hands. Mark Hignett - when he did score, it usually mattered. Richard Curry - brought the luck of the (Northern) Irish. Niels Hagglund - left back when the team traveled. We all got by with a little help from our friends.

In the summer of 1996 we had the thrill of seeing our first child graduate from High School, which is such a rite of passage in America, and not such a big deal in Scotland. Shona was always somewhere on the Honor Roll, and in a class of about 500 kids she graduated twenty first, which helped gain her entrance to the University of Virginia, one of the best rated universities in the country, and a mere one hour and five minutes easy driving from our home. When the day came for Shona to pack her belongings into the trunk of our car and leave home, it was such a wonderful yet sad event in all our lives. Shona and Cassie had always been best friends, and our four person nuclear family suffered an emotional assault that was challenging to us all. This inevitable fork in the road that took Shona to another place was a painful experience for us, and yet so right that it became manageable as time went by. The empty chair at the dinner table was a poignant reminder of how much we missed her.

Meanwhile, life at Signet Bank was a challenge, and as things played out over the course of the next couple of years, I was not up to it. We re-organized, and then re-organized the re-organization, in a continuing quest to transform our bank into a regional star that would enable us to ride the wave of national banking into a regional and then national player, with the concomitant benefits of a higher stock price and recognition as a leader rather than a follower. This was not to be. We were eventually acquired by First Union, a North Carolina Bank, in 1997, but not before a consulting project that lasted several months, and ended up with a host of employees at all levels of the organization let go. The way this was engineered was actually quite clever, and you have to credit the consulting firm with the way they manipulated the process (and Executive Management) to accomplish the primary goal of significantly downsizing the company, and justifying their fee. As an Executive Vice President, with around 300 or so employees under my management, my responsibility was to analyze the entire scope of how we inter-related with every other part of the organization, then find ways to eliminate processes that were unproductive, enabling a reduction in the headcount of employees throughout the entire system. Having identified across the board cuts in people, then the next obvious step is to refine the management structure to eliminate expense in the entire command and control function, to use military terminology. I set out as one of my recommendations a new organizational structure that eliminated my own position, as did many of my peers. Now, this was one of several scenarios that the project allowed for, but the beauty of the exercise was that top management could pick the combination of plans that accomplished the downsizing goal, and present it as a bottoms-up reorganization plan. In the process there were cuts at all levels of management, and I like to think that I was a statistical casualty of the process, and that there was nothing personal about it that might impugn my own sense of self worth. The fact is that in my case my then boss was nothing like me, not in any way shape or form, and here was the perfect opportunity to remove an obstacle to his success. It is not by accident that his own background was consulting, and for him banking was just a combination of business processes that could be analyzed, categorized, simplified, and dispensed. A far cry from what I learned in my apprenticeship with the Royal Bank.

However, the reality of it all is that I came into work one day in the Spring of 1997 and met with my boss to be told that my position was being eliminated, and that I would be leaving the bank in a few months. It was actually a bit of a relief, because the company had changed so much in the previous few years that it was no longer the organization that it was. For me the only downside was to accept the fact that I had failed, after a lifetime of advancing through every organization that I had worked for and always being identified as a productive and loyal employee. I was also cognizant of the fact that in many cases over the previous years it was me who was doing the firing, of employees who were often friends and inherently good people. All of this was processed many times over as I made the journey home to arrive unexpectedly and tell Ann the news. Of course, she was absolutely supportive, and concerned for me, not so much about what it would mean. I remember driving home that day, and I couldn't wait to get there, and tell Ann. I suppose I just wanted to feel the comfort of her telling me that everything would be alright. She did, and it was.

There was so much going on at the bank, and so many people impacted, that it all seemed fairly routine. It was particularly difficult for my Secretary, Pauline Tracey, who was a Lancashire lass and had worked for me for many years. One of the nice things Pauline did was to give me as a going away gift an office ornament which happened to be a sculpture of a gray wolf. I told her that if ever I had my own company in the future I would name it Gray Wolf, and sure enough within a few months of leaving the bank I set up a consulting company, Gray Wolf Associates, and still do business under that name. Most people that I meet with professionally like the name, and mistakenly assume it has to do with the color of my hair.

In the time honored process of disengagement from the bank, I was provided with the services of a professional counselor, and I was set up to visit with him once a week to ostensibly help me through the process of separating from my employer. While I enjoyed the first few visits, and the first time experience of having someone try and get inside my head with a view to adjusting the tension wires and improving the balance, I soon realized that this was not really necessary, so I stopped the assignment. I had no real issues to deal with, and in fact was impatient to begin the next phase of my life, whatever that might be. In large part this was due to the reality that in my career at the bank I had accumulated company shares and stock options at fairly modest prices, and various types of bonus and incentive payments that had been prudently invested, so from a financial perspective I knew that I would not have to go back into the job market. Whatever was out there for me was still to be defined, but it would never again be an employer. In the few months that all of this was going on, there was also much happening behind the scenes at the bank. When the top management of the bank directed the huge downsizing effort involved in the consulting project, there also came the recognition that the road ahead as an independent financial institution was a rocky one, and a test that not even the Chairman and President were up to. There was a lot of consolidation going on in the banking industry at that time, and banks all across the country were having to take a position on being a survivor, by aggressively acquiring other banks, or acknowledging a reality that perhaps the easy way out in selling to another bank was the best bet. The hard way ahead would have been to put stakes in the ground around a corporate mission of survival, and then manage the organization for growth and profitability at high levels of achievement. The easy way ahead was the road taken, which was to quietly solicit interest in an acquisition from a few likely suitors, and cut a deal at an attractive share price that would ensure support by the Board and the Shareholders. This was the "elegant solution," as memorialized in the words of the bank's financial advisor, the investment banking firm of J.P. Morgan. The acquiring bank would acquire an organization that had already gone through the hard part of a painful restructuring and downsizing process, and when the additional combinations of systems and management with the new parent company were applied, there would be profits aplenty to justify the attractive price that First Union paid to buy Signet Bank.

One of the nice things about the sale of the bank was the generous financial terms, and soon after the deal was announced I met with an accounting expert from the bank's auditing firm Ernst and Young, in order to review all of my stock option positions and map out a plan for exercising them in order to "cash out" of my investments. I had no ambition to stay invested with First Union, and was happy to exercise all my options for cash, which would provide me the capital to put into whatever business ventures that I might get into in my future. I also sold all of my accumulated shares in the company, and by the time it was all done I remember having taxable income over several hundred thousand dollars. I have always taken the position that paying taxes is not a problem, because you only pay them if you have enjoyed either income or capital gains. I have paid a lot of taxes in my life here in the United States, but that one year was a big check to Uncle Sam.

All of a sudden the organization had to regroup around a divestiture process that would take several months, due to the complex regulatory issues that had to be dealt with before the deal could actually be done. Instead of leaving the bank in the summer months, I was asked to stay on until the deal was "closed" so that I could help with a project that involved selling a number of bank branches. Selling branches was not just a real estate transaction, it meant that we would sell the entire book of deposits held by the bank, so the acquiring organization was essentially buying customers as well as the physical premises. This suited me fine, as I continued to be paid as before, and it gave me plenty of time to plan for what might happen when I drove out of the building for the last time. This would take place in December 1997, on the day that we were legally acquired by First Union. Accompanying me on the way out of the building on my last day were the Chairman, and the President, along with just about every other executive level manager in the company. We were all fired at once.

CHAPTER **16**

# Real Estate and Stuff

BY THE TIME I "retired" from the bank I had already developed a long and friendly relationship with a local businessman, Morton Zedd. Mort was a few years older than me, and had heard about my familiarity with the Cayman Islands, where he had visited with his wife Leslie and their three children. Mort was a real estate developer and over many years had acquired a number of apartment properties, which he had upgraded and held as long term investments. When I first met him he had just turned forty, and was independently wealthy, thanks to the accumulation of valuable real estate properties that he had developed since setting up as an independent investor straight out of college. Mort had young children by the time I met him, and he told me how he would put on a shirt, tie, and suit each morning to have breakfast with his kids, so that they assumed he had a normal job like all the parents of their friends.

The reality is that he was a one man real estate development enterprise. He had a law degree, so he did his own legal work. He had a Broker's Licence so that he could share in the commissions that he had to pay to people who represented him on property acquisitions. This enabled him to a refund of 50% of the commissions on every property that he bought or sold. He had an insurance licence so that he could get return commission on any business that he directed to Insurance Agencies on his properties. He also hired managers to live on all his properties, and did not tell them that he was the owner, just that he was employed by the owner. This made it easier for him to say no to whatever things the property managers brought up with him, without there being any personal blame on him. He really had it all figured out, and that is why he was financially secure at forty years of age. He was a great mentor to me in my early days of financial freedom after my retirement from the bank, and in many respects was my inspiration to get into property development. I could never quite do it the way he did it, but it was such an advantage to have someone like that in my corner when I first got into real estate as a source of income to support our household while the girls completed their high school and college experiences.

However, while property development would become an interesting and profitable business for me over the course of many years, my first inclination on leaving the bank was to set up as a financial consultant, in the hope that I would be able to turn my knowledge about money and finance into something that I could sell. I incorporated my consulting company as Gray Wolf Associates, the associate being my wife Ann. She used to say that she had fifty percent of nothing, but I have managed to generate a fairly erratic but nonetheless profitable level of consulting engagements since I incorporated, and will continue to do so based upon how I feel when I get up in the morning.

My first deal was to set up a Letter of Credit transaction through a Japanese bank and a New York bank to finance the shipment of a brick office building from Richmond to Japan. A soccer playing pal, Gerry Canavan, had asked me to help figure out how to structure the financing of a project that he had lined up as his first deal going solo as a general contractor in commercial construction. One of his former clients was married to a lady from Japan. She had a group of Japanese doctor friends who loved to visit Virginia, and had been impressed by the architecture in Colonial Williamsburg. When they decided to build a medical office building outside Tokyo, they thought they would try and figure out a way to have it designed and built in the colonial architectural style, and asked their friend in Richmond if it was possible. Gerry figured out a way to have it designed in conformity with the relevant building code, and then arranged for all the materials to be shipped by container to Japan. He then dispatched one of his project managers to Japan for six weeks to manage the group

◂ THE BOG, THE BAHAMAS, AND BEYOND

of Japanese construction workers while they built it. My job was to line up the financing with a local bank, and I used two large international banks, one in New York and the other in Tokyo, as financial conduits so that title to the goods was passed on payment of the purchase price, and then the funds were transferred through the banking system to Gerry's account in Richmond. With International Letters of Credit the most important aspect is control of the title documents to the shipment. The actual merchandise is easy to deal with. It gets placed in a container, the container moves through freight forwarding channels across the oceans and to the destination port, and then is unloaded, cleared through Customs, and delivered to the site of the buyer. The title documents make their way from the packing and shipping origin to the work-site destination, through the banking system, and at the control point when the documents pass from the bank of the shipper to the bank of the buyer, the sale proceeds must be either wired to the buyer's bank, or guaranteed to be provided at some future date if there is any form of buyer financing involved. The deal worked well for everyone. Gerry was able to put the profits directly into his new construction business in Richmond, and the Japanese doctors had a distinctive office building like no other in Japan.

My next deal was to help another soccer pal, Jim Brady, get bank financing to enable him to start up a software development company that would develop internet based systems to help doctors deal with the administrative aspects of their medical practice. It was a small deal, and easy enough to put together. I was impressed enough by what Jim was doing that I invested in his company, and he would ultimately sell the business for about fifty million dollars to an English Health-care organization several years later. Not that it was all downhill to the finish line. One of the realities about becoming involved in the operations of a start up enterprise, especially when the principal is a friend, is the tendency to become not just an advisor but a sponsor, especially in the early days when money is short. In a banking career as long as I had you get used to saying no to people who want to borrow money, so I never had a problem in saying no. However, now and again you see inside a business and can feel the potential, and in Jim's case it was clear to me from early on that he had something that was going to be really good, and had a business plan that would prove to be viable. Because of my own financial situation after my retirement from the bank, I had ample investment funds, and was in a position to step in and provide some temporary relief when there was not enough money in the company's bank account to meet the weekly payroll. I was happy to do this for Jim, and it enabled him to get through at least one rough patch on the way to financial stability. My rather modest investment of a few thousand dollars was multiplied several times over when the company was sold, and paid for our daughter Shona's not inexpensive wedding, for which we are eternally grateful to my pal Jim Brady.

A couple of months or so after my last official day of employment I was contacted by the Personnel Department of the new bank about a pension account in my name, which had a balance of about two hundred and fifty thousand dollars, being part of a package of benefits, including stock options, that accrued to me with my retirement and departure from the bank. I completed the appropriate paperwork and made arrangements for the funds to be transferred to a new investment firm, so that the money would continue to be invested on my behalf. Two years later I was once again contacted by the bank asking for my instructions to close out the pension account. I told the person that I had closed the account shortly after I retired, and so no further action was needed. The personnel officer told me that the account was still open, with a balance even larger than the original due to ongoing accruals of interest. After our call, I didn't think too much about it until I had another call from a different personnel officer again asking for my transfer instructions. This happened one or two more times, and eventually I asked that a senior officer of the bank give me a call. The call ended the same way, with me protesting and the banker supplicating, so there was no real resolution. By now I am beginning to think I should go ahead and accept the account balance, so I called my lawyer, gave him the scenario, and asked him what I should do. His advice was to keep the money, put it into a separately identified account, invest the proceeds in US Treasury Bonds, and see what happens. If a few years go by past the statute of limitations, then I would be quite entitled to keep the funds or spend them as I see fit, as they would represent my money and not anyone else's.

## THE BOG, THE BAHAMAS, AND BEYOND

It so happened that a family dinner the next weekend included Shona's boyfriend Chris, and Cassie's boyfriend Kurt. Both boys were at College, and their relationships with the girls were on track for engagement and marriage, which eventually transpired. I was interested in what my girls and their guys thought I should do. Across the board there was no hesitation. "Keep the money, just like the lawyer says".

I called the bank again, and told them to keep the money, as it was their money and not mine. It just wasn't my money to keep.

There was one consulting deal that came out of nowhere, and resulted in my having a long association with a start up Pharmacy Benefit business that continues to this day. I had a call out of the blue from a guy named Bob Oscar, who had been referred to me by his bank manager, Ron Davis, a former colleague at the bank. Bob had an idea to create software that would help health care providers who paid the bill for their employees' prescription medications that were covered under their Health Plan. The unusual structure of the business model governing these drug benefit plans was a function of the lack of control by the buyer of the product, and the absence of price competition at the point of sale. Here's how it works. The employer contracts with a pharmacy benefit management company (PBM) to design a health care plan for its employees. The plan provides the menu of drugs that can be prescribed for the various medical conditions covered by the plan, and typically would have the different drugs manufactured by different drug companies for every possible medical condition. This menu is known as a Formulary. The plan specifies how much each drug will cost, and how the price is split between the Health Plan and the employee, with the employee typically paying a standard co-payment of around $10 to around $25, and the Health Plan paying the difference. Because each drug manufactured by the different drug manufacturers is priced differently, the choice of which drug to use determines the cost of the medications that is paid for primarily by the Health Plan. However, the PBM, which charges a fee to the Health Plan for creating the Formulary, receives additional compensation from the drug manufacturers for including their particular drugs in the plan, which is nothing else but a form of bribery to induce the sale of their products.

So, let's say a female employee covered by the Health Plan goes to the doctor, and is diagnosed with high blood pressure. The doctor prescribes a particular brand of medication, so the patient goes to the pharmacy to buy a month's worth of the pills, and essentially becomes a customer for life, buying the pills every month, paying the co-payment, and not really caring that some other entity, the Health Plan, is paying the balance of the cost of the drugs. Here is a situation where the person who places the order to buy a given product, the doctor, has no idea what it costs, and so is indifferent to whatever price is paid. The person who picks up the order, the patient, likewise has no idea what the drug costs in total, only what she pays for the co-payment. The Formulary separates the amount charged to the patient from the much higher amount charged to the Health Plan, but neither party see it, and no one involved in the purchase and sale of the product really knows that there are alternatives in the Formulary that could be less expensive. The Health Plan essentially has a series of inter-related people making decisions about what the Plan will actually spend to provide medicine to its employees who are sick. No wonder the cost of prescription medication doubles every ten years, and the profits of the drug manufacturers rise in tandem.

Bob Oscar is a pharmacist by education and profession, who somewhere along the way became the geek who liked to work on the administrative side of the business, in between dispensing drugs over the counter. He eventually set up his own one man consulting business, and created a computerized system for tracking all the drugs in a Health Plan, listing the cost of the co-pay and the cost of the balance of the price paid by the Health Plan for every drug in the Plan, which normally is comprised of several hundred drugs from multiple manufacturers. This is computerized and updated daily with every transaction for every drug purchased by the Health Plan members and is made available on a web site that can be accessed by each employee. For the first time a member can see what the choices of drugs are on her plan for a given condition, what the relative costs are, and can print off a copy of the Formulary to show to the Doctor. Now the patient can ask if the monthly prescription can be one of the less expensive drugs on the menu, and assuming that the doctor

◀ THE BOG, THE BAHAMAS, AND BEYOND

has no medical issues with that particular drug, then there would be no reason not to prescribe it every month from that point on. In this scenario, a lifetime commitment to buy a product every month can incorporate the normal elements of price and quality in a competitive environment that are basic to almost every other purchase decision made by that consumer. Magic!

I helped Bob almost from the start of his new company, RxEOB. Bob was able to raise almost two million dollars to get the company off the ground, and for the next several years I provided financial consulting services to the company. One of my neighborhood pals, Gene McKeown, had recently been part of a technology company that had been acquired, and Gene was now in a position to invest in other businesses. I introduced him to Bob and Gene soon became an investor along with me, and has been involved in the many stages of development of the company over the years. Each time there was a cash crisis we would create another way to borrow the money that would keep the business going while new customers could be found to grow revenues. As I did with Jim, I invested in Bob's company, and although the company has not been sold or acquired by someone else, it is a viable business that is now very profitable. Whether the future is a sale to a larger company, or continued growth as a stand-alone business, it is a success story and a tribute to the entrepreneurial spirit of a pharmacist who created a paradigm shift in the way employees could become part of the purchasing decision on their own prescription medication needs.

Ann finally received the phone call from Agnes that she had been dreading for some time. Her Mum - Gran Louden to her grandchildren, had passed away in her sleep at her home in Glasgow. It is the odd stories and recollections of all four of her grandchildren and expressed from time to time in normal family conversations that serve to keep these memories alive, and a source of happiness in the family. This is really what defines a life well lived.

I became a Landlord once I started down the path of acquiring apartment buildings and rental units to satisfy some kind of entrepreneurial instinct that led me towards the acquisition of real estate. The very first transaction I did was essentially a "dry run" whereby I decided to buy a two bedroom townhouse in a condominium project about a mile from our home, in a well established area of the suburbs, close to the leading private school in Richmond. I thought that this would be a way to take a modest amount of risk and see what it would be like to go through the entire process, from negotiating the purchase, arranging financing, preparing the unit for occupancy, and finding a credit worthy tenant. The whole thing went rather well, and I was able to find my tenant, a middle-aged lady who had moved back to Richmond from California. She could have afforded to buy a place of her own but she just did not want the responsibility, after a messy and financially difficult divorce. She was quite happy to pay rent, and as apartments here are typically leased on an unfurnished basis, she moved her furniture from the West coast to the East, and settled in quite easily. In the eight years or so that I owned the apartment I never had a bit of trouble. When I finally decided to sell the apartment, I found a buyer on my own, negotiated a sale arrangement that gave her plenty of time to move into a new location, and sold the unit for twice what I paid for it. During the years of ownership I had a modest cash return from the rental activity, tax write-offs against earned income, and an eventual capital gain on sale. In real estate investing, this is the "trifecta", and perhaps the gambling analogy is a good one, as it is generally not without risk.

All in all, my first year as an entrepreneur, making my living from selling my knowledge of financial matters, and dipping my toe in the property market, was all I could ask for, although it took a while for Ann to get used to me being around the house. Apparently this is a common occurrence when a spouse "retires," but after a while it began to seem natural. I set up my office in a spare bedroom upstairs, but within a few months we called our original builder and asked him to design and build an addition to our home that would include a new office on the ground floor for the budding enterprises of Gray Wolf Associates. Not all attempts to find consulting clients were successful. The first opportunity that I worked on was fun, but cost me a few thousand dollars of time and money in pursuing a project that in the end did not materialize. My lawyer Tom Eubank called me one day and said that a client of his was interested in talking to me about the

## THE BOG, THE BAHAMAS, AND BEYOND

Cayman Islands. This guy and his partner ran an investment fund from an office west of the city, and supposedly was mega wealthy thanks to an impressive record of investment successes on behalf of his clients, which were all run through their office in the Cayman Islands. They had acquired profits in their offshore subsidiary, and apparently those profits would be taxed in the United States unless they re-invested them offshore. They were interested in acquiring property in Cayman using their accumulated funds, but did not know how to go about it. I quickly put a consulting proposal together, and Ann and I had fun running off all the photocopies on our new home office copier, and putting the proposal binder together.

My strategy was to go to Grand Cayman, and check out potential commercial office projects. I flew down to Cayman and met with an architect, a construction contractor, and a real estate agent, all friends from our time on the island. I came back with a lot of information, which I sorted out and organized into a recommendation for action, which naturally included my fee for services. In the nature of things, things changed, and within a few weeks of tendering the proposal and following up with my potential client, I came to the realization that the deal was not going to happen. It turned out that their investment funds were in trouble, due to their exposure to Russian Bond investments at a time when Russia had a severe financial crisis and defaulted on its debt. My potential client quickly went into self preservation mode, and the last thing they wanted at that time was to take on a new project offshore when their bread and butter business here was going downhill fast. So, my first deal cost me a few thousand dollars of expenses, for no return, but I did get to see my pals in the Cayman Islands, and it was a nice dry run for Ann and me to work together on a project again after so many years since our time together in the Cayman office.

My friend and mentor Morton Zedd died suddenly in the Spring of 2000, after a short battle with pancreatic cancer. It was a shock to find out he was sick with cancer, and then to learn in a few short weeks that he had passed away. He was an incredibly successful businessman, who had built his fortune as a one man real estate developer, without any partners, and without the benefit of any institutional support

## REAL ESTATE AND STUFF

system. He was a wonderful person, and I have often asked myself what Mort would have done, whenever I had issues to deal with on the apartments or office buildings. Ann and I were in the car travelling to his funeral in Williamsburg, where he had only recently settled with his wife Leslie to enjoy their retirement years. Williamsburg was the capital of Virginia in colonial times, and although since then it has played second fiddle to Richmond, it is now a major tourist center, and also an upscale retirement community. While I was driving the car to Williamsburg, Ann was reading the latest edition of the Scots Magazine, which is required reading for those of us with Scots blood in our veins who reside overseas. She came across a posting in the Classified section, and read out to me the invitation, asking for a couple to spend two weeks in the Summer Isles, managing a small tea-room and a connected post office, while the owners of the island were on holiday. There was no remuneration, just free lodging in a croft (cottage) and a few hours a day handling the tea-room/post office. All we knew of the Summer Isles (after consulting a map) was that they were somewhere off the coast of Wester Ross in the northwest of Scotland, opposite the mainland village of Achiltibuie.

Once back in Richmond we immediately telephoned the owners and registered our keen interest in spending two weeks in August, and we made sure to tell them that our 30$^{th}$ wedding anniversary was August 21 and how nice it would be to spend that time on their island. We must have been the first responders, because we were 'hired' without any fuss, and we then set about organizing our August flight to Scotland, and the onward journey to the Summer Isles.

The history of the Summer Isles is scant indeed, although the sheltered bay on the east side of the largest island, Tanera Mhor, was known to Viking seafarers in the latter part of the first millennium as the "Island of the Haven." Vikings used the large deep water bay as a hiding place after their raids on Celtic villages on the mainland. The island acquired some strategic significance in the fifteenth/sixteenth centuries, with the exploitation of the Loch Broom herring fishery. This enterprise had developed when the Dutch came to this part of the world with advanced fishing technology, following the path of the shoals of herring that passed between Tanera Mhor and the mainland

◄ THE BOG, THE BAHAMAS, AND BEYOND

on the way to the head of Loch Broom, about twenty miles away. This annual migration had been known for several hundred years, and was the primary reason for the establishment of the "new" port town of Ullapool in the late seventeen hundreds, on the mainland. With the end of the Jacobite Rebellion in 1745, and the Highlands generally "quiet" it is no surprise that the Highlands began to figure in the plans of business-men from the South. The harbor area of Tanera Mhor was bought in 1784 and a merchant from Stornoway, Mr. Murdoch Morrison, was installed as manager and given the resources to build an extensive fishery factory and outbuildings in the land contiguous to the harbor. As is the way of nature, she can turn capricious when least expected, and over the course of the next few decades a change in the migration patterns of the herring caused the economic failure of the enterprise.

From the mid 19th century onwards there was activity on and around the island, as it apparently made a secure base from which to engage in smuggling ventures, with sea voyages to the continent to bring in silks, tobacco products, and wine. These would then be safely stored, then later moved to the mainland for distribution. Thereafter, the building of several crofts, or dwelling-houses, and a stone built schoolhouse, are testament to a permanent population of 119 people spread among several families, who finally left the island for good in the 1920's. Perhaps the most famous resident of Tanera Mhor was the British ecologist, ornithologist, farmer, conservationist, and author, Sir Frank Fraser Darling, who lived on Tanera Mhor for several years from 1939 until around the end of World War Two. He wrote about his experiences in his book "Island Farm" and tells stories of a time that is evocative to a native Scot like me, and of a way of life that has little in common with the world of today.

At the beginning of September we arrived in Achiltibuie for our appointment with the owner of the island, who met us at the pier and loaded our stuff into his small outboard engine powered craft to take us over to the island, a journey of about ten minutes. This was our first day of a magical two week adventure. Bill Wilder and his wife Jean bought the island a couple of years before, having sold their extensive farming operation in the south of England and moved to this remote part of the British Isles to live a different lifestyle, for that very reason. Their kids were up and out at university, and they wanted a change for the second half of their lives. In part, this was a reflection of the change in farming in the south of England, which had become a highly competitive business while at the same time less productive from a financial perspective. It was either double up on production by becoming bigger, or walk away and begin again, with a version of farming that was far removed from world that they knew in the green fields of Dorset.

Our mission was fairly simple. Ann managed the tearoom and I was the Postmaster. Each day around 12 noon a boat would arrive at the pier with a passenger contingent of anywhere from about a dozen people to as many as fifty, all intent on their destination - a rectangular building that functioned as both a tearoom/sandwich shop and a post office. Inside the building, I was behind the post office desk in the corner, ready to dispense the rather unusual and scarce postage stamps that carried the motifs of the Summer Isles, by virtue of a licence granted by the United Kingdom Government a long time ago. Just like the Isle of Man, and the Channel Islands of Guernsey and Jersey, the Summer Isles are able to print their own unique postage stamps, which are recognized as a valid postal marque all over the world.

At the far end of the building Ann was behind the counter, with urns of tea and coffee and an assembly line of sandwich offerings ready to dispense to the thirsty and hungry visitors. Were it not for the lure of the postage stamps, the daily yield of tourists from the Ullapool boat would not be enough to turn a profit at the teahouse. However, small though it is, the stamp collector world is made up of serious practitioners, and for many of our guests this was a trip of a lifetime to be able to buy Summer Isles stamps, and then affix them to a postcard, which was then mailed to the home address, so that the stamp will have the embossed seal of HM Post Office (this was my part in the proceeding), thereby creating an authenticated used Summer Isles Postage Stamp. The captain of the boat would call me on the ship to shore radio at eleven each morning to give me a headcount of the passengers, which determined the quantity of tearoom offerings. Ann had about an hour to make the right amount of tea, and bring it to the boil at just the right time. Sandwich production was also determined by the headcount, but still a difficult skill to get absolutely right, so I suppose Ann had the harder of the two jobs. It was fun to stand by the door of the shed and watch the group file off the boat in an orderly manner, then take off in our direction in pursuit of the person ahead of them, only to draw up in confusion at the door, when they then had to make the choice of food first and stamps later or stamps first and food later.

By one thirty in the afternoon the boat had left our pier to return to Ullapool, on the mainland. However, there was also one more landing most days, around four o'clock, although this was a small craft with usually between five and ten people, and they were limited to soft drinks, whatever sandwiches were left over from lunch, and an unlimited offering of stamps from the smallest post office in the United Kingdom. I loved getting the call from Captain McLeod giving me the heads up on the number of visitors en-route. He had that wonderful Highland lilt to his voice as he would tell me that there were "just a few passengers today, Les, well actually four, so it's not too many I suppose, although I believe it might be better tomorrow." Once I had sold the few stamps to the faithful, I would head on down to the boat and chat for a while with Captain Duncan McLeod. He was a retired sea captain who kept himself busy with the few tourists who would show up at his jetty in Achiltibuie, and it must have been a far cry from the days when he sailed in the island steamers that serviced the Western Highlands and Islands of Scotland.

The only Gaelic speaking people of Scotland live in and around the Inner Hebrides, some fifty five thousand or so out of a population of around five million. These are the descendants of the Kingdom of Dalriada, left over from the Highland Clearances of their forefathers, who were evicted from the crofts in the late nineteenth century. The economics of large scale sheep farming transformed what was a tenant farming society struggling to achieve a marginal existence, with maybe enough to pay a modest tribute to the wealthy landowner, into a world of sheep at pasture, over thousands of acres, and providing a better return on capital for the owners. What they did in evicting the crofters, then shepherding them on to boats bound for Canada and America, was a shameful chapter in the history of Scotland. All the more so when the perpetrators were the leading families, former Clan Chiefs, who in previous generations would never have violated their own people.

Since the Union of the Crowns in 1707, and particularly since the failure of the Jacobite Rebellion of 1745 when Bonnie Prince Charlie's army was slaughtered at Culloden Moor, the ways of the clan system were exorcised by the Union Government, and the Clan Chiefs became landowners now beholden to a governmental system that was run from London. In time they would move south, and turn over their local affairs to Factors, who were tasked with maximizing the yields from the vast acres of land owned by this nouveau riche aristocracy. The Factors were paid handsomely, lived in relative comfort, and used their delegated powers with impunity. Contributing to this perfect storm were the effects of the Napoleanic Wars, which interrupted food supplies ordinarily imported from the continent, and so there was economic pressure to increase British production of farm products. In the vast highland estates the productive land was normally closer to the coastline, and farmed by the crofters, with only a modest by-product of rents paid to the Landowner. Suddenly there was a realization that sheep farming was so much more profitable, and a more disciplined form of land use. The role of the Factor provided the perfect excuse for the absentee Landlords to look the other way, and the result was a massive de-population of crofting communities, perpetrated by Factors working within the rule of law. The ruins of those crofts lie scattered across the landscape of the Western Highlands of Scotland, and every one a testament to a way of life that is lost in the mists of time.

For two wonderful weeks in the late summer of 1999, this was our world. We lived in Murdo's cottage, a small croft on a hillside overlooking the bay, and one of only five houses on the island. There were no roads. There was a salmon fish farm in the bay, which was really just a series of netted enclosures moored to the bottom of the sea, where the salmon were reared on a diet rich in protein and fed on a regular basis by the two or three workers who lived in a couple of the other cottages. The "big house" at the far end of the bay was the home of our employers, from where they conducted their island farming operations, and kept an eye on the fish farm. Once every few weeks a Russian ship would enter the bay, and take on supplies of fresh salmon from the fish farm, although we never saw them in our short stay there. The farm had working supplies of sheep and cattle, and the owners were also trying to encourage the growth of trees, which they had planted and supported with wooden stakes in a sometimes losing battle with the winds. We assumed that when we arrived they would leave to go on vacation, but in fact they really just wanted some time to themselves on the island away from the daily requirements of the tea-room/post office activity.

In a place where winds and rain are the order of the day, we somehow managed to be there when the sun shone from morning till night, and it never rained. In the evening we would have dinner at the croft, and then walk up to the top of the nearby hill to the summit marker of stones, where we would open our chosen libation, invariably wine for Ann and beer for me, and enjoy the quiet time watching the sun sink into the Atlantic Ocean. After a while we would walk down to the cottage, sit in the front porch, and watch the sky put on a show. If we looked to the east we would see the village of Achiltibuie. To the north lay the mountains of Wester Ross, where the setting sun chose a crimson colored palette with which to illuminate the sleeping mountains in this most beautiful of landscapes. To the west were the other islands in the group of Summer Isles, which one by one would sink into the ocean as the light gave way to dark.

As is normal for members of our family on "holiday" we soon attracted a crowd. My Mum and sisters Betty and Connie showed up unexpectedly at the pier at Achiltibuie, and somehow there was enough room for them to spend the night with us at Murdo's Cottage, after Bill Wilder had made a special run to pick them up. Then a few days later we had a visit from Ann's cousin Adam and his partner Alison, who arrived in Duncan McLeod's boat one afternoon in the hope that they would find us. On the journey over they enquired of Captain McLeod about Ann and Les Hunter, and the good captain was quite protective of us, and not in a hurry to give out information. They had to drag out of him the fact that we were staying at Murdo's

Cottage, and that perhaps it would be all right if they were dropped off at the Tanera Mhor pier without making the return journey. Our final house-guests were our long time friends Jim and Janette Marshall, from Kilsyth, and they both were co-opted to work the next day shift with us at the boathouse. Janette, whose baked goods are highly desired edibles back home, duly conjured up a special batch of Scottish shortbread. They were attractively priced to sell, but that day's boatload of visitors happened to be a contingent of German tourists, who are famous throughout Europe for always packing their own lunches. The local seagulls were the beneficiaries of the paucity of the German wallet and our own largesse, as we shared the plentiful supply of shortbread from the picnic table by the water's edge. When our two weeks were up, we reluctantly packed up our belongings and were ferried over to Achiltibuie, and our waiting car, for the trip back to Glasgow.

Sometime after Gerry Canavan and I worked together on the Japan office building contract, we went into partnership on the purchase of an office building at 2310 West Main Street in Richmond. The property had came to my notice when I had lunch with the owner, Mark Kittrell, whose late father was a family friend of Ann's cousin Helen and her husband James, from Chichester, after they had met on an educational conference. When I saw the property, an attractive two story brick former townhouse in a nice business district west of the town center, I called Gerry and suggested that he relocate his growing construction business in the building. There were a couple of offices on the ground floor that were already leased, and the second floor was perfect for the needs of Canavan Construction Company, so Gerry and I went 50/50 on the deal, and set up a corporation, which we named Dalriada LLC, to take title to the building. The name was inspired by the ancient Scots kingdom of Dalriada, which was created when the Irish settled in the north west of Scotland. As Gerry was born in Ireland, and I in Scotland, it was an inspired choice. We also added some much needed administrative and secretarial support when Ann decided that she would like to take a part time job, so she was quickly recruited to work in the office. With both of our girls away at University there was a vacuum in Ann's world, and we all know that

## ◄ THE BOG, THE BAHAMAS, AND BEYOND

Nature abhors a vacuum, so in the natural order of things Ann joined the consulting world, and was now a contributing member of Gray Wolf Associates.

In the summer of 1999 I bought my first apartment building, in the heart of the university district at the edge of down-town Richmond. A friend of mine, Ronnie Adolf, whose daughter Robin was our daughter Cassie's best friend, called me and asked if I could help him sort out a piece of real estate that he and a partner owned, arising out of a failed business transaction. Ronnie owned a leading Jewelry store in the West End of Richmond, and was not really in a position to actively deal with this problem property. He described it to me as a yellow colored building at 918 West Grace Street, and as I drove along West Grace I saw an ugly bright mustard colored building in the distance, and assumed the worst. However it was not the actual address, so I drove another couple of blocks and there on my right was a mellow yellow colored brick building that was my actual destination. The building had 5,600 square feet of commercial office space, with a restaurant space in the English basement. It was in general disrepair inside, and had not been occupied for some time. As I looked at the possibilities, I inevitably thought about buying it from Ronnie and developing it into apartments that could be rented to students, with some form of commercial tenant in the storefront basement. I talked to Gerry and we agreed to form a partnership to develop the property, assuming we could strike a deal with Ronnie. This was duly accomplished rather quickly and easily, and Gerry and I went 50/50 on the project. I named our partnership 'Mellow Yellow LLC" as an acknowledgement of the color of the paint on the property, but the legal assistant in my lawyer's office made a mistake in the submission of the documentation, and we ended up with a corporation called "Mello Yello LLC". We then went about the process of hiring an architect and pricing out the construction requirements, which was Gerry's bailiwick. I dealt with the financial matters, the most important of which was construction financing for the project.

Gerry and I would repeat this process on another property, Double Decker LLC, which we bought in the Fall of 1999. This was a building in the university area that had six apartments on the upper two floors, and two retail premises on the ground floor. The building had not been occupied for several years, so once again we established a 50/50 partnership, and began the development phase with the construction work needed to restore the building. One of the things we discovered in the acquisition phase was a serious environmental problem in the attic. Our building inspector was a Mr. Ben Blanks, and during the course of his inspection Ben brought his trusty step-ladder and stuck it through the attic trap-door, then ventured up the steps and stuck his head into the attic space. He quickly ducked back down, finding it hard to believe what he had found. He offered me the chance to take a look for myself, so I stepped up and pointed his flashlight into the dark space. The floor of the attic had about a two or three feet thick covering of pigeon shit, that had accumulated over the previous twenty or so years that the building had been unoccupied. There was a colony of pigeons that had made their home in the attic, and this was the result. The pigeon shit is actually a serious health hazard, as the toxic dust can get into a person's throat, and the disease can be fatal. Ben advised me of this, and told me that we would need to get a special firm to remove the toxic contents from the attic before any other work could be done. We hired a company to do the nasty work, and I remember watching a crew of Latino's all dressed in protective clothing and headgear make their way up the stairs to tackle the job. The first thing they did was hang protective plastic sheets in the stairwells, and then they proceeded to bring down the ceilings and scoop the stuff into large bags, to be removed to an environmentally approved site.

That was the bad news that we had to deal with at Double Decker. However, the financial aspects of the deal were really attractive, because we were able to take advantage of Historic Tax Credits to offset about 20% of the total construction costs of the renovation. Basically the U.S. Government and the State Government both have tax credit plans in place that provide an attractive incentive to develop old properties that lie in historic districts, which this one did. The Tax Credits are given to each developer personally, so I was issued with Federal credits which I used to offset against future income. I also received State credits, and they are actually marketable, as they can be bought

⊰ THE BOG, THE BAHAMAS, AND BEYOND

by a third party and used to reduce their own tax liability. Gerry and I were able to sell our credits through a broker in New Orleans.

At the same time that Gerry and I became partners in the building ownership, I also started a financial consulting relationship with him that lasted several years. It had lots of high points and quite a few low points, largely because of Gerry's penchant for sailing close to the wind on financial matters. This would become clearer to me over time, but for the first few years he seemed to be a good operator, and clearly knew a lot about commercial construction. He managed to start his construction business without any significant operating funds, and built up an impressive list of clients, and projects. There came a time, a few years later, when Gerry needed a source of cash infusion in his business to keep his dream alive, and at that point I bought him out of Dalriada, Mello Yello, and Double Decker, which gave him much needed cash to capitalize his construction business, and gave me total control over the three commercial buildings that we had heretofore shared. By then, all of the construction related improvements had been made to the buildings, and the emphasis shifted from construction to ongoing management and leasing. This was my world, not Gerry's, so our agreement to divide and conquer made sense for both of us.

In the Spring of 2000 Ann and I made plans to travel to Spain for a week of celebration with Ann's cousin Agnes Smith, and her husband John. They had retired to Marbella after John sold his business in Scotland, and had made a comfortable and enjoyable life for themselves in their beautiful villa in the hills above the town. On the day before we were due to fly out of Washington Dulles to Madrid, Ann decided to call Spain to see if her sister Agnes (Brown) had got there safely, only to be told that John had died suddenly just a few hours before. Instead of a lovely week of family and friends on the Costa del Sol, we had a very different situation to deal with. By the time we got there it was all about the funeral arrangements, and who needed to be contacted, and where to put everyone. John was such a popular man, and a wonderful person. His funeral service was held in a nearby town, and I volunteered to represent the family and speak about John's life, from his upbringing in a beautiful part of the central Highlands of Scotland, until his untimely death at the age of 60.

Thankfully, there was one very uplifting and important piece of family business to take care of that summer – Shona graduated from the University of Virginia with a Bachelor's Degree in English and Social Studies. The "Class of 2000" has an especially nice ring to it, and Shona left her university with a first class education and the inclination to teach, which took her to Washington DC. She and her college room-mate Laura rented a townhouse in Alexandria, and were fairly quickly absorbed into the labor force with full time jobs. Shona was hired by a "Charter" school in Washington to teach kids whose parents had jobs that precluded them from being there at the end of the regular school day, so the kids were collected in an after schools program that ran from 3pm until 7pm each day. The school was located north of the down-town area in a part of town that was predominantly African American, and the kids were mostly from single parent homes, and without the benefit of a conventional family structure. You can imagine how wired these kids were after a full day of regular school, only to be cooped up for a few more hours in the school building. On her drive to and from work Shona had to run the gauntlet through what can charitably be described as a mean part of town. She stuck it out for about six months, but inevitably she had to resign and find some other profession where she would be able to contribute to society without threat to her personal safety.

She very quickly joined Envision, a company that put together courses and seminars for high school students all across the country. Through their network they were also in a position to get funding for those students whose family situation did not allow for the expense of getting to the nation's capital, and spending a week or two weeks on site. In her travels back and forward between Richmond and Washington DC she met Chris Colglazier, an acquaintance from her high school years, and began their own wonderful journey in love and life together. Chris spent part of his final college year studying in Paris, and was able to spend time with my sister Connie's family and Shona's cousins Axelle, Virginia, and Remi. Later that year Chris graduated from James Madison University, with a degree in Finance, and he was able to find a job with a Defense Contracting company, and an apartment near Shona.

### THE BOG, THE BAHAMAS, AND BEYOND

As for me, not only did I gain a prospective son in Chris, I also acquired a terrific football playing partner. Chris played one summer with the Pink Panthers before he moved away, and he and I managed to play together in many other pick-up games and friendly matches over the years, until I hung up my boots when I turned sixty. Chris was a high school star and went to university on a soccer scholarship, but couldn't stand waiting on the bench as a young college freshman, and transferred to James Madison University to pursue academics. He still likes nothing better than to head across the road to the soccer field opposite his apartment, and kick around on his own and juggle the ball in the way that can only be appreciated and understood by other fellow football fans – like me. He now has two sons and the opportunity to instill in them his love of the game, and maybe having a grandfather that is equally fanatic about football will provide an extra motivation that will see the boys excel in this athletic and cerebral sport.

CHAPTER 17

# All's Well That Ends Well

FOR THE FIRST few years of the new century I managed the rental properties myself, and dealt one-on-one with tenants. I eventually had around twenty plus rent checks to collect each month, as well as the physical aspects of maintaining the properties in good condition. I must say that my experiences with almost all of my tenants, and I must have had about 100 or so over the years, were positive, and I had almost no rent arrears to speak of, or bad experiences with tenants, save for two situations at Mello Yello. These two situations were quite bizarre, since they both involved dead bodies.

The first was pretty much over and done by the time I was aware of it, so there was no personal trauma for me as such. A young couple who had rented a two bedroom apartment split up a few months after they took occupancy, and unfortunately the female was the more trustworthy partner, and I was left with the more challenging of the two as the remaining tenant. He did pay his rent on time, so there was no real problem, but I was uncomfortable with his financial situation, and rent day was always a trick. Then one day he called me to tell me that he had left the apartment, to move back to California. Apparently, a few days before the call he had picked up a friend of his who had flown in from California to spend some vacation time with him in Richmond. Either before or during the flight, he had taken the drug Valium, and had a reaction to it during the journey. He somehow made it to Richmond, where my tenant picked him up and they went back to the apartment. After drinking and ingesting other drugs, the

## THE BOG, THE BAHAMAS, AND BEYOND

friend passed out on the spare bed. The next morning my tenant went to wake him up, and discovered his dead body, where it lay undisturbed from the previous evening. He called the police who took care of the situation. It seems that the combination of Valium, the flight, and the previous evening's drugs, were enough to cause heart failure. By the time I got the call the body had already been moved to a mortuary. My conversation with my tenant was short and to the point. I did not have a Morals Clause in my lease, but I acted as if I did, and he went away without any fuss. I had the place cleaned up and rented in short order, as that particular unit in the building was easy to lease because it had the extra bedroom. My normally prescient instinct about prospective tenants had let me down in this case, but I figured that the loss of one month's rent was a small price to pay for what could have been a lot worse. Little did I know what was in store for me the next time I had to deal with a corpse on the premises.

One of the Gray Wolf deals that I did was such an odd "one off" situation but was fun to work on, and really solved a problem for the couple who came to me for help. It was a former banking colleague who sent them to me, as he had turned them down for a loan at his bank because of their difficult financial situation. They owned a house that was worth about $200,000 and had a mortgage on it of about $70,000. The husband was out of work, and his wife had sold her hairdressing business on credit to a friend, and the friend had ran it into the ground. She had financed the buyer and now the loan had no source of repayment, as the business had failed. There was no income coming into their household. They had decided to sell the house to get access to the substantial equity that they had in it, but in the meantime they had defaulted on their mortgage and the mortgage company was about a week away from fore-closing. They needed somehow to borrow enough money to bring their mortgage current and enable them to live for as long as it took to sell the house and recover the equity, then they would have some time in which to get new jobs lined up, and start over again. I liked the couple from the outset, and with some elementary due diligence by telephone I quickly determined that they were good people in a bad place, and so I put together a proposal that gave them enough money to satisfy the

## ALL'S WELL THAT ENDS WELL

mortgage company, and meet their household budget for the next six months. I set them up with a real estate broker to market the property for a quick sale. Everything went according to plan, and within four months they had sold their house, I had been repaid in full, and they were now in a position to plan their future without the threat of financial ruin over them.

This was a situation where the couple was caught between a rock and hard place in dealing with conventional sources of financing. Their situation was too far gone to get a bank to step in at the last minute. I knew from the outset that the loan they needed was not of enough size to create any significant income for me. After I had reviewed their situation, and we sat down to talk, I suggested a scenario that would incent me to help them. Rather than pay interest on a loan, I would do it for a one-time fee, of a few thousand dollars that would enable me to pay for a nice trip for Ann and me on a cruise to Alaska. That was the deal. We get a nice trip, and they solve their problem. If it turned out that they had trouble selling the house, then I would be strung out on my loan, and would just have to weather the storm along with them. However, it all went rather smoothly, Ann and I had our "free" trip, and the couple moved on with their lives. I love those win-win situations, but you can never say it's a win-win until it is over. This one was.

We flew to Vancouver in Canada along with our mainly British contingent and spent a couple of days there before picking up our cruise-ship. On entering our hotel room, my first task was to grab the local phone directory and look for an entry under the name "Leslie Hunter." I found about six references to either Leslie or "L" Hunter and set about trying to locate my Dad's cousin, after whom I am named. He had emigrated to Canada around 1950, and his father was a brother of my grandfather, "Pop" Hunter. There had been no contact for about fifty years, but armed with a name and a bloodline I called all the possibilities, and when I finally got one who was about the same age, he still had his London accent, and felt bad about telling me his parentage, which was indubitably English. The only thing I know about the Canadian Leslie Hunter is that he was a ballet dancer, and that is the extent of the knowledge I leave to my descendants, plus my hopes for a bit more success should they one day try to locate my namesake in Vancouver.

As regards the actual cruise, it was actually a bit of a let-down. The inland sea was smooth as a billiard table, so there were no complaints of sea-sickness, but we found the Alaskan townships where we docked to be rather seedy, and not really attractive. Once you turned your eyes inland towards the mountains the scenery was glorious, but you can't really get there from the ship. On the day that whales were spotted on the starboard side of the ship, I was on the port side, and when the next sighting was on the port side......well, I think you know where this is going. So all in all it was a bit disappointing. Our friends Terry and Rose O'Neill of Penny Lane Pub were celebrating their sixtieth birthdays, so we had a great time with lots of laughs, but I find the cruise vacation to be quite structured, and not my cup of tea. However, Ann loves to cruise. Fortunately, so do her "Glasgow" girlfriends, and they have often chosen a cruise together to celebrate many of the special birthdays that occur within the group. Their other preferred method of shared experience is to hike, or trek, or merely walk trails, and the ninety six mile journey along the West Highland Way that they did together in 2006 was probably the seminal group experience. Or maybe it was their "walk" into the wild country of the Knoydart Peninsula, where there are no roads, and where the mountains protect the village of Inverie from an east wind that is spent by the time it gets there. Inverie's remote location at the head of the sea loch provides access to the daily boat to Skye, and guarantees an easier way out than in, but to get there the girls had to hike across the moors, camp for the night, then head up and over the mountains and down into Inverie next day. It is a challenging trek, and the one pub in the village does earn the tee shirt tribute to the remotest pub in Britain. I wear the tee shirt but have yet to taste the beer.

The event against which all other world happenings in the first ten years of the new century have been measured - 9/11, hit us all smack in the face in 2001. We watched the incredible developments on live television, as they happened, and even now it is hard to imagine that the twin towers which symbolized all that was biggest and best of New York were brought to the ground by a few fanatics with a modicum of training in aviation. It was the flash report from Washington about the apparent crash of a plane into the Pentagon that made this our issue in a very potent and scary way, knowing that Shona worked in down-town Washington DC, where reports were coming in about a possible explosion in the offices of the State Department, not far from her office on 17th Street. Most cell phone activity in the DC area was frozen for a while that morning, as people everywhere, just like us, tried to reach out to their loved ones. It was about four hours later that we were able to talk to Shona and find out that her building had been evacuated. The employees split into groups and headed out of the down-town area by whatever road they could find that was still open. But while we and countless other tens of thousands of families were affected one way or another by the events of that day, it was in the larger arena of world politics that the consequences of 9/11 would be played out, as the search for Osama Bin Laden and the causes he espoused somehow translated into an opportunity for the Bush Presidency to frame the event in a larger context. Within a year he managed to make the case that Saddam Hussein in Iraq was close to achieving nuclear weapons capability, and that the national interests of the United States required a military response. Iraq was eventually invaded once again by mostly American forces under the pretence of locating and eliminating Iraq's weapons of mass destruction, in a costly and controversial war.

The other situation that involved the death of one of my tenants was a sad affair, and I am often haunted by the circumstances of her death. I had rented a one bedroom apartment in Mello Yello to a fifty year old African American woman, who was going back to Virginia Commonwealth University (VCU) to complete her degree, after a long time in the workforce in New York. She was well spoken, and I got good references, which I checked out by telephone and they were all fine. Her income was in the form of a Government (Student) loan, and she earned some additional money by reporting on the VCU student radio station. Her gross income was still a bit below the minimum that I had established for qualification, but I felt that she deserved a chance. She was with me for several months, and because of the periodic loans from school, I received the rent check ahead of the due date. After a period of not quite a year, she was getting ready for the start of school after the summer, and I tried to contact her to make arrangements to get the financial aid check that would cover her rent for the next Semester. She failed to meet me as agreed a couple of times, and then when I went to meet her at the apartment she came outside the door and we conducted our conversation in the hall. I began to get a bit suspicious that all was not well, so next time that I met her at the door for an update, I told her I needed to come in for the annual inspection of the premises that was provided for in my lease document. When she opened the door I stepped in to a living room floor that was absolutely covered with brown paper (grocery store) bags, filled with all sorts of books, newspapers, discs, house-hold products, and all sorts of rubbish. This was my first and only experience with a hoarder - someone who has a compulsive need to save everything they possess or acquire in the ordinary course of life. I picked my way across the room, past the kitchen, along the hall, and into the bedroom. There was no spare area of floor whatsoever. It was unbelievable.

    I told Vicky that she had to move out as soon as possible, as the apartment was a fire and safety hazard, not just for her but for the other residents. I said that I would come back to help her pack up all her stuff, and would transport it for her for storage or to wherever she relocated to. While I felt bad about the short notice, I just had to get her out the building. It did not help that her air conditioning was not on, and in the ninety degree temperature that is late summer in Richmond, the smell was palpable. I told her to start looking for a new place right away, and that I would return in a couple of days with cardboard boxes that we could use to pack all her stuff. A few days later I called at the apartment to drop off the boxes, and to get her mobilized into action. There was no answer. Although I had a key, I had a rule that I would not enter a tenant's apartment without permission, so I left a hand written note for her and went on home.

    A few days later I received a phone call from my tenant in the clothing store located in the English basement of the building, to say that there was a strange smell in the shop. I went down to investigate, and after talking to my tenant I went up to the apartment hall to check out the rest of the building. The smell hit me as soon as I went in the

## ALL'S WELL THAT ENDS WELL

door and up the stairs, at the top of which was Vicky's apartment. I knocked on the door again, but there was no answer. This time I felt I had no option but to break my own rule, so I unlocked the door for entry. I pushed open the door and it stuck against a chair that was positioned close to the door frame. When I put my head round the door to investigate, there was a naked dead body on an armchair that was positioned in front of a computer desk. The consequence of death in that heat had caused the body to distend and arch. The body was unrecognizable as male or female, even though it (she) was naked. It had swollen because of the heat to probably twice its size, the hair was all straggly and disheveled, and the smell was of death and decomposition. The expression on the face was horrific, which was not necessarily a precursor to her death but more likely as a consequence of the swollen body fluids. The heat had actually caused the body to burst, and the body fluids had dripped to the floor, and entered not just the carpet but the wooden floorboards below.

I ducked back into the hallway to gather myself, then forced myself to look one more time before I relocked the door. It happens that the VCU Police Station is located at the other side of the adjacent parking lot, so I hurried across to the station to report. One of the policemen came with me, so once again I followed the smell up stairs, unlocked the door, and motioned for the policeman to look in. He took one look, and immediately ducked back in to the hallway, just as I had done. He used his mobile phone to call the Richmond City Police, since this was clearly not something that was within the Campus Police jurisdiction. He stayed with me, and within a few minutes the building was a crime scene, with detectives, police officers, and sundry official personnel milling about the building trying to determine if in fact a crime had been committed. Naturally enough I was the key witness, and for all I know I may have even been a suspect. The whole thing took about six hours till finally a mortuary vehicle came and took the body away. The detective in charge told me that there would be an autopsy to determine the cause of death, but it looked as if it was from natural causes, or perhaps suicide.

I did have to wait a few days while her parents and family drove out from Kansas to deal with her remains, and they came over to the apartment to take her personal effects. At that point nothing had been disturbed, so they saw the place as it looked when I found her. I can't imagine having to smell the body of your child or sibling, but there was no way for them to avoid it, and thankfully, after removing her computer, they were away within a few minutes. It took my handyman and his clean-up crew two weeks to get the place in a fit condition to be habitable again. The floorboards had to be replaced where the body fluids had penetrated, and the whole place needed cleaning and repainting. During the rental process I took pains to tell prospective tenants what had happened in the apartment in case it would affect their decision. I was surprised that no-one seemed that concerned about it, and had a young graduate student sign a lease after a few weeks of no rent.

I followed up with the detective on the cause of death, and in fact it took the police several weeks before they were able to get all the reports they needed to designate her death as being of natural causes. I felt all along, and still feel to this day, that it is more likely that she committed suicide. It just seems too much of a coincidence that she would happen to die in such a strange way, while her life was subject to changes over which she had little control. Such a conclusion, if true, would lay some element of responsibility at my door, and it sits in my mind as an open question, to be asked of myself in odd moments of self examination. It is probably the one instance in my life as a landlord that I truly regret. I know that I did as much as I could to welcome her as a tenant, working with her on funding her rent, and applauding her for going back to school, but it seems a poor tribute when weighed against the outcome of the loss of her life, and the abuse of her body after death by the circumstances of that death.

The month of September 2002 brought a welcome relief from the vagaries of apartment management, with the arrival of Ann's crew of girl friends from Scotland, who had to delay their 2001 trip one year because of 9/11. For some reason the trip began with the name "Odyssey" in 2001 so it was quickly re-defined as Odyssey 2002, and Ann flew up to New York to meet the girls and spend a few days there before heading for our home in Richmond. In New York they ticked all the boxes for what the British tourist likes to see in the city, which

## ALL'S WELL THAT ENDS WELL

are all the usual sights plus the Dakota Apartment Building in the Upper West Side where John Lennon was shot. They discovered a little known band called "Fourplay" from a CD played by the clearly illegal alien who drove them from the airport to their mid-town hotel, and it soon became the "national anthem" of their trip, to be played on the way to do something, and then on the way back. In Richmond the house was ready for them, and to make the sleeping numbers work I put a mattress in my office, and retired each evening ahead of the crowd. Ann's pal Marolyn Clarke, who lived at the time in Atlanta, came to Richmond to join the gang, having spent time with them when they all walked the West Highland Way a few years prior. With side trips to Virginia Beach and Washington DC we kept them on the run, and I am pretty sure they enjoyed this little slice of Americana.

It was Bryan and Marolyn's turn to reciprocate the following January, when they invited us to Atlanta to stay for a few days and participate in their "Burn's Supper" party at their beautiful home in the north side of town. This was pretty much an annual event in their lives, and is a testimony of sorts to the Scot's blood in Marolyn's side of the family, who lived in Fife until Marolyn was about fourteen, when they moved to Leeds. The Clarke's Burn's Supper was one of the few events that I could count on to be able to wear my kilt, the other's being weddings of close family friends, and Hogmonay (New Year's Eve).

While we were en route back to Richmond from Florida, we got news of the Space Shuttle Colombia disaster, which killed all seven Astronauts when it disintegrated during re-entry into the earth's atmosphere. The accident was actually caused during the launching process, when foam insulation designed to protect the vehicle from the intense heat generated from atmospheric friction on re-entry broke away, and struck the leading edge of the left wing. The thermal protection system (TPS) had been compromised at the beginning of the mission, and failed to protect the craft during the critical re-entry phase. While the headlines told the story in countless versions over the succeeding days and weeks, I was reminded of a story that I had heard several years before, that made a pretty interesting case for a link between the size of the Booster Rockets on the Space Shuttle, and the size of the space between the wheels of Roman Chariots! It goes like this.

The standard railroad gauge in the US is 4 feet 8 1/2 inches. Why such an odd number? Because that was the size of the gauge in England, on which the US designs were based. Why was that the gauge size in England? Because that was the gauge size used for the precursor of the train – the tram. The tram was built using the same jigs and tools that were used to build wagons. The wagons had that particular gauge size because otherwise their wheels would break on some of the old long distance roads in England, due to the spacing of the wheel ruts. So who built those old rutted roads? Imperial Rome built them for their Legions, and over time the ruts were formed by the Roman Chariots, which were made with a standardized spacing between the wheels, based on the width of the back end of the two horses that pulled the Chariot. That general gauge size, originally measured by the back end of two horses, became standardized at 4 foot 8 I/2 inches.

The designers of the booster rockets for the US Space Program, who were based in Utah, had to restrict the width of the rockets so that they could be transported by train to the launch site in Florida. The railway line happens to run through a tunnel in the mountains, and they had to fit through that tunnel. So, although they would have preferred a bulkier design version for the Booster Rockets, they had to conform to the width of the tunnel, which was determined by the gauge of the track. In other words, the world's most advanced transportation system was determined over two thousand years ago by the width of a horse's ass! This makes a great story, although without general academic support, is at least a tribute to someone with a better imagination than me.

It was Cassie's turn to graduate in 2003, and she did so in style with a Bachelors degree in Finance from JMU. Also graduating that year was her boyfriend Kurt Wolfe, who was one of the original group of "roomies" assigned to the same dormitory in their freshman year. Just as we drove fairly often to Charlottesville to see Shona, we also made the somewhat longer trek up to Harrisonburg to spend time with Cassie while she was working her way through college. Kurt and

Cassie graduated together, and both of them came to Richmond to begin the next chapter of their lives. While Cassie joined a financial organization, Kurt immediately signed up for Law School at the University of Richmond, and embarked on the three year ordeal that is the study of Law.

This was the year of Shona and Chris's wedding, and what should have been a wonderful time for me as a proud and happy father and father-in-law was spoiled somewhat by my first real experience of being ill on a regular basis. For some reason I developed a kind of stomach pain that had the symptoms of Acid Indigestion, yet did not respond to the many treatment options, all of which I tried, but in vain. I was referred to Gastro-Enterologists by my family doctor, but all they succeeded in doing was ruling out a progressive litany of scarier and scarier potential causes. I soon became grateful for all the diseases that I did not have. I even tracked down a lady near Perth in Scotland while on vacation that summer, who claimed to be able to identify low levels of certain obtuse chemicals in my blood caused by eating modern food! Somehow she expected me to change to a diet of vegetables that were not grown in twenty first century soils. It was all a bit 'new world" for me so I gave up her supplements after a couple of weeks and somehow it felt better not to feel better, as if the threat of a lifetime of eating under those terms and conditions was just a bit too much to bear. When Shona was married that September I weighed 147 pounds, which was about ten to fifteen pounds less than I normally weigh, and although I tried to be the beaming and loquacious father of the bride, I fell a bit short, although not for lack of effort. It was still a fabulous day for the Hunter family, and I am sure it was the same for the Colglazier's. The happy couple headed to Barbados for a few days of honeymoon, and then it was back to the real world and the prospect of married life in the nation's capital, Washington DC.

Both the Hunter and Louden families from "across the pond" were well represented at the wedding, and our next door neighbors John and Susan Claytor surprised us by delivering a full ice chest of wines and beers to our deck, which they topped up every day. We have been so lucky in our lives here in Richmond to have had wonderful neighbors wherever we lived. Between the Eubank's and the Coleman's at

### THE BOG, THE BAHAMAS, AND BEYOND

Raintree, and the Claytor's and the Lovette's in Georges Bluff, life in the suburbs has been good for us, and to us. The beauty of making deep and personal friendships along the highway of life is that the bus continues to take on passengers, and few get off. We have friends going back to our Nassau and Cayman days that we have not seen for many years, yet they still sit comfortably in our minds, ready to join us in moments of introspection, and occasionally the subject of our conversations if something pops up that triggers the recall of moments from the past.

Ann and I had a week or two to get back to a more normal routine, then it was time for Ann and a few of the stalwarts of the British Women's Club in Richmond to head to Las Vegas for a long weekend. Celine Dion may have headlined, but the worth of the trip was self generated, as Ann and a bevy of (mostly) post menopausal women put on their make-up and went out to enjoy America's party city. Back in Richmond, no sooner was the make-up off than it was time for both of us to prepare ourselves for a party celebration in Scotland, to be held in Airth Castle near Falkirk, in the form of a Ceilidh party for Shona and Chris. This was a way for friends and family who were not able to come to Richmond to attend the wedding to meet Chris and his family, who all flew over for the occasion. The Ceilidh Band got everyone involved in the highland dancing, and even our two American boys, Chris and Kurt, wore kilts, and Shona got to wear her wedding dress again.

Before the year was out, Ann and I had yet one more trip to take, and it was to South Africa, to spend time with Ian and Rosie Laurie, around the occasion of their son Tom's 21st birthday, on January 1, 2004. The trip involved a seven hour flight over the Atlantic to London, a six hour lay-over, and then a ten hour flight to Durban. The accommodation in Business Class helped, and we soon got over the jet lag and entered into the protracted celebrations for Tom, most of which took place on a farm in rural Natal Province owned by a family friend of Ian and Rosie's.

This was a time in South Africa when the country had emerged with a sense of nationhood and self confidence from the pre-Mandela era of apartheid, to the post Mandela coming of age of their new democracy. At least it seemed that way out in the country, but we had yet

## ALL'S WELL THAT ENDS WELL

to visit Johannesburg. Ian and Rosie's house was close to the village of Botha's Hill, with wonderful views across the Valley of One Thousand Hills, which form around the valley of the Mngeni River and its tributaries, and is the heart of the Kwazulu people. We also took off for a few days on our own, driving to the Drakensberg Mountains, where we were reminded of the hills of Scotland.

After leaving the Laurie's we flew to Johannesburg, to spend a few days with Irene and Donnie MacEwan, in their gated community in the suburbs of the city. Irene and Donnie were from Hillington, and Irene was one of Ann's closest friends growing up. After a couple of days in the city the four of us headed for a week-long trip to the Kruger National Park. We stayed at a lodge at the edge of the Park, but within the fenced areas, so there were no barriers between us and the wild animals save for the topography of the land. We were perched on a ledge overlooking a riverbed and watering hole, which guaranteed a superb view of the animals as they headed for the water in the evenings as the sun set. We were up early each morning to head out into the park along the system of interconnected roads, driving slowly and looking for signs of any of the "big five" – elephant, lion, white rhino, buffalo, and leopard, and over the two or three days we saw all but the leopard. However, we did come across a pack of wild dogs, and duly notified the hotel ranger when we returned of the location of the sighting. We had been forewarned to do so, as they are a rare and declining species, but it did seem rather odd to get excited about seeing dogs in the middle of the World's best known wild animal preserve.

When we got back to Johannesburg we never did visit the city center, as it was deemed to be too dangerous. Their neighbors were mostly white South Africans, and were accustomed to living a life of privilege until it all started to change with the abolition of Apartheid, and the onset of black majority rule. A few days later we flew back to Virginia, and I had to quickly come to grips with all the goings on in the apartment buildings, but thankfully there were no disasters to deal with, natural or otherwise.

As the winter weather beat the retreat in the face of a beautiful mild and sunny Spring in Virginia, I was determined to find a way to deal with my ongoing stomach problems, and had by now outlasted the specialists, plus the lady from Perth with the mineral supplements. The only logical thing to try now was Acupuncture, so I did some research on practitioners in the area and found Dr. David Groopman, who had his medical office just a few miles from our home. All I knew about Acupuncture was what my sister Rena told me some forty or so years before, when she went to an Acupuncture guy in Falkirk to try and get some relief from neck pain. While she was being treated, the Chinese Medicine practioner, who was in fact Chinese, noticed that Rena had nicotine stains on her fingers, and asked her if she wanted to stop smoking. She replied "not really" but agreed that he could go ahead and do some additional procedures with the needles to address that particular condition, as well as the strategically placed needles that were there to treat the neck pain. After her treatment, Rena went out to her car to drive home, picked up the pack of cigarettes that was lying next to the gear lever, then put it back down again. Her neck pain treatment didn't work, but she never smoked a cigarette again.

The fact that Dr. Groopman was a medical doctor gave me some comfort, and when I went for the first time he was very easy to talk to, and pretty unequivocal about the prospect of success. He told me that Acupuncture does not necessarily cure, and often helps reduce pain and discomfort, but sometimes has no remedial impact at all. He said that if there was no significant response to the treatments after seven or eight sessions, it was probably not going to work. After the weekly sessions were completed there was no apparent relief, and so we sat down to talk through my symptoms again. David told me that he did not think that I had a stomach problem *per se*, and that he believed it was more likely to be linked to the central nervous system. In short, my stomach problem was being created by some form of disruption in neural transmissions between the brain and the stomach. Although stress can cause this type of abnormality, I did not otherwise show any signs of stress, and certainly from my personal point of view I had nothing going on in my life that was causing me to feel stressed.

Putting on his "MD" hat, and pulling out his prescription pad, he proceeded to write me a prescription for an old line drug called Amitriptyline, which is often prescribed for un-diagnosed pain. It was originally an anti-depressant, but had long since been replaced by more modern drugs for that condition. However, it is still used by many doctors when nothing else works. Well, I picked up my first prescription of 30 tablets and took one pill in the evening, around 6 pm. There were two immediate effects from the pill. It made me sleepy, so I just started taking it later in the evening, and it gave me a dry mouth, so I began to put a bottle of water on the bedside table, within easy reach in the wee hours of the morning. Within a few days the stomach pain was gone, and it has been that way ever since the good doctor decided on a course of treatment based on a hunch.

I still go back to David's medical office for an Acupuncture treatment every three months, and I do so out of loyalty more than anything else. He cured me when the best in the business couldn't, and even though he insists that Acupuncture helps to sustain my resistance to stomach pain, I happily spend $125 that is not recoverable from health insurance, and endure the discomfort and sometimes pain of sharp needles in my body out of a sense of gratitude and loyalty to someone who made a difference in my life.

The most popular Holy Father of modern times died in April of 2004, and it seemed as if the whole world was in mourning for the passing of Pope John Paul 11. While the passing of a Pope does require a modicum of sympathy and mourning, even for a non-Catholic like me, I was reminded of what happened in 1978, when the sitting Holy Father Pope Paul V1 died , and was succeeded by Pope John Paul 1, who in turn died after only 33 days in office. That was when Pope John Paul 11 was elected by the College of Cardinals. I happened to be on a business trip to the Bahamas at that time, and had tuned in to Bahamas Television to watch the news in my hotel room. The news reader for Batelco, the local TV station, was reading his prepared script, and began his broadcast by saying "the weather in the Bahamas today was beautiful. As usual the Pope died in Rome." The newscaster had merely paused at the end of the line of script, took a breath, and then went on to the next line as a new subject. Unfortunately, that's not the way the script was intended, but it made good theater, and in a broadcast television company that is not all bad.

In the summer of 2004 we planned our usual summer trip to

◀ THE BOG, THE BAHAMAS, AND BEYOND

Scotland, and we were both excited as always, and full of ideas for what we might get up to for the next few weeks. With Ann's family based in Barrhead (Glasgow), and mine in Falkirk, we typically would spend a few days with the Brown's and then make our way through to Falkirk to be based with Mum for a few days. Although we had a firm plan that one day we would buy a home in Scotland that would be our base for our regular visits, we had no real time-frame in mind, although we always kept up with the property market through the "Glasgow Herald" and the "Scotsman" weekly property guides. Ann had got to the Glasgow Herald before I did, and spotted an interesting property that soon got both our attention – an apartment in a castle. The ad did its job, which was to generate excitement and interest, and we had lots of both, so we immediately planned to stop by the next day (Sunday) on our way to Falkirk.

Bridge Castle is located about three miles from the country town of Bathgate, in the County of West Lothian. It is no more than a one hour drive from Barrhead, and a twenty minute drive to Falkirk. In other words it passed the first test of a potential home for us in Scotland, and that of course is proximity to our nearest and dearest. We found Bridge Castle on a sixteen acre parcel of land off a quiet country road. It sits on a rocky elevated area at the bend of the Barbauchlaw Burn (a "creek" in American terms) which runs from the hills behind the nearby village of Armadale down to the River Avon, and from there it joins the River Forth and in its small way contributes to the confluence with the North Sea. But that is a mental reach to someone sitting by the edge of the burn, enjoying the view of Bridge Castle, which is where I found myself that day, enchanted with the thought that maybe, just maybe, we might be able to buy the apartment. Because it was the weekend, there was no way to locate the real estate agent for a formal viewing. All we could do that day was to look through the one window that did not have a closed curtain or blind, and what we saw was enough to instill a certainty of purpose that became an obsession for a few days, then a reality when we actually signed a contract to buy Number 2 Bridge Castle House. We looked into the "Drawing" room which was about forty feet long and twenty wide, with a curved ceiling that we would learn was actually a "barrel vaulted ceiling" and typical of any fortified building from around the fourteenth/fifteenth century. It was the ground level apartment, and the curved ceiling supported the other floors and battlements above. We knew from the ad that there were two bedrooms, two bathrooms, a kitchen and living room, a central hall, and of course the spectacular Drawing Room. All the elements were in place for us to buy the property. The location was perfect, the price was reasonable, and the sixteen other family homes that were scattered around the sixteen acres, including the outbuildings and stable properties that adjoined the castle, meant that we would be able to lock it up and leave it unoccupied for months at a time, in a small and secure neighborhood. I knew that we would need help negotiating the legal system, and securing a contract to buy. It only took one phone call, to our old friends from the Cayman Islands Steuart and Diane Howie, who had returned to Edinburgh many years ago, where Steuart was senior partner in the venerable law firm of Russell and Aitken.

I spoke to Steuart that evening, and he promised to get on it first thing on Monday morning. It turned out that the solicitor who was acting on behalf of the seller was a friend, so he was able to cut right through the formalities and get to the essence of the deal. In Scotland when you sell a property you ask for offers over a certain amount. This leaves it up to the buyer to "guess" what might be the right number. It is almost a silent auction, with all the advantages accruing to the seller. Steuart nailed down the price, made sure we were happy with it, and then exchanged contracts that day with the seller's solicitor. Just like that, we had bought an apartment in a castle. We had set aside the funds for our 'future' home in Scotland, so it made it so much easier to deal with as a buyer, as there were no major conditions to be met on our side. Just show up with the money, which we did, and the title passed on November 30, 2004. On my to-do list on a future trip is to visit the Land Registry office in Edinburgh, and access the title deeds to the property. All such title deeds in Scotland prior to a certain date (sometime in the 1800's) are kept centrally, so you don't actually get to see your title deeds when you buy property that is older than the cut-off date. As ours go all the way back to the late 1300's, it will be quite a thrill to look through the old deeds and see the chain of title, that begins with the Stewart family, from nearby Linlithgow.

### THE BOG, THE BAHAMAS, AND BEYOND

The castle dates from the early fifteenth century. Originally known as the Fortalice of Little Brighouse in the Barony of Ogilface, it stands on an outcrop of rock overlooking the Barbauchlaw Burn in the parish of Torphichen. The founders were the Stewart family, one of whom was a steward to the Royal House at Linlithgow, the center of the Scottish monarchy at that time. The original building was a plain tower, or "keep" five storey's high, and was built of stone and rubble. Access from one floor to another was by an outside stair. When one of the Stewarts married a St Clair, the dowry that came with the lady allowed for an addition to be built to the tower, including an inside stair. Later in its history the castle passed to the Sandilands family (Lords of Torphichen) whose seat was at Couston, giving rise to the legend of the existence of a tunnel between Couston and Bridge Castle. The Sandilands had close connections with Torphichen and the Order of St. John of Jerusalem. One of the family members was the librarian of the Order and it is thought that at the time of the Reformation, records and documents from Torphichen Preceptory were hidden in and around Bridge Castle. During the 18th century workmen discovered a hidden stairway leading downwards, but the cavity was immediately bricked up.

The claim is made that Oliver Cromwell spent a night here (after laying siege to Linlithgow Palace). As is typical of many of the lesser known castles in Scotland, there is so much more unknown than known. Because our apartment is the entire ground floor and lowest level of the castle buildings, we are fortunate that many historical features are actually in our apartment. The stone carved crest of the Sinclair (St Clair) family is embedded in the stone wall facings of our family room, and we have two barrel vaulted rooms, one of which is the main Living/Dining room, and the other is the guest bedroom, the latter being probably the quaintest room in the apartment. The blocked up passageway, if it exists, is under our Drawing room floor. There is also an historical feature in the guest bedroom that is protected by the rules governing listed buildings (Bridge Castle being a "B" listed property) – an aperture in the wall of one of the early stone entranceways that is funneled in shape and would have been a defensive feature that gave the person on the inside of the castle wall an expanded field of vision of the outside from a relatively small opening.

It is many years now since we bought the apartment at Bridge Castle, and it continues to give our family much pleasure. The nearby Bathgate Hills provide a lovely rural backdrop to our home in the heavily populated central belt of Scotland, and so far the little hamlets and villages around us have stood fast against commercial development.

My daily run is no less a habit in West Lothian than it is back in Virginia, and the bracing winds and frequent showers of Central Scotland are as nothing compared to the ninety degree heat and humidity of summer that challenge me on a routine basis in Richmond. I am lucky that I still enjoy running, and for me it is not something I do just for health and fitness, it is a mental exercise as well. There are times when it is hard work, usually because of weather conditions, or sometimes when I have missed a few days due to travel or other commitments, and need to add a mile or two as penance. There are occasional surprises that lighten the mood. On one of my runs past a wooded section of our general neighborhood I noticed a fairly pungent smell of what was unmistakably a dead animal. The smell was still in the air for the next couple of runs, but then one morning as I passed the area all I could smell was the fabulous perfume of honeysuckle. As any dedicated runner knows, the ability to be introspective when running is not just good for the soul, but it passes time otherwise spent unduly focused on the difficulty of the run, or the unpleasantness of the conditions. It struck me as I contemplated this unusual and uplifting experience that a believer in God would no doubt attribute it to being God's way of reminding us of the power of good to overcome bad, and would take great comfort from such a personal representation of His goodness. I prefer to take such matters at face value, so that I hold my nose when the odor pervades my space, and breathe in deeply when the gorgeous scent of honeysuckle comes my way.

The end of summer in 2005 brought an unusual event in Richmond. Hurricane force winds that were the remnants of "Gaston," a Category 1 storm that had made its way up the south-eastern coast of the United States, swung inland, then hovered over central Virginia for several hours. I remember that day, but Ann has perfect recall. After lunch I decided to drive to down-town Richmond for something I had to attend to at an apartment, and suggested to Ann that I might take her car instead of mine. I brushed aside any concerns about the gathering storm, and she reluctantly handed me the keys to her pride and joy, a current year model Mini Cooper. About two hours later I was heading for home, in the midst of a significant storm, with rain battering down and a feeling of trepidation as I made my way through the down-town area. Roads were suddenly becoming flood zones, and I was caught at an intersection on the aptly named River Road when I had to stop the car in the middle of the low area of the intersection. As I slowed to a halt, there was a torrent of water that came off a side street, and the Mini stalled. I stepped out into about two feet of rising water and was able to enlist the help of a couple of guys to help me push the car back along the road to a higher level. I somehow got it started again, then drove for about a mile through city streets looking for a way home when the engine just gave out. I had no option but to abandon the Mini, and then I walked for about a mile, in some parts wading through streets, until I got to Cassie's apartment, where I was able to dry out and hang out for a few hours. The car was a total loss, and although Ann was able to pick out a replacement car, identical to the old one, she was less than thrilled with the consequences of my afternoon jaunt in her car. Hurricane Gaston was a precursor to Hurricane Katrina, which hit the Gulf Coast in late August, and in that context was but a passing breeze.

My September 13th birthday in 2006 was a significant day for me, as I had decided, at age 60, to hang up my football boots and no longer play competitively. While I had enjoyed a lifetime of playing the game, with a minimum of injury, the fact was that as I got older I was increasingly subject to sore hamstring muscles and tendons, particularly in my right thigh. It became a choice. I could play football once a week, and then spend a few days recuperating and not able to have my daily run, or give up the tendon challenging sport of football, and run pain free on a daily basis. It was time to stand down. To celebrate the occasion, Ann and Shona organized a six-a-side tournament at an indoor sports complex in Richmond, and invited many of my long time playing pals, and a few adversaries. We put four squads together, and after a couple of hours of football, we all enjoyed pizza and beer in the clubhouse. The game that for most of my life had kept me fit, and given me so much pleasure as a performer, was now to be enjoyed vicariously through television, and the odd attendance at a game in Scotland when home on holiday. I do still miss it, and now I juggle the ball with my grandsons, and hope to pass along a few tricks to help them appreciate the incredible joy to be had as a young boy with a ball at his feet, and goals to be scored. I once calculated the approximate number of goals that I had scored in matches that I played since I was a schoolboy back in 1957, and it was comfortably more than the holy grail of 1,000 goals. While it could never pass an audit, the fact is that I have always measured my progress in every league that I played in against the standard of twenty goals a season. I think it is fair to say that in almost every team that I played for, I was usually the top scorer, or close to it, as I usually played in a striker position. Of course, I also included the many years of competitive 5 a side leagues that I played in, as for me football was a year round sport.

Cassie and Kurt were married in October of 2006, just a few months after Kurt graduated from law school. The wedding was held in the grounds of a riverside property that had once been a mill, and was now the location of a beautiful country house that specialized in weddings. It was a 30 minute bus run from our home in the West End of Richmond, and we had a houseful of family and friends here to celebrate their wedding. Kurt's Grandfather, known to us all as "Grandaddy" is a retired Methodist preacher, and he came out of retirement to perform the wedding ceremony. The medical issues that I had to deal with at Shona's wedding were now history, and so I was able to enjoy the occasion and participate liberally in its execution. The lone piper provided the musical backdrop to the occasion, and there was a strong representation from the Glasgow and Falkirk sides of our families, as there had been at Shona's. In accordance with the first chapter of their life plan, the happy couple flew to London so that Kurt could take an additional year of law studies at the London School of Economics. Cassie was quick to produce her UK Passport, and therefore qualified to enter the workforce without need of any kind of work permit. Through a friend in Richmond she was introduced to a financial company headquartered in Nottingham, with an office in London. In Cassie style she talked her way into the job with a minimum of fuss, and shortly thereafter began her work in the world of consumer debt, and the process by which portfolios of consumer debt obligations are parceled together and traded among financial investors, mainly institutional. Before long she was negotiating with buyers throughout the country and setting up auctions when there were multiple buyers of a given portfolio. Kurt's mission was to acquire a Master's Degree in European Law, and so they set up home in an apartment in Islington, and got on with their life together in the wonderful city that is London.

We had our first visitors from Richmond to Bridge Castle when Gene McKeown and his family flew over to join us, and it was as much fun for us to host as it was for them to experience a pretty unusual vacation. My sister Connie just happened to be over from France for a short break, and we were able to have the McKeown's feel like part of our family for a few days. Gene is Irish American, as he was born in New York of parents who were both from Ireland. His son is named Patrick and his daughter is named Claire, and their names speak to their connection to the land of their ancestors.

My activities as a landlord were now greatly simplified, as I had sold off the residential apartment properties and now held one remaining piece of investment property, an office building and parking lot at 406 West Franklin Street in the City of Richmond. During the years after retirement from the bank, when I was busy acquiring and re-habilitating rental properties, I managed to pick up a basic level of competence in some of the skills that an owner of multiple properties must have, unless he is willing to hire tradesmen every time there is a leak in a roof, an obstruction in a toilet, a coat of paint looking for a subject, or for any of the other little things that are sent to complicate the life of a landlord. I keep an office in the basement of the building, which is really more of a storage space for tools and equipment, but it gives me a place to operate from when I visit the building, which I do on a regular basis. My financial plan for the building when I bought it was to hold it for a number of years, and generate income through rentals, then finally sell once I was fed up with the responsibility. With the passing of about seven years of ownership, I am still *au fait* with the management responsibilities, so in no particular hurry to sell, but in any event this current market is not a place to be a seller, on the back of the recession of 2008/2009 and the anemic recovery since then. I will ride out the business downturn till the inevitable pick up in the local economy, and it remains to be seen if asset prices for commercial real estate revert to the mean and turn back up in the next business cycle.

In April 2007 we headed once more up Interstate 95 to Washington DC, only this time there was a special purpose to the trip – the imminent birth of a grandson. Shona delivered a healthy boy on schedule, and we were all happy to be around them at this special time in their lives. Graysen Hunter Colglazier is his name, and as I write this he has acquired a brother, Callum Watson Colglazier, who just had his first birthday. The two boys are both a bundle of joy and a truckload of trouble, depending on all the usual variables that go into rearing children these days. The statistics show them to be but two specs of humanity in a globe that has almost seven billion souls, but for Shona and Chris, and the rest of the immediate family, they are just lovely wee boys who interfere with our rest, demand all our attention, diffuse our recriminations, and fill our hearts with joy.

We organized our summer trip to Scotland to culminate in a visit to Cassie and Kurt in London, and help them close up their apartment, then travel back with us to America at the end of their one year stay. Kurt acquired his degree, and Cassie came back as something of an expert in the specialized world of consumer debt. They had decided to move to Washington DC, in a move that seemed to make sense for a number of reasons. Kurt's European Law accreditation would more likely be recognized in a major international business community such as Washington, and this proved to be correct, although it took several months for Kurt to find the right spot in the right firm, given the state of the economy when they returned. Cassie began a new career in Healthcare, working for a consulting and software company, and her clients are all major hospital groups or individual hospitals across the entire country. She is able to use her specialist knowledge of consumer debt in helping hospitals deal with this by-product of their business, when they are obligated to provide all sorts of specialized medical services to critical care patients who do not have the financial resources to pay their bills. They decided to rent an apartment in Pentagon City just a few hundred yards from the Metro, ensuring easy access to the city, and conveniently just two minute's walk away from Shona and Chris, who live in the same complex. Our routine trips north to see our family are so much easier because they live so near to each other, and we will enjoy this good fortune until they inevitable move up the property ladder, and probably in different directions.

2008 was the year that the financial markets faced a virtual collapse, as the financial losses in a medium sized investment bank in New York, Bear Sterns, were translated into something symptomatic of a larger problem lying beneath the surface of the American, and indeed the Western, financial system. We were all to learn about sub-prime mortgages, which heretofore had been a little noticed but readily apparent financial product, whose intrinsic qualities as a debt instrument that would follow predictable price movements proved to be a dubious assertion. By the time it was all over, the financial system in the United States and in Europe was exposed to a vulnerable underbelly of huge losses in financial firms, followed by commercial firms who had relied upon too much financial leverage in the go-go years leading up to the crash.

For Ann and me, 2008 was an auspicious year, as it marked the first time that we had exercised our right to vote in America. I think it was the activism of Shona and Cassie that carried the day, who both for some reason decided that it was time for Mum and Dad to put a stake in the ground, and take a political position that was embedded in action at the voting booth, rather than verbal abuse directed to the TV screen, which was our usual form of political action. Our political views are liberal, and in the West End of Richmond we live in an enclave of conservatism, so that on the rare occasions when political discourse happened during a social event, we were quickly branded with the 'L' word, and for our own welfare were placed by our dear friends and neighbors in a "do not disturb" category. This is probably

## ALL'S WELL THAT ENDS WELL

the best thing, so that there is no longer the chance that the party of the month (small "p") might end up in a conversational controversy between people who are in fact really good friends.

When election time came we went to Maybeury Elementary School early on voting day and pressed the buttons that got Barack Obama elected as the 44th President of the United States. We really felt good about it, and that had much more to do with the candidate of choice, as against the exercise of voting as a responsibility of citizenship. For Ann and for me our citizenship in America is something we acquired for reasons other than the norm, and has always been a card that we hide behind our back, to be played when it is convenient. But this time was different. I do think that we both were fully engaged in our right to vote, the process of voting, and the consequences of our action. The first three years of Obama's Presidency has not been easy for him, and it remains to be seen whether he will prevail in 2012, but he can be assured of at least two votes from the West End of Richmond.

For a majority of the citizens of this country to vote for a black man to be President was almost unthinkable, until it happened, and yet when it happened it was so patently obvious that it was time to take this road less travelled. There was such a spirit of positivity in the country when he and the First Lady to be took the stage that night, and the reality of what had just happened was beginning to sink in. It was fabulous for them, but it was so much more for America. This country was founded in an age when colonization was an accepted policy of elite nations. America was built by mainly white Europeans, but relied upon the marginalization of the indigent people, and the exploitation of an imported people to support an agrarian economy. It took several generations after Slavery was abolished for black Americans to achieve legal parity with whites, and then the actuality had to work its way through the prejudices that racism had embedded. If ever a tide had risen in the affairs of men, it was during that liberating election of 2008, when the emancipation was as much for the conscience of white Americans as it was for the coming of age of black Americans. It was the first time that Ann and I had entered a ballot box, and it felt really good.

## THE BOG, THE BAHAMAS, AND BEYOND

The bloom came off the rose pretty quickly, as Obama took over the White House amid an economy and a stock market that was in freefall. He hardly stood a chance, and he has had to deal with so many problematic issues that have resulted in more losses than victories, at least as measured by the response of the private economy. Aside from a victim of bad timing, he is also a victim of modern economic theory, which directs that government needs to run budget deficits in order to stimulate the economy into growth again, which eventually creates enough momentum to turn the economy around. Unfortunately there was already a latent but highly evident budget deficit built into the economy, inherited from his predecessor, George Bush, and indeed the larger issue of aggregate government debt was beginning to overwhelm the debate about short term policies.

Having accomplished our mission in helping to elect Barack Obama as President, we did something rather unusual, and travelled back to Scotland for Christmas and New Year. It was truly a family affair, as we were joined by Shona, Chris, and Graysen, and Cassie and Kurt. While it was a wonderful family time together, there were also moments of sadness, due to a death in the family that had just happened a few months before. The baby boy of our nephew Ashley and Claire had died in the womb, and Claire had to deliver the stillborn baby, whom they named Oliver. This had happened in September, so Ann and I had flown back to Scotland to be with them for the funeral. It was such a sad time in all our lives, but devastating for Ash and Claire. Now we were back together again to celebrate Christmas, and somehow acknowledge all the happiness that this time of year brings, yet also grieve for baby Oliver.

In May of each year the Scottish Cup Final is played at Hampden Park in Glasgow. In the one hundred and thirty or so years that Falkirk Football Club has been in existence, this year would mark only the fourth time that the club would make it all the way to the final. Our opponents were the mighty Glasgow Rangers, and when I got news of Falkirk's semi-final victory, I called Ian in London and quickly made plans to fly back to Scotland, and hook up for the big event. Ian arranged the tickets, and on the morning of the game we congregated in (Ian's sister) Kathryn's home in Grangemouth as the departure point

## ALL'S WELL THAT ENDS WELL

for our train trip through to Glasgow. Ian's son Jason, nephew Robin, and son-in-law Scott joined us for the trip. Our initial taxi destination of Falkirk High Station, after some price negotiation with the driver, was quickly changed to incorporate the thirty mile journey through to Hampden Park, and we got there an hour before kick-off to join in the chorus of happy Falkirk fans chanting the latest fan favorite – We are the steeple! – as a sharp parody of the Ranger's standard – We are the people! It was a great day, but a bad result, as Rangers scored the only goal much against the run of play. Our sorrow lasted not much longer than it takes to consume a few pints of Tennant's Lager, and after a pub break of a couple of hours to let the traffic die down, we caught a Glasgow taxicab and surprised the driver with his first ever trip to Falkirk. It was a great day, a busy weekend, and a long trip back to Virginia, but it was worth every penny. Just to be in Hampden Park was a thrill for me, as it brought back memories of 1962 when Ian and I travelled in the luggage compartment of a train to see Scotland defeat England before 134,000 spectators.

The annual "Pink Drink" at Penny Lane that year was yet another standout celebration of the football team that was the binding agent for me and so many of my pals in the Richmond area for years. Each year the list gets longer, as new players are added to the club, and others fall by the way, only to show up again for the Pink Drink around the Christmas season. We always raise a special glass to one of our originals, Albert Jones, who died in his Pink Panther shirt at half time of a summer league game in the early years of the club. "Bert" was built like the side of a house, and had probably the least amount of pure football skill of anyone who ever donned the Pink Shirt. But he tried, and he had some memorable moments, usually involving a rugby style tackle on a rival player. He was handicapped by a terrible stutter when he spoke, and yet he was a lawyer by profession, and regularly represented his clients before the Bar. He was a fellow member of the German American Sports Club, and spoke excellent German, without any stutter at all. He had a Pink Panther tattoo on his chest, and took it to his grave. We miss you, Bert.

Shona's second pregnancy produced another beautiful wee boy, Callum, who arrived on time and intact. His middle name, Watson,

## THE BOG, THE BAHAMAS, AND BEYOND

acknowledges his Edinburgh connections through my Mum's family, and in one of these strange twists of fate, he has red hair. It turns out that my Mum's brother, "Uncle" John, had red hair as a child, and it turned fair as he got older. His children - my cousins Sandra, Kitty, and Gordon also had red hair in childhood. Callum is on track to emulate those red-headed Watsons, and time will tell if he follows the familiar trail or takes a turn in another direction and stays red for life.

Our air travel plans in April were interrupted by the eruption of a volcano in Iceland, although while we merely had some flight time adjustments, and no real inconvenience, it was a major headache for European air travel in general. The previous eruption was in the nineteen twenties, and before that in the eighteen twenties, so this latest event should not have been unexpected. Not that it really affected our vacation, as the volcanic ash turned out to be more of a threat to the Scottish mainland than a reality, and the sun shone through enough to give us alternatives in how to spend our days.

In the month of August 2010, when our forty years of married life were about to be celebrated by a long weekend holiday in an exclusive resort in the Caribbean, we were dealing with an issue of a very different nature, when Ann found out that she had breast cancer. Through self examination she had found a small lump in her breast, and went to her doctor, who arranged for a biopsy as a precaution, but told Ann that it was probably nothing to worry about. Several days later Ann and I visited with the specialist, who told us that the biopsy had tested positive for cancer, and that the prognosis called for a full mastectomy of her left breast. The good news was that she had found it early, and that she should respond well to the typical treatment that involves radiation and/or chemotherapy after surgery, depending on what the surgeon finds on the operating table. The surgery was scheduled to take place in September, after we returned from our holiday in Anguilla.

There was nothing left to do other than jump on the plane and have a few days of rest and recreation before the surgery. We put a good face on it, and headed for the Cap Juluca resort, which was everything it was promised to be. We had a villa on a private beach, and nothing to do but enjoy the sun and sea during the day, and then cocktails and dinner at the clubhouse in the evening. Although disappointed to have our anniversary compromised by the strange and frightening situation that we found ourselves in, we both took comfort in just being together, so that the few days of immersion in each other's time and space was the perfect opportunity to think, reflect, hope, and talk about what was about to happen to Ann. We came back home from our trip ready to deal with it head on, and duly prepared ourselves for the upcoming surgery. Shona and Cassie were first and foremost in our thoughts as this whole situation unfolded, and from the first moment that we knew about it, we had told the girls, when we arrived unexpectedly at their homes in Pentagon City right after we were given the news.

The tests that were administered prior to the actual surgery did not show any other areas of cancer. Any progression of the disease normally shows first in the lymph nodes, and while they had tested negative prior to surgery, there was another test during surgery that would answer the question. That test revealed clear lymph nodes, so the surgery was restricted to the removal of the breast. While the post operation healing process was painful and traumatic, Ann followed all the rules, and within a couple of weeks could feel herself getting stronger. There was one additional test that would determine whether or not she would have to have chemotherapy, and much to our relief it revealed a low incidence of genetic contribution to the disease. Her cancer was estrogen related, and may in fact have been caused by the estrogen drugs that she had taken after menopause, in accordance with conventional medical protocols at that time. Since the remaining live tissue in her body that would continue to be at risk is in her other breast, then the course of treatment to prevent a recurrence of the disease is a daily pill of a substance that effectively blocks the estrogen from harming the remaining live tissue. She will take this medication for five years, and assuming she remains clear of cancer at that point, need no longer take it.

In the year since Ann's cancer was diagnosed, two of her friends have been diagnosed with breast cancer, and in both cases the progression of the disease required a prognosis that called for more radical treatment. For Julie and Angela the fight goes on, and although they are both responding well to treatment, the physical and mental tolls exact a heavy price. When a person moves over the divide and becomes a cancer victim, the fear and anxiety if not outright terror at the implications of the disease for one's self and for one's families must be mind boggling. The rest of us, who are companions to the disease but (thus far) immune from its grasp, can be a salve for the pain, but the cure is beyond our scope, and this must create a feeling of singularity in the victim that must add to the challenge.

Ann was able to recover enough from the surgery to join me in our annual trip to Scotland to celebrate Mum's 90th birthday, and as usual the one with the least apparent emotion about the whole affair was the subject. It so happens that Cassie, her cousin Ashley, and his wife Claire all celebrated their 30th birthdays around the end of October/beginning of November, so Ashley organized a party at the Grangemouth Rugby Club, for "three thirties and a ninety," although because of work requirements Cassie was not able to make the trip. However, the rest of us and a bunch of family and friends enjoyed the disco, and even Mum was able to hit the dance floor with an invite from Claire's grandfather.

In December I had the usual Christmas lunch at Penny Lane with several of my former colleagues from our days together at the Bank, and naturally enough we gathered in the "Hunter" room at the pub, so named because of my services to Terry and Rose as an unofficial advisor on their business operations. It was great to see the guys again, every one more a friend than a colleague, but it was also sad to learn that my former boss and mentor, Don Just, had been diagnosed with Parkinson's Disease. You could not tell it from his appearance. He was every bit as energetic in conversation as he used to be in the old days when he joined the cocktail party and "worked" the room as if everyone was there for him, and he wanted each person to know he valued their presence. Don and I had always connected on a different level, and somehow we shared a sense of humor, perhaps even comedy, that enabled us to find a way to laugh in just about any situation. Don is a "Type A" personality with an intellect that few can match, but he is always grounded in reality, and I think he got as much out of our relationship as I did. I hope so, because his friendship and "sponsorship,"

## ALL'S WELL THAT ENDS WELL

especially in the early years of our life here in America was the difference between settling down for a life that has been nothing but good, and giving up on life here and moving on somewhere else. We rarely see each other now, but when we do it feels like it always did. I think in a way that's the test of friendship – it never really ends.

One day while Ann was out Christmas shopping, she stopped in at the local camera shop. She was served by the same employee who has been there for years, and who normally has a fairly cold and uninterested approach to customer service. As he was looking through the portfolio of pictures to identify the one that needed to be edited, he noticed a photo of two battleaxes and a long-sword that are on display in our apartment in Bridge Castle in Scotland. All of a sudden he was full of chat, and wanted to know all about the medieval weapons, and why we had them. It turns out that he is an amateur collector of (American) war memorabilia, and even makes Indian arrowheads for reproduction pieces. Ann came away with her edited photo, and an Indian arrowhead gift from her new found friend. Everybody has a hot button, but finding it is more often luck than judgment.

The purchase of the two battleaxes was the result of a quiet rendezvous I had with the Glasgow Herald one fine summer's morning, as Ann and I relaxed around the small flower garden at Bridge Castle. There was an article about the forthcoming auction of a medieval battleaxe that ostensibly was used at the Battle of Falkirk in 1298, and had been on display for centuries in a castle in Stirlingshire. The collection was broken up some years ago and had only just found its way on to the open market, hence the auction. I called directory enquiries to get the number of the auction house, and managed to get hold of the owner of The Lanes Armoury in Brighton, England, specialists in Fine Arms, Armour, and military objects. I negotiated a deal for the larger battleaxe, and also a smaller hand carried battleaxe from the "Wallace" era, but not linked to a particular battle. They were sent by courier to my sister Betty's house at Ashbank, and we all gathered there a few days later to open the box and inspect the contents. Well, they are certainly battleaxes, and they look to be very old. Not the shanks of course, which are modern wooden replacements, but the metal heads, in the "bearded" style of construction that was prevalent

### ⊰ THE BOG, THE BAHAMAS, AND BEYOND

in medieval times. They are now on display in the central hall in our apartment at Bridge Castle and are an impressive testament to a time and a place that is evocative of the rich history of our part of Scotland. Although dated to the late thirteenth century, the purported link to the Battle of Falkirk is somewhat tenuous, as the exact site of the battle has long been a source of controversy among historians. I am just happy to have brought them home.

This is the year that welcomes me into its fold as a man of sixty five years of age. Introspection on the past inevitably leads to speculation about the future, and what it will take to beat the marker set by the actuarial tables. Since there is nothing to be gained from the prospect of an early demise, I shall do my best to make this year another pleasant interlude in the journey of life, and a reason to trust in the motto of the Clan Hunter, which is "Cursum perficio" meaning "Stay the course." It has become fashionable for people in their late middle age, around retirement time if they are lucky, to prepare a list of (usually ten) things that they absolutely have to do in the rest of their time on this earth. A robust "Bucket List" will have such things as travel destinations, a book to be written, a mountain to be climbed, a voluntary service goal, an old sweetheart to track down, an estranged family member to re-connect with, and so on. Some people have fairly modest goals that stand a good chance of being met, and others set the standard pretty high, which gives weight and excitement to this quite personal examination. Having observed this phenomenon in other people over many years, my sense is that more often than not the challenge loses intensity with the passage of time, and the list is modified accordingly. I advise people to have two lists, a Bucket list, and another list to be compiled from the discarded dreams, the name of which is phonetically similar to the original, and involves the easy substitution of the letter 'F' for the letter 'B'. A couple of years ago my pal Ian Laurie and I were inspired by Ian's daughter Taryn to plan some day to join her in climbing the highest mountain in Africa, Mount Kilimanjaro. This particular mountain is vulnerable to rank amateur climbers, like Ian and me, as long as there is a decent level of overall fitness. This became the first item on our respective Bucket Lists, but after we had talked ourselves into the possibility, out of the blue Ian began to have severe discomfort from an old knee injury and eventually had to have reconstructive surgery. Unfortunately, he is left with a knee that functions fine on a daily basis in getting from point A to point B, but would not stand the stress of a journey up an eighteen thousand foot mountain. Since this was going to be a team effort, I have given up on this particular dream. That's one transferred to the other list.

A wedding in Las Vegas provided me with a chance to add a whole new challenge to the list, and mark it as completed. The Stratosphere Hotel, our destination for the visit and the wedding, sits at the end of the "Strip," and attached to the hotel proper is the 108 story tower that is the signature building of the property. Our room looked over to the tower, and from the window we could see people jumping from a platform, attached only to a couple of wires, and plummet to the ground with a controlled landing that dropped the person gently in the middle of a bulls-eye. I decided that this was something that was a bit different from my usual recreation activity, and was definitely list-worthy. Next day I excused myself from the pool in mid afternoon and headed up to my reservation at the top of the tower. After payment of $100 and numerous initials and signatures on the waiver documents, I was strapped in to a jump suit and led out to the exposed platform that is 855 feet from the ground. The young lady attendant clipped me in to the guide wires and the control wire, which presumably is the one with the braking mechanism that makes it all possible. After a three count I jumped out of the tower, and was instantly in a free fall for several hundred feet, and landed safely about twenty seconds or so later. It was on a path along a cliff in Sicily when I first experienced a feeling of vertigo many years ago, and I have generally been rather leery of heights since then. This was a chance to test my resolve with something that had really bad consequences in the event of failure, but had a statistically low probability of that happening. The odds were properly weighed, as the jump went quick and easy, and I left with a DVD to show my grandchildren.

It is now over a year since Ann had her cancer surgery, and her prognosis continues to be excellent. The several months of breast reconstruction surgeries finally ended in September, and to all intents and purposes she is back to where she was before the onset of cancer. The dark tunnel that we entered when the medical concern was first raised, through diagnosis, surgery, and post operative procedures, is now behind us, and the way ahead is clear. Ann has managed her illness with courage and grace, and dealt with the pain as if it were a slight inconvenience rather than a potent adversary.

With forty one years of marriage behind us, and time with which to contemplate the hope of many years ahead, we are both so lucky to have found each other when we did, to have supported each other when we needed to, and to have enjoyed everything that we created together. We came of age in the Sixties at a time when the world was on the move, and the happenstance that put us in the same stone building in Glasgow – a city girl and a small town boy – also conspired to pick us out as a couple that would see life through the same prism, and thrive in the beautiful reflections of that reality. It is many years since I shared a budding romance with Ann Louden, but the passage of time and experiences since those early days in Glasgow are still held in thrall by the love we found in our youth, and never lost.

In any family story there is always a compunction for sons in particular to compare themselves to their father, and while I had never ever thought much about it before, I now find myself doing exactly that, as if the very fact of writing the history of our family requires that I tick off certain boxes, this being one of them. I hope my writings reveal that my Dad was an innately intelligent and clever person whose station in life and accomplishments probably did not epitomize this. In boxing terms, he punched below his weight, which is perhaps unfair, as it implies a criticism that he did not get the most out of his capabilities. His childhood took place in the post World War One society, where there was no familial or societal expectation levied other than to get out of school as soon as possible, get a job of any kind that brought a weekly wage into the household, and ideally a trade that would hold the promise of a lifetime of employability. In this regard, he was off to a good start. Once married, my Dad settled in to a life that was pretty much pre-ordained by his social class and his job as a tradesman. To move into our newly built council house in the Bog Road in 1948 at twenty eight years of age must have seemed to him an incredible achievement. He had a respectable trade job as a plasterer, a wife who was a full time mother to their (then) three young children, and the key to the door of a three bedroom home with a garden and an inside toilet. This may have been a relatively greater leap than that subsequently achieved by his six children. If the job of a parent is to give their children the opportunity to rise to a yet higher level of social standing as measured by their relative progress through a life that has an educational foundation, a moral compass, and the ability to prosper, then I have to give Mum and Dad full credit, because that is in fact what transpired. If the measure of my Dad's contribution as a father is to gauge the standing of his six children, then in this respect, I would say that the Hunter children, all six of them, would be pluses on any reasonable report card in terms of their evolution as citizens, and their progress in life through education, society, and parenthood.

When I put myself through this examination, I believe there were times when I stood up to this scrutiny and did all right, and others when I perhaps settled for less that I was capable of. I realized a long time ago that I had academic capabilities that were not challenged enough in High School, and this was evident in my subsequent rapid and successful progress through the professional qualifications that I earned. When I came to America and joined the ranks of young professionals in our bank, they were all university graduates, and many with a Masters degree. Because I came to the organization with such an unusual background, and perhaps because I was British and therefore imbued with a certain assumed quality that put me no less than level with my contemporaries, I was never pressured to acquire academic credentials in the US. While this would have been detrimental had I ever lost my job and had to find another one, it was never an issue in the bank, and I was given executive responsibilities and remuneration on a steadily upward track right up until the last year of our survival as an independent organization. But perhaps, like my Dad, I left something on the table in my progression through life, and it may be that my lack of a formal academic education compatible with my peers in the bank was like a governor on a car engine, that restrains the potential from being fully realized.

I came across a quotation in some long forgotten book that

crossed my desk, which I think may have been a proverb from Israel. It read "The veil that hides the future from us is woven by an Angel of mercy." This is a potent admonition of the frailty of the human being in dealing with the uncertainty of the future. If I am honest with myself, I lived a long time within the comfort of the Angel's majesty, and just assumed that whatever the future held had to be good, because all that had gone before was not bad. Along the way, and perhaps as a function of just growing wiser rather than just becoming older, I changed. It's not that I suddenly woke up with the thought that I needed to have a "Life Plan." It was more of an attitudinal shift, when I seemed to realize that my own perceptions and opinions on matters large and small had been tested enough over a long enough period of time that they no longer needed to be shrouded with the veil. My opinions became more public, my actions less private, and my decisions better informed. I was no longer the boy from the Bog, following the crowd and doing just enough to keep up. Or was I?

As for my Mum, well, I hope she knows how much her love meant to me over the fullness of life as a child, and the later majority years as an absentee son growing to manhood in a faraway country, and pursuing a life that only allowed her access on our annual family holidays in Scotland. She made the choice even before I made the decision that my road ahead should lead to a faraway place, and an opportunity to develop outside of the constraints that were embedded in the life of the small town of Falkirk. In this respect Mum was a visionary, and I have her to thank for giving me the confidence to seek the challenge of the unknown, and for bearing the sadness that she must have often felt at the absence in her life of her son, her daughter-in-law, and our children. When you add to that the fact that three of her remaining six children moved overseas after marriages, and raised their kids - her grandchildren - far, far, away from the family home in Falkirk, only then can you appreciate the sacrifice that she made as a mother and grandmother.

Our journeys led us to a quiet suburb on the outskirts of a city that is a long way from the land of our birth. We came to Virginia to find a way out, to whatever might lie ahead for a young couple blessed with the naivety of youth and inexperience. The brand new house that we bought was no more than a vessel to carry us along in safety and comfort while we pondered the future, and where it might be, rather than what it could be. Somewhere along the way we became parents, and the existence of our first born, Shona, and her sister Cassie became the life that we wanted. There was no grand announcement to our world that, as parents, we had come of age. As time went by we just felt more complete, more secure, less impulsive, and recognized the change in the horizon as a result of becoming Mum and Dad to two wonderful daughters. Chris and Kurt are the sons I never had, and part of our family that now includes two magical wee boys, Graysen and Callum. Scotland was our past, and America is their future. Ours is a story told so many times.

Today is September 13, 2011, and is both a beginning and an ending in this journey through my life. It is a convenient time to bring this narrative to a close, now that I have reached the socially auspicious 65th birthday. I can put down the pen, and focus on my remaining life as a daily progression of experiences that will hopefully give pleasure to me and my family. It is just over a year and a half since I woke up one day with a mission to write about my journey through life, the people with whom I have travelled, and the family that have given it meaning and purpose. If my story is read by those who know me, there should be no surprises. For others who happen to read my story by chance, I hope it strikes a chord that is at least in tune, and resonates.

THE END